HARDY DEVELOPMENTS LTD

HARDY DEVELOPMENTS LTD

Text and cases in management accounting

Graham Ray
Senior Lecturer in the School of Management
at the University of Bath

Joe Smith
Senior Lecturer in the Management Centre at
the University of Aston in Birmingham

John Sizer

MANAGEMENT COST ACCOUNTING

Gower

Published by
Gower Publishing Company Limited
Aldershot, Hants, England

British Library Cataloguing in Publication Data

Ray, Graham
    Hardy Developments Ltd.
    1. Managerial accounting-Great Britain
    I. Title   II. Smith, Joe
    658.1′511′0941   HF5635

    ISBN 0 566 02251 6
    ISBN 0 566 02252 4 Pbk

Typeset by Activity, Salisbury, Wilts
Printed and bound in Great Britain
at The Pitman Press, Bath

Contents

Preface   ix

PART I: HARDY HEATING CO LTD 1948–1968   1

Introducing the company   3

1   The accountant – the information manager   11

     Case study no. 1 – the job of chief accountant   19

     Case study no. 2 – Sam Howell, works director –
        'I'm in charge'   22

     Case study no. 3 – the appointment of the
        chief accountant   24

2   The balance sheet   27

     Case study no. 4 – the balance sheet of Hardy
        Heating Co Ltd   36

     Case study no. 5 – the balance sheet should show
        what the business is worth!   41

     Case study no. 6 – 'the strength of the company lies in
        its plans'   46

3   The profit and loss account   49

     Case study no. 7 – the profit and loss account   57

     Case study no. 8 – where has all the profit gone?   60

Case study no. 9 – 'more detail, more often, please'   67

4   Accounting ratios   71

Case study no. 10 – a first attempt at ratio
    analysis   80

Case study no. 11 – inter-firm comparison   85

Case study no. 12 – ratio analysis in planning   89

5   Cost classifications and product costing   91

Case study no. 13 – the product costs   100

Case study no. 14 – department overhead rates   103

Case study no. 15 – a job well done?   105

Case study no. 16 – a further classification re-
    quired?   109

Case study no. 17 – cost–profit–volume relation-
    ships   110

6   Accounting in planning and control   113

Case study no. 18 – planning by objectives   123

Case study no. 19 – budgeted ratios?   126

Case study no. 20 – standards of performance   128

7   Standards and flexible budgets for control   131

Case study no. 21 – compiling the standard cost of a
    product   139

Case study no. 22 – flexible budgetary control and
    standard costing in operation   143

Case study no. 23 – variance analysis   148

8   Planning for operations and profit   151

Case study no. 24 – break-even analysis   160

Case study no. 25 – the accountant and the economist
    discuss cost-revenue-output relationships   163

Case study no. 26 – a new product   169

Case study no. 27 – limiting factors   172

9   Planning for funds   175

Case study no. 28 – depreciation: a source of
    funds?   185

Case study no. 29 – preliminary analysis of finance
    planning   186

Case study no. 30 – finance and the new product   189

10   The planning and control of capital expenditure   193

Case study no. 31 – a capital expenditure
    decision (1)   200

Case study no. 32 – a capital expenditure
    decision (2)   204

Case study no. 33 – a capital expenditure
    decision (3)   208

Case study no. 34 – the cost of capital   211

Case study no. 35 – a complete evaluation of the new
    fan project   218

PART II: HARDY DEVELOPMENTS LTD   221
From Hardy Heating to Hardy Developments   223

11   The design and development of management
    accounting systems   235

12   Performance reporting of various activities   245

Case study no. 36 – profit centre reporting   247

Case study no. 37 – departmental budgetary control 261

Case study no. 38 – reactions to budgetary control   277

Case study no. 39 – the control of administrative
    costs   285

13   The measurement of product profitability   299

Case study no. 40 – product profitability (1)   301

Case study no. 41 – product profitability (2)   315

14 Management accounting and investment decisions   327

Case study no. 42 – takeover negotiations   329

Case study no. 43 – capital investment in new
      venture   344

15 Management accounting and corporate planning   363

Case study no. 44 – aspects of corporate planning:
      1 Preparation of plans   365

Case study no. 45 – aspects of corporate planning:
      2 Cost structure analysis   384

Case study no. 46 – aspects of corporate planning:
      3 Setting financial objectives   393

Case study no. 47 – aspects of corporate planning:
      4 Pricing policy   399

16 Major financial issues since flotation   405

Bibliography   413

Preface

Whatever happened to Hardy Heating? This is a question which has been put to us on many occasions. Happily the combination of text, case studies and a BBC television series seems to have committed to memory the development of management accounting at the small firm of Hardy Heating Limited; and the initial viewing in 1968 and 1969 has been reinforced subsequently by the availability of ten films which correspond to the ten chapters in the original text. The text and cases were deliberately written in a style which, judging by the BBC's sales, appealed to the non-accountant, and after the BBC relinquished their interest the original text, when published by ourselves at Midland Consultants Publications, has continued to enjoy healthy sales.

We have always answered the question as to the progress of Hardy Heating by saying that it was on its way to a public quotation and that the saga would eventually be brought up to date. Meanwhile thousands of students have had their first introduction to management accounting by examining the details of the small Black Country firm. In our own teaching at the Universities of Aston and of Bath, we have been developing material which takes the student to a more advanced level and we have retained Hardy Heating as the vehicle for this. Some of the material has already been published in the journal *Management Accounting* in the form of case studies and we have now developed a format which describes the development of management accounting at Hardy Heating from 1969.

Except for some minor modifications, we have decided to retain intact, as Part I of this new book, the original text and cases which we produced for the BBC. We have used this material for the last twenty years in various forms and we know from our own experience and from welcome comments by other lecturers and students that it works well as a basic introduction to management accounting, particularly for non-accountants.

We have now added a Part II which allows the student to be involved in an extended range of management accounting problems; this material has been specially developed for second stage courses, assuming that the basic introduction from Part I has been covered. In Part II Hardy Heating expands its operations and becomes Hardy Developments Limited, a public company, and we have presented twelve case studies which deal with key issues in management accounting. We have tried to retain a style which is appreciated by the non-accountant and we have introduced a commentary on each case study in which two executives reflect on their experience. We have also used two interviews with the executives to expose students to other issues. Our intention has been to retain the realism and vitality of the original publication and to continue the saga in a similar vein.

Anticipating the question 'Whatever happened to Hardy Developments Limited?' we are now following through the management accounting implications of international operations and there are rumours that the company will become 'Hardy International'. We shall see what the future brings.

In the meantime, we shall be glad to receive comments from lecturers, students and businessmen on the updated work.

We, and our families, have literally grown up with Hardy Heating and Hardy Developments. We thank our families for their forbearance and patience as they have watched, heard and read about these developments, in what to us has always been a fascinating firm.

Graham Ray
Joe Smith

July 1981

PART I

HARDY HEATING CO LTD 1948–1968

Introducing the company

In 1948 Jack Hardy, an enterprising young man of about 30, started his one-man business, an electrical shop, in Wolverhampton. He purchased the shop outright, including its stock-in-trade, for £3,500, and ran it himself, without assistance, for the first four months. Then he started to employ two sales assistants as business improved. It was a variable sort of trade, full of ups and downs, mainly prompted by changes in the supply of credit and in the supply of certain lines. But Jack Hardy was satisfied—he was his own boss at last, and the business was reasonably profitable. Before this venture, he had been an assistant works manager in a factory in Walsall where large quantities of electrical accessories were made. What he really wanted was a factory of his own, but this shop was the first step, a venture which he hoped would provide the necessary build-up of capital. As a sole trader, Jack Hardy got a great deal of satisfaction from administering the business, changing the stocks and dealing with both customers and suppliers. Though he did not make a great deal of money, the profit return was better than his previous salary in industry, and Jack was careful. All the net profit of the business, after tax, was saved as additional capital, waiting for the day when Jack could get involved in his true love, manufacturing.

Sam Howell, the works manager at the company where Jack had previously worked, was ten years older than Jack Hardy, but they had kept in close touch over the three years since Jack had opened his shop, and Sam, being a cautious man, had accumulated some savings. It was late in 1951 that they got to discussing a partnership which would extend the activities of Hardy's business. Sam was ready to leave his present

3

employment as soon as possible in order to extend the shop into the next-door premises. This meant that the range of goods offered could be increased and the total volume of sales could be doubled, they estimated. By now, the total capital employed in the business was around £35,000. Hardy and Howell became a well known partnership in the district and offered such good service that all serious competition in the neighbourhood was quickly mopped up.

It was a slow process building up the business to the sort of capital figure the two partners believed was necessary to make manufacturing possible. In fact, it took them seven more years. During this time they bought three more shops, and by 1958 the staff employed had reached ten.

In the July of that year, the bold step was taken. Hardy and Howell had accumulated over £20,000 of their own and were prepared to sink this in a manufacturing business. Just the sort of premises which they required became available, and it even had some plant which they felt they could put to good use. In some ways they were disappointed that they could not purchase the land and premises, because Jack Hardy was a great one for 'being the landlord', but they rented the factory at what they considered a reasonable rental, so saving their capital for other things. Unfortunately, the lease was not as long as they would have liked. The shops were sold, though neither Hardy nor Howell liked making the sale. They would have preferred to retain them as one point of distribution, though they recognised that manufacture—to be economic—would have to be at a greater volume than could be taken by their shops alone. But no one else in the industry maintained their own distribution outlet, so Hardy and Howell guessed that this was not practicable.

Manufacturing started in a small way with just a few workpeople. It was a scrappy hand-to-mouth and badly organised affair at the beginning, and it was fortunate that output was restricted to five standard plugs, made in one colour only, and four standard sockets, just in brown. These were designed by the two directors themselves, based on their experience at the Walsall factory. In the ten years since then there has been a steady increase in the range of products offered, more or less in line with the product lists of competitive manufacturers. Quite early on the plugs and sockets were offered in an alternative colour, and the sockets were manufactured in the shuttered type as well as plain. Lampholders and battenholders were introduced within twelve months of starting the business, and it was a momentous decision late in 1960 when ordinary switches of six different types were put into the catalogue. The more modern rocker switches followed in 1966, and only a few months before their introduction the proprietary products—convectors and electric fires—started to roll off the assembly benches. No one, least of all the two founders, would call it an adventurous business.

The product list has been steadily building up, but very much in line with what competitors have to offer. Though they have progressively diversified their products, no original or unique lines have been introduced.

Originally the new premises were adequate though old. Now they are a mixture of the old and the new, numerous attempts have been made to modernise them internally. The factory is a bit of a rabbit warren and this complicates the production processes, making transporting, delivering and handling of products and components quite difficult. But it has been possible to departmentalise the factory into its several production and service departments, although because of the present level of production activity, there are now considerable space restrictions.

In spite of the nature of the premises and these restrictions, the company is quite an efficient unit. Both Hardy and Howell were well trained in the manufacture of electrical products and this has stood them in good stead. They have made a point of keeping abreast of the latest methods of manufacture, though they have not always considered it necessary to buy nor in any case always been able to afford the very latest manufacturing plant and equipment. Neither would claim to be a trained manager, but both have by now been through the mill of experience of running a business. Howell is a man of considerable production management abilities, while Hardy's abilities quite clearly lie in the field of co-ordinating all the various departmental activities. Hardy, in particular, has taken the opportunity to learn about current thinking in management. They have both been invited to attend university short courses, but while both profess enthusiasm, Hardy usually goes while Howell never gets there. From various sources both have learned a lot about the tools and techniques of management and have given thought to their use within the company. One front upon which the business is particularly strong is work measurement.

Bill Twist joined the company five years ago as work study engineer. He had worked at his last company initially as planning engineer and then on the work measurement aspects of work study. He was therefore experienced in the computation of operation standard times for incentive scheme purposes and for planning and machine loading. Bill reckons the work measurement for production operators is virtually complete, save for measuring additional operations made necessary by new products, the regular review of times, occasional method changes and regular examinations of efficiency and performance against standards. He had, however, done little work measurement for non-productive or indirect employees. When, in 1965, the work force reached 150 people, he took over responsibility for some of the job recruiting and inducting of new labour and in fact found himself landed with the job of personnel manager. He now deals with the administration chores necessitated by the Training Act and recommendations to directors on the training of all staff, save senior management. Bill finds the labour market is very tight and he, in particular, is having extreme difficulty over wage rates.

Inevitably over the years the company has had to specialise in its management functions as part of its growth. Wilfred Appleby is the sales manager and joined the organisation just a fortnight after Bill Twist. His previous experience was entirely in the accounting machine field in which he had done some pretty hard selling. Wilfred Appleby has to get out and about a lot, since Hardy Heating sells to both wholesalers and retailers, and in addition there is a small industrial market for a limited number of the products. Wilfred is not in the office more than a day and a half per week since the job of selling out in the field is so demanding. Export sales amount to almost 20 per cent of the company's business, all done through agents. The export sales activity has been built up from nothing in the last three years, a particular brain child of Wilfred. It is to his comfort that Jack, his managing director, takes some of the sales load by dealing with two of the major wholesale customers, one which takes only proprietary products and the other which takes the accessories. The only problem which this allocation of the sales activities has caused, one suspects, is that perhaps undue emphasis has sometimes been given to Hardy's own customers.

In his conversations with the directors, Wilfred has not disguised his dissatisfaction with the sales set-up. He argues that they need a proper sales force, and that if they had it, sales coverage could be much greater and the volume of sales substantially increased. He also argues that the company is approaching the size when it needs a sales manager who manages, not sells, and that he is not able to give any large amount of time to planning and developing the marketing activities of the business, considering the alternative channels of distribution, and extensions and modifications to the product range. This last point is a particular bee in his bonnet, since his contact with customers and potential customers suggests many new items which he believes should be considered. His conversations with the two directors about this have so far gone no further than to consider the strength of competition there would be in some new markets.

The present organisation structure is clear from the organisation chart and the chart of production and service departments (see Figures 1 and 2). Jack Hardy is both chairman and managing director of the company, and Sam Howell, who accepts responsibility for managing the factory, is the only other director. Reporting directly to Hardy are Wilfred Appleby, Ken Newell, the chief designer, Paul Kenton, the buyer and Mrs Jean Wilkins, who deals with accounts and wages and generally supervises the office. Not all the people answering to Jack Hardy have the same managerial status. Sam Howell is in a unique position as a founder director of the company who also has a managerial

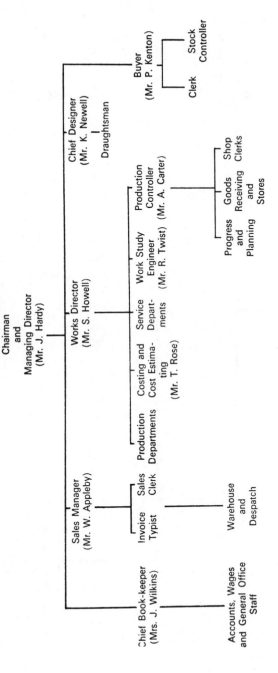

Fig. 1 The company

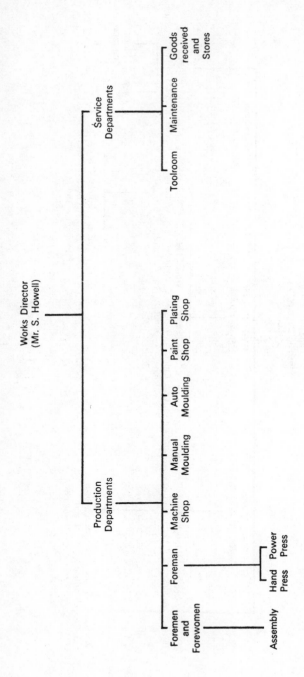

Fig. 2   Production department

role to play. Wilfred Appleby, though a key man in company operations, is not a man who is expected to grow very much more with the company, and Sam Howell in particular regards him as a doubtful case for any further promotion. Ken Newell and Paul Kenton report to the managing director more because of his particular interest in these functions and his desire to keep a grip on them than for any other reason. Though Jean Wilkins accepts responsibility for all general office and administrative chores, Wilfred Appleby supervises the invoicing of all sales. The costing and cost estimating activities are carried out by Tom Rose, and although he keeps close contact with Jean Wilkins on accounting matters which affect costing, he reports to Sam Howell, the man responsible for the bulk of the costs in the company, namely those incurred in the factory.

The two directors have experienced the usual small business difficulty of detaching themselves from specialist functions. This is particularly true of the area of product design where the chief designer, a young man, is a recent appointment. Paul Kenton is both buyer and material controller, though he has an elderly man acting under him whose duties cover the important area of material stock control.

Turnover in the last trading year was a little short of £356,000, an increase of 13 per cent on the previous year's figure of £317,000. Three years ago, when the rocker switches and the proprietary products were introduced, turnover grew by £63,000 in the year, an increase of almost 25 per cent on the year before. Both the directors feel that the growth rate of the company is likely to settle at no more than 5 per cent to 7 per cent per annum unless new products are introduced in the near future. On the other hand both feel that a bigger growth in profits is possible, because there is better machinery to be purchased, and other cost savings can be secured.

Table 1 presents an analysis of the company labour force into the various departments, showing the distribution of the total labour force between direct, indirect and other employees, and between male and female workpeople. The labour force increased on average by less than 20 per annum until 1966, but in the last two years it has risen by 30 per annum, mainly accounted for by the additional labour requirements of the proprietary products. In the early days there were virtually no male employees in the factory, but the ratio of male to female employees has increased in recent years, since the firm decided to stiffen up the permanent labour force and to undertake the manufacture and repair of the tools required by the business; work they had previously sub-contracted.

To get some idea of departmental manning in the company, it will be useful to look at the most recent manning list produced by Bill Twist.

Table 1
Manning list

	Male	Female	Total
Managerial and administrative			
Directors	2	–	2
Executives	3	1	4
Others	8	9	17
	13	10	23
Direct factory employees			
Assembly shop	2	50	52
Press shop	3	15	18
Machine shop	3	7	10
Manual moulding	2	8	10
Auto moulding	1	2	3
Plating	4	–	4
Spray shop	2	4	6
	17	86	103
Indirect factory employees			
Foremen assembly	2	1	3
Foreman press	1	–	1
Moulding	1	–	1
Toolsetters, presses	2	–	2
Progress and planning	4	–	4
Goods received and stores	4	–	4
Shop clerks	–	3	3
General labourers	10	–	10
Despatch/warehouse	2	1	3
Maintenance	5	–	5
Toolroom	14	–	14
Inspection	3	18	21
Development (models)	2	–	2
Office cleaner	–	1	1
Canteen	–	2	2
	50	26	76
Totals	80	122	202

1

The accountant – the information manager

The purposes of the accounting system

In almost any organisation the accounting system acts as an important information network. The accountant in industry might therefore be called an information manager. He is responsible for the supply of information both within the organisation and also outside it. The accountant, in a sense, is two-faced. Through the directors, he faces outwards to the shareholders, the Inland Revenue, and the Registrar of Companies. He also faces inwards to the management of his company. The first face is concerned with financial accounting, and the latter face, when looking inside the company, is concerned with management accounting.

The distinction between financial and management accounting

Financial accounting

Financial accounting is concerned primarily with reporting historical information to interested parties outside the company. The information which is reported is governed by generally accepted principles, and the overall intention is to portray to outsiders a true and fair view of the financial affairs of the company. The main documents which are used to supply this information are the balance sheet, the profit and loss account and the Directors' report.

The generally accepted financial accounting principles are not codified in any act of parliament. Accounting principles are unlike the principles of natural sciences: they are not deduced from basic axioms but represent a generally agreed way of presenting information on a business problem. Recommendations from the professional bodies of accountants are not binding on their members but represent guides to action. The accountant within a company has some latitude in the ways in which he applies these guides, since there may be a number of equally acceptable ways of providing information on the financial affairs of the company. The auditors of the company, for their part, act as 'watch-dogs' on behalf of the members of the company to ensure that the application of the guides to action produces information which gives a true and a fair view of the financial affairs of the enterprise. The auditors have a considerable part to play in the development of ways of providing information to parties outside the company, and thus in the development of accounting principles.

Management accounting

The emphasis in management accounting is quite different. Here the main test is not, 'Does the information conform to generally accepted accounting principles?' but 'Is the information useful to the management of the company?' Financial accounting is concerned with providing historical information to external parties in a consistent and objective manner. Management accounting must be concerned with giving information on what has just happened, and also giving estimates of what will happen in the future.

Management is concerned with making efficient use of limited resources. The resources are sometimes called the four Ms: men, machines, materials and money. A binding agent is required in the form of information to ensure that the relevant facts are known when management is planning and controlling the use of these resources. In order to know what has happened, is happening, and what may happen to a business, management needs a system continually supplying relevant information on which to base its decisions.

The relationship between the accountant, management and external parties

The relationship between the accountant, the management and external parties is shown in Figure 1.1. The left-hand side of the chart shows the cycle of planning and controlling by management. Management decides what is required, and also when and how it is carried out in accordance with established standards of performance. The next step is to execute

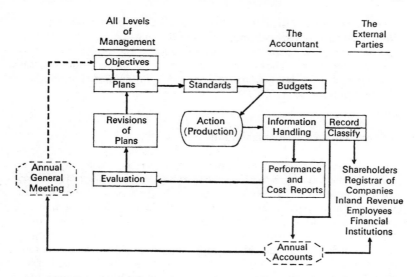

Fig. 1.1   Relationship between accountant, management and external parties

the plan, and to follow this with an evaluation of how well actual performance conformed to plan. A feedback exists, following evaluation, so that new plans can be drawn up which take into account the experience already gained. 'Action' and 'evaluation' cover the management process of control.

The middle column shows the role of the accountant. Management planning of the resources of the company is 'expressed' by the accountant in the form of budgets. When preparing budgets, he will give advice about how the efforts of managers could be co-ordinated. Management control is then aided by performance reports prepared by the accountant. To produce these reports, the accountant must record and classify actions as they occur.

The right-hand column shows the connection between external parties and the accountant. The external parties receive historical information after the accountant has recorded and classified activities.

In one sense the management and the external parties both receive performance reports. Management receives performance reports as part of its management planning and control cycle: such reports should include reference to the standards of performance which have been set by the management, and might well be received on a daily, weekly or monthly basis. External parties receive an account of stewardship at relatively long periods of time and standards of performance are not built into this reporting system which is concerned only with historical facts.

Performance reports with built-in standards of performance give information to the manager about how he is doing and what problems he should look into. Information is often supplied by the accountant for use in long-range planning and also in making special, non-recurring decisions, such as whether to make or buy, add or drop a product, or replace equipment.

The accountant in the organisation

The accountant's job, as information manager, is similar in some respects to the job of production manager; he is responsible, however, not for the production of components but for the production of information. The physical characteristics of a product must be specified by a designer, and similarly the accountant must design a management information system. Standards of performance must be established for production operators by the production manager, and the accountant must also build up standards of performance for the activities within his control. Strict time schedules must be worked to by both the accountant and the production manager.

In addition to his production job as information manager, he acts as the interpreter of information to other managers. His job includes explaining reports to all levels of management and giving advice on financial and economic alternatives. The management team must take the responsibility for decisions which affect its functional areas, but such decisions are made within a framework of information and advice given by the accountant.

There are dangers in any organisation that this framework may result in a management control system which is too rigid, and can seriously affect the vitality of the unit. In such cases there is a real danger that the accountant may become a production manager with a product that he cannot sell to his customers, the management team, and consequently he may have little opportunity to influence and advise them.

The qualities of the accountant

The qualities required to perform the financial accounting responsibilities of the accountant are very different from those required to carry out management accounting duties.

For financial accounting, it is necessary to have a good understanding of company law, and also of auditing practice; to know what is the generally accepted accounting practice on a wide range of reporting problems, and to recognise possible alternative treatments. Naturally, an intimate knowledge of taxation law and procedures is also required.

Like a lawyer, the financial accountant must have a knowledge of precedents, be able to deal analytically with difficult technical problems and negotiate with auditors and civil servants.

In management accounting, the accountant is required to design, implement, control and maintain a management information system. A thorough appreciation of the problems faced by his fellow managers is required. In a technical industry the accountant must have a good understanding of the technology which is being applied, and preferably some practical knowledge of work study and other specialised management techniques. The techniques of data processing must be mastered if the accountant is to be a successful information manager.

A management accountant needs the imagination and ability of the designer to create a communications framework for information and to specify its characteristics. He needs considerable analytical ability to give relevant information and advice on a wide range of management problems. The ability to co-ordinate the efforts of a team of managers is inherent in good budgetary control, and the accountant needs the persuasive skills of the salesman when he works as interpreter and adviser. The abilities of the production manager to obtain output at satisfactory quality and cost are needed to fulfil the role of data processing manager, and the accountant must also have the ability to analyse past events, and sense the information requirements of future situations.

There can be little wonder that an accountant who fulfils all these requirements is able to command a very considerable salary.

The accountant, the firm and its environment

As interpreter of information and adviser on the financial aspects of problems, the accountant must understand fully the nature of the firm and the environment in which it operates. It is useful to regard the firm as a system of parts, interrelated and working together to achieve a common purpose. The role of top management is to bring into balance the various sub-systems, such as manufacturing, selling or accounting. Each sub-system may have its own purpose, values and standards of action which need to be reconciled one with another to form a viable total system.

The firm can also be regarded as one of a large number of sub-systems of the total society of the country. Other sub-systems include nationalised industries, trade unions, government departments, educational, social and cultural institutions. Figure 1.2 shows the firm and its environment as systems within systems.

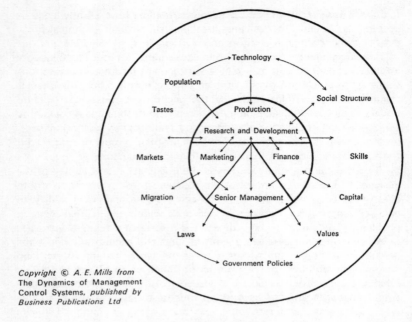

Fig. 1.2   The firm as a sub-system

Case study no. 1 – the job of chief accountant

Jack Hardy considered his one-foot putt at the eighteenth hole. Taking slow and deliberate aim, he stroked the ball towards the hole. It spun round the rim of the cup and finished nearly two feet past the hole. 'Just my luck! That's typical,' he complained. 'One pace forward and two back.'

His golfing partner, Peter Hall, smiled and confidently tapped home his putt. 'My game, I think, Jack. Buy me a drink in the club.' Over drinks Jack Hardy, Chairman of Hardy Heating, talked about his problems to Peter Hall, senior partner in Lilleshall, Hall and Co., Chartered Accountants.

'You remember when you first acted for me? Then I used to employ 10 men, could operate my own machines, and acted as salesman and buyer myself. I even kept the books when I got home at night. And I knew everything that was going on in the business. I didn't need any fancy management techniques and controls. I could tell how we were doing just by looking. Now I employ more than 200 people and I seem out of touch. I don't feel as if I'm in control. Every time I try to get on top of things, I just seem to make matters worse. It's just like that putt on the last green. Now to crown everything, my bookkeeper's husband has been killed in a car crash and she will be away for some time. If I don't have the wages ready next week, I shall have a strike on my hands. For two pins I would sell out.'

Peter Hall smiled and said that the business was certainly worth more than two pins. 'I think that you've got one basic problem here. I've told you for some time that you need to plan the production of information and paperwork, just as you plan your products. I'll send someone round from my office to look after your bookkeeping for a time but you need to make a proper investigation before you can deal with this problem of management information. As a matter of fact we have entered into a consortium with other firms of accountants and now offer a management consultancy service. Let me arrange for Ian Tooday to visit you.'

Jack Hardy said that he didn't believe in paperwork, but that he'd let Ian Tooday spend a couple of days examining the organisation, production and administrative methods of the company, and then have a look at his report.

After two days' intensive investigation, during which he interviewed all senior members of the staff, Ian Tooday reported back. He came straight to the point. 'I feel strongly that the time has come to appoint a chief accountant who would also act as company secretary. Mrs Wilkins, your book-keeper, has done an excellent job on the routine financial recording side, but your management information system is virtually non-existent. This system needs to be planned and controlled. The company will suffer if you try to use the same planning and control procedures which worked well when you were first setting up in business on a very small scale. I've drawn up a specification of the job as I see it should be done. If you decide to advertise and recruit to this specification, we shall be glad to help you choose the right man.'

Job specification of chief accountant and company secretary

Responsible for:

1 The planning and control of all expenditure connected with the financial policy laid down by the board of directors.
2 The administration of a system of budgetary control covering all activities of the company.
3 The design and operation of a management information system, pertinent to the planning and control of the activities and resources of the company.

4 The design, planning and control of data processing within the company.

5 The maintenance of adequate records and accounts of business transactions, and preparing annual accounts for presentation to the board and shareholders.

6 Passing all accounts for payment.

7 Receiving, banking and accounting for all money received.

8 Ensuring adequate provision for collecting money due to the company in respect of sales of products.

9 Keeping statutory records regarding salaries, wages and national health insurance.

10 Acting as company secretary in the fulfilment of the company's legal responsibilities under the Companies Act.

11 Preparing agenda, minutes and other documents for meetings of the board of directors and of shareholders.

12 Dealing with the issue and transfer of shares together with the maintenance of share register.

13 Ensuring that the assets and interests of the company are adequately insured.

14 Advising the board on legal matters and conducting legal negotiations.

'It sounds a bit elaborate to me,' said Jack Hardy, 'the chap will have to work as part of our management team. I'll have a word with Sam Howell, our works director, and let you know what we decide.'

Required

1 Should the company recruit on the basis of this job specification?

2 Outline the main personal qualities which are required to carry out the job specification.

3 Assuming the appointment is made, who will be responsible for 'planning and control'?

4 Outline the main characteristics of a management information system applicable to this company.

5 Assume that you are appointed to this position. What could be the main problems during the first year and how would you deal with them?

Case study no. 2 – Sam Howell, works director – 'I'm in charge'

'I am thinking of appointing a chief accountant,' said Jack Hardy. He tossed a copy of the job specification to Sam Howell and asked for his reactions.

'Just what are you up to Jack? We've built this business together and you're thinking of cutting down my job. What are you trying to do?'

This outburst surprised Jack Hardy. He pointed out that he was only proposing to appoint a chief accountant, not a production manager. Sam replied that he had always been in complete charge of the production side of the business, but it seemed that the chief accountant would have some responsibility for cost control. He had always adopted the principle that costs should be controlled at source; therefore the proper man to control costs in the production departments was the man in charge, Sam Howell. Sam remarked that neither chief accountants nor paperwork produced electrical components of satisfactory quality at the required time and at an economical cost.

Jack Hardy reassured Sam that he was not trying to undermine his position. In fact he was trying to ensure that Sam was provided with the information necessary to carry out his difficult and responsible job of production management. The new responsibility for providing information would be taken up by the new chief accountant.

22

'Look, Sam. Let's say you're the driver of the car, and the chief accountant designs the instrument panel. You need that panel when you're driving; and without the control his information gives you, you can't drive effectively at all.'

'If you design a car control panel, you ought to know something about cars. This accountant will know nothing about my production problems,' snapped Sam. 'He'll take the credit when things go well, but he'll never share the blame. I can't stand "back seat drivers", and that's what you're putting on to me.'

At this point one of the foremen came in to tell Sam a machine had broken down again. 'Will this new chap give me some useful information on this?' Sam muttered as he dashed out.

Required

1   Outline the organisational relationship of the chief accountant and production manager.
2   What information can be supplied to the production manager by the chief accountant?
3   Who should be responsible for 'cost control' in production?

Case study no. 3 – the appointment of the chief accountant

John Marsh had applied for the job of chief accountant and secretary of Hardy Heating. He had attended a preliminary interview with Ian Tooday, a management consultant, and Sam Howell, and the final interview had been arranged and chaired by Jack Hardy.

Although John was well qualified by examination—both a chartered accountant and cost and works accountant—at 30 he was a little lacking in managerial experience. Ian Tooday pointed out that John did not fully match up to the specification which had been drawn up for the job. Indeed the job as specified was not yet in existence within the company, and an essential requirement of the successful candidate was the ability to design and implement a management information system. Ian Tooday stressed that this job required not only technical knowledge of finance and accounting, but full appreciation and understanding of all the financial aspects of management. This meant that the successful applicant should be able to understand the problems of his fellow managers, and should be able to communicate effectively with them. He would have to be a salesman and an educator in the financial aspects of management.

John Marsh was a little surprised that the qualities of a salesman were required, but was eager to be involved in a situation which clearly demanded the use of imagination, ingenuity and tact.

Jack Hardy was impressed by the enthusiasm of the young man, but could not help wondering how John Marsh would fit into the management team alongside Sam Howell, the works director, and other senior managers. He judged that although John did not fully meet the specification, he had the ability to grow into the job.

To the surprise of John Marsh he was offered the position at a reasonable salary, which included an annual review.

John accepted the offer with his characteristic enthusiasm.

Required

1   Assume you are Jack Hardy. How would you introduce your new chief accountant into the company?
2   Assume you are John Marsh. Outline your main steps on taking up your appointment, and give a weighting to the priorities.
3   Do you agree that the accountant should possess some of the qualities of a salesman? If so, why?

2

The balance sheet

THE PREVIOUS chapter presented accountancy as a system for providing information, viewed both from within the organisation and from outside. Financial accounting is concerned primarily with reporting historical information to interested parties outside the company. This chapter concentrates on the balance sheet, which should give to outsiders a true and fair view of the financial affairs of the company. This is supported by the profit and loss account in Chapter 3.

The balance sheet of an individual

If an individual wishes to summarise his financial affairs, his first step will probably involve listing the items which he owns. The accountant would say that he lists his *assets*.

	Items owned or assets	1 January £
	House	22,000
	Furniture	8,000
Assets	Car	3,500
	Caravan	2,000
	Boat	1,500
		£ 37,000

In addition to describing the items which he owns, a money figure has been added. The selection of the appropriate basis for measurement of items shown in the balance sheet is a fundamental accounting problem. Unfortunately for most people, the above list does not represent a complete summary of their financial affairs, since it is likely that there will be claims which must be set against the assets. We therefore need a list of claims, drawn up at the same time.

	Claims or sources of capital	1 January
		£
	Building Society loan	18,000
	Hire purchase on furniture	2,000
Liabilities	Hire purchase on car	1,500
	Loan from father-in-law	6,000
	Bank overdraft	1,500
	Owners' claims (capital)	8,000
		£ 37,000

The list of claims represents the sources of capital which have been used to finance the assets, and the two lists together form a balance sheet which shows, at a particular point in time, the assets of the enterprise and the sources of capital used to finance these assets.

The two lists do not necessarily represent a complete statement about the individual. For instance, the fact that he has a wife and two children is not recorded. Perhaps the individual cannot decide whether to include them in the list of assets or in the list of liabilities and even if he decides on the appropriate list, perhaps he cannot decide on the money figure which should be shown.

The balance sheet of a manufacturing company

Assets or capital in use

The balance sheet of the individual can now be extended to that of a manufacturing company. There must once again be a list of capital in use, or assets. In preparing such a list the accountant finds it useful to distinguish between fixed assets (relatively permanent items) and current assets (items changing from day to day and which are eventually converted into cash).

Assets or capital in use 1 January
Long-term or fixed assets
                    Land and buildings

       Plant and machinery
       Motor vehicles
       Fixtures and fittings

Short-term or current assets
       Stocks of raw material
       Work in progress
       Stocks of finished goods
       Debtors
       Bank balance and cash

This initial division illustrates a basic management problem. The company must decide how much to invest in fixed assets and how much to invest in current assets. This will depend to some extent upon the technology of the industry and also the sources of capital available to the company.

The heading 'current assets' covers an important operating cycle within the company which is vital both for profitability and liquidity. In this cycle cash flows out of the business up to and including the point where the customer, or debtor, takes delivery of the finished goods. When the customer pays, cash flows back, and if the goods yield a profit, the current assets increase. We can think of a child pushing a snowball through the snow, hoping to make a much larger ball, and the increase is profit. The faster the child pushes the snowball, the quicker it grows. The frequency with which the company turns over the current assets is a vital factor which influences the amount of profit earned. The amount of current capital will increase all the time in a profitable company, subject to periodic withdrawals from it. These withdrawals are:

1   expenditure on fixed assets
2   tax payments made annually
3   dividend payments
4   other investments outside the company.

Claims or the sources of capital

In order to complete the balance sheet, a list of claims or sources of capital is needed. As in the case of assets, the accountant should classify the sources of capital on a time basis (long, medium, short).

Claims or the sources of capital on 1 January
Permanent or long-term

       Share capital (ordinary and preference)
       Retained profits

Medium-term

  Loan capital
  Debentures

Short-term or current

  Bank overdraft
  Creditors
  Special creditors

  The main problem in practice is securing a balance between the various sources of funds. This raises the problem of capital gearing and debt capacity.

  The list of assets and the list of claims together comprise the balance sheet of the company, and the connection between them is illustrated in Figure 2.1.

Accounting guidelines

Chapter 1 stated that the information which is reported is governed by generally accepted accounting principles. We need to view the balance sheet in the light of five main guidelines which underpin its construction.

Guideline 1 measuring in money

The balance sheet expresses in monetary terms certain facts relating to the assets of the enterprise and the claims against those assets. That is to say, certain facts have been reduced to the common denominator of money. Accounting deals only with those facts which can be expressed in monetary terms, and in consequence accounting reports may not include many important facts about a business. For instance, a balance sheet will not report that industrial relations are very strained within the company, nor that there are no immediate replacements for several key senior managers who are due to retire shortly.

Guideline 2 the business as a separate unit

Each business enterprise is a separate entity for accounting purposes, and accounts are kept for each separate entity. In the case of sole traders and partnerships, there is no distinction in law between the financial affairs of the business and the financial affairs of the individuals. For accounting purposes, however, the business of the sole trader and of the partnership are held to be accounting entities, quite separate from the personal affairs of the individuals. In the case of a limited liability company, the company has a legal entity separate from the shareholders who own it. Once again, accounts are kept for the

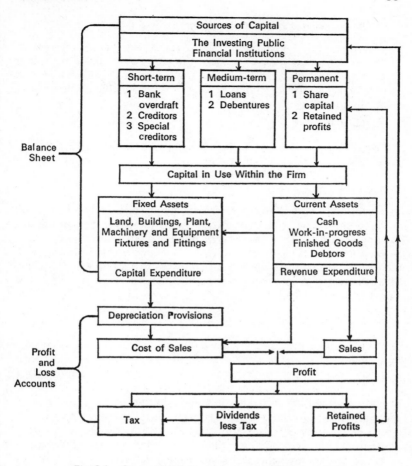

Fig. 2.1   Connection between a company's assets and claims

business entity of the limited liability company as distinct from the
shareholders who actually own the business.

Guideline 3   claims = assets

The firm's assets are financed from two sources: its owners and its
creditors. The claims of the creditors are called liabilities. It is clear
from the example of the individual's balance sheet that the assets of the
business are claimed by someone, either the owners or creditors. At
the same time the total claims against the enterprise cannot exceed
what there is to be claimed. We can express this relationship in an
equation:

Owners' claims + liabilities = assets.

This relationship holds good continuously, so that an increase in owners' claims must always be accompanied by an equivalent increase in assets or a reduction in liabilities. The claims of the owners are the residue, equal to the difference between the sum of the assets and the total liabilities:

Owners' claims = assets — liabilities.

Owners' claims in a limited liability company will be represented by issued share capital and retained profits.

Guideline 4   the going concern

In accounting, the business is viewed as a going concern, one that is not going to be sold or liquididated in the near future. This implies that the existing resources of the business, such as the plant and equipment, will be used in order to produce goods, and not simply sold in tomorrow's market. If this concept were not used, the accounting reports might instead attempt to measure what the business is currently worth to the owner at market values, but that is not current practice.

Guideline 5   measuring in actual cost

The resources of the company are shown at their cost and not at current values. The amounts shown against assets listed in the balance sheet of a company do not aim to show what those assets could be sold for. If anyone wants to know the current value of a business, then the balance sheet will not provide the answer. In this respect the economic snapshot shown on the balance sheet always deviates from that which would be given by an up-to-date assessment of asset values, but it does ensure that objective evidence is the basis for recording transactions.

An up-to-date assessment involves making estimates, and it is always possible that informed people and managements will disagree about the right estimate. In the absence of an acceptable system which will provide objective evidence to assess the effect of changing price levels and asset values, accountants have decided at present not to take any action to revise the cost concept. As a compromise, when it is clear that asset values have increased, many companies periodically revalue their assets and incorporate the adjustments in the balance sheet. This represents an in-between stage, and does not ensure, even in those cases, that the balance sheet accurately shows the current value of the business.

The accuracy of the balance sheet

The desire for objective evidence extends beyond the accounting problems of changes in the price level and affects the recording of many transactions. For instance, if the company pays nothing for an item it acquires, the item will not usually appear in the accounting records. The goodwill built up by a company as a result of successful trading is not shown on the balance sheet. Yet the valuation of this item is vitally important when a company is considering selling the whole or a part of its enterprise.

Other resources are also omitted from the balance sheet. Leased assets are not included, although it is possible for a company to acquire most or even all of its capital in use by such arrangements.

The balance sheet is a statement of stewardship and therefore expresses historical costs. The purpose of the balance sheet is not to show future worth, and so the statement is not shown in present values.

The equation: claims = assets gives an impression of accuracy which can be misleading unless the basic assumptions used in the construction of the balance sheet are thoroughly understood. The fact that the total of the list of assets exactly equals the total of the list of claims is no guarantee that a complete snapshot of the activities of the company is on view. In taking the snapshot the accountant has used a camera with a limited viewfinder and built-in filters. Other accountants, using cameras with rather different viewfinders and filters, can produce very different impressions of the same subject. Yet each snapshot could quite reasonably be justified by its accountant as representing a true and fair view of the affairs of the company.

Case study no. 4 – the balance sheet of Hardy Heating Co Ltd

Mrs Jean Wilkins had proved quite a surprise to everyone. As John Marsh said to his managing director one day, 'I'm not surprised that she made a good job of learning all about the books of account, and how to keep them, but she's also made an excellent job of preparing the year-end financial statements, and I reckon that that's really something.' 'Yes', said Hardy, 'but it's one thing to prepare them, and quite another to understand them, as I know to my cost. Or perhaps you feel that having done all the detailed work of preparing them, she's bound to have understood most of them.' 'Well, no. I wish I could say that, but it wouldn't be true. Accountants are not always as good at analysis and interpretation as one would like them to be, and I feel that it often stems from an insufficient understanding of these statements,' replied Marsh.

But he thought about this a little more when he was back in his own office, and in particular he wondered whether Jean Wilkins viewed a balance sheet in the way that he did. He decided to ask her. 'I suppose that my overall view of the balance sheet is of a statement of liabilities and assets', she said. 'Fair enough', said John, 'or you could look at it as a statement which tells you the sources of the capital in use in the company, and where it is invested by the company. Let's get the balance sheet out and take a look at the sources of capital first.' 'Do you mind if I ask a few questions as we go through?' queried Jean. 'Of course not', was the reply.

'To start with, looking at the balance sheet (see Figure 2.2), it would seem that the total amount invested in the company is £260,345.' 'You could say that', replied John, 'though accountants normally take the view that the current liabilities are not really money invested or capital employed. In which case, the total invested in the company would be £175,113. And do remember that this is a balance sheet figure at a particular point in time.' 'How would you classify the total money invested? I ask this because my technical college teacher was always talking about classification in accounting.' John replied, 'There is permanent capital and debt capital, or shareholders' funds and borrowed funds. The first classification is obvious enough, as long as you remember to add in the reserves, or profits which have been retained. And debt capital is all the rest, that's capital borrowed from or owing to ordinary or special creditors. Of this, some is more long-term than others. In our balance sheet, for example, the future tax liability is not payable for 21 months, and the loan capital has 10 years to go before redemption is required; neither of these items can be thought of as claims which will arise immediately, so there is the reasonable argument that these should be kept quite separate from current liabilities.'

Jean took up the discussion again, 'Isn't it a pretty fine line between future taxation and current taxation when there's just 12 months' difference between payment dates, and couldn't you argue that even current taxation is very different from creditors, which, in theory, are payable at next month-end?' 'Yes, true, and it's even further complicated by the fact that bank overdraft may become a permanent feature of the capital used by a business. You see, we've incurred an overdraft for the first time in this accounting year, but for all I know at the moment, we may live on overdraft in the future. In other words, it may become long-term capital, but it will always be immediately repayable. What about the assets which are represented by all this capital?'

Jean said that she saw the need to write down the fixed

1967				
£	£		£	£
		Authorised capital		
	10,000	10,000 6% pref. shares of £1 each		10,000
	50,000	50,000 ordinary shares of £1 each		50,000
	60,000			60,000
		Issued capital		
	10,000	10,000 6% pref. shares of £1 each		10,000
	50,000	50,000 ordinary shares of £1 each		50,000
	60,000			60,000
		Retained profits		
35,000		General reserve	45,000	
11,534	46,534	Profit and loss account	16,613	61,613
	106,534			121,613
	10,800	*Future tax liability*		13,500
	30,000	*Loan capital:* Electrical trades		
		Finance company (5%)	30,000	
		ICFC (7%)	10,000	40,000
		Current liabilities		
47,146		Creditors	52,143	
–		Bank overdraft	16,689	
3,290		Dividends due	3,290	
12,460		Current taxation	13,110	
	62,896			85,232
	£ 210,230		£	260,345

Fig. 2.2   Hardy Heating Co Ltd — balance sheet as at 30 September 1968 (two-sided)

assets by providing for depreciation, but that she had some reservations about how the fixed percentages for the different types of fixed assets were determined. John replied that it was, in any business, a matter of making an intelligent guess at the lives of individual machines and other equipment, and that you never really knew what depreciation had been until the plant was scrapped or sold. 'Of course,' he said, 'there are some similar problems, aren't there, with putting a value on stocks for balance sheet purposes? Not quite the same, but what I mean is that they have to be valued and one has to decide the basis.' 'I suppose so,' said Jean, 'but it

1967

		Fixed assets	Original cost	Accum. depn.	WDV
£	£		£	£	£
29,648		Plant and machinery	78,599	40,718	37,881
3,370		Motor vehicles	4,151	1,818	2,333
4,050		Fixtures and fittings	6,594	2,964	3,900
37,068			89,344	45,230	44,114

		Current assets			
	89,427	Stocks	125,515		
	81,643	Debtors	90,600		
	2,092	Bank balance and cash	116		
173,162		/			216,231
210,230					260,345

doesn't give us much trouble, because we've got some well-established rules, agreed by Mr Hardy with the auditors. I gather these were fixed way back. Wouldn't it be fair to say that to be consistent is the main thing?'

'Yes, but accuracy is as important as consistency. I wouldn't like to think that we were consistently wrong, would you?' Jean's reaction to this was to say that at least one could be pretty sure about the physical aspects of the stock-taking, since the factory was always shut down for two days each year for a complete stock-taking, and she knew that this job was done under the close supervision of Sam Howell, who showed great enthusiasm for it. John's reply was to the effect that it was a great pity that there were not adequate records of certain parts of the stock so as to preclude the necessity of shutting down. 'When you are studying accountancy in the early phases, you just do not realise the link which exists between physical activities in the factory and the financial statements for which the accounting department is responsible,' said Jean. 'For instance, the balance sheet, being partly a summary of the company's assets, reflects things which are out there in the factory. On the other hand, it does not reflect the most important assets which the company has, namely people and their skills. One cannot deny the fact that this company is a successful one, and I know that its success depends to a considerable extent on how effectively the assets are utilised, but it is the skills of people like Mr Hardy and Mr Howell which make for this effectiveness.'

'That's enough of that. We can't have someone who should be concerned mainly with the figures becoming philosophical,' joked John Marsh. 'Our job is very much to conserve the company's assets. There is still one figure on the balance sheet which we haven't discussed yet. That's this big figure of debtors. Is that a sensible figure?' Jean explained that this figure came straight out of the debtors' ledger, and that great care was taken to satisfy herself that the debts were all safe and sound. 'Fine, that means that the balance sheet is as realistic a document as it can be,' said John; 'after all it is only a list of balances, detailing the assets and the claims against those assets, and we shouldn't claim that it is anything more than that.' Jean's reaction to this comment was swift, 'Does anyone ever suggest that the balance sheet portrays more than that, then?'

Required
1   *What impressions do uninformed people have of the balance sheet?*
2   *Devise a form of balance sheet which brings out more clearly the 'Claims and assets' aspects.*
3   *Explain the value of comparative figures in the balance sheet.*

Case study no. 5 – the balance sheet should show what the business is worth!

John Marsh explained to his managing director that in his opinion Mrs Wilkins had a good knowledge of the balance sheet, and that this knowledge would improve now that she had mastered the basic bookkeeping and could spare a little time to consider the concepts and philosophies, rather than just concentrate on the mechanics. 'Well, if you are going to talk as broadly as that about one of the bits of paper which you prepare, perhaps you would care to clear my mind a little about the balance sheet. Shouldn't it show the value of the business?' said Hardy. John Marsh explained that the balance sheet was basically a simple document, a list of balances from the ledgers, taken out on a particular day. It could not show the value of the business, he said, because it was kept in actual cost terms, not in values. The managing director felt that needed some explanation.

'There are many examples of this,' Marsh replies. 'For instance, we do not own any freehold land, but many companies do. Often this land was purchased many years ago, quite cheaply by comparison with present day prices, and normally the balance sheet will show the land at its cost, not in any way reflecting the current worth of this asset.' 'But there have been many instances in recent years, surely, when

41

companies have revalued assets, not only land, but buildings, plant and equipment. In these cases, wouldn't the balance sheet more truly represent the value of the business?' John Marsh said that this was true, but it was normally a spot re-valuation for some particular purpose, such as prompted when the Companies Act 1948 came into force, or when the directors of a company felt, perhaps for an imminent take-over reason, that the balance sheet should more truly reflect the value of the assets. In these instances revaluations were infrequent, so that it was only once in a while that the balance sheet could be considered up to date. 'And in any case, accounting statements never reflect factors which are not properly quantifiable. For instance, a company builds up goodwill as a result of its reputation for products as well as its profitable activities, and this is not shown in the balance sheet. I mean, when and how should one put a value on good-will?'

'There's even more to it, I suppose. You've had a good look at the business by now, and I don't know whether you consider that Sam and I are assets or liabilities, but we do have some assets in the way of people with particular skills, and they're not valued in the balance sheet, are they?' queried Hardy. 'No, this is just another example of the fact that the balance sheet is no more than an accounting report which tells us what assets we own, at their cost or market value, whichever the lower, and from what sources the money has come to purchase those assets. On the other hand, having said that the balance sheet is an accounting report, it is as well to remember that it can be presented in different ways. By now, you are very used to the two-sided balance sheet, but I would like you to see a vertical balance sheet, which I think por-trays the picture much more clearly.' Having said this, John went away, to return with the new draft shown in Figure 2.3.

Required

1   *What limitations does a balance sheet possess which neither Hardy nor Marsh has mentioned in this conver-sation?*

2   *Are any of the limitations of the two-sided balance sheet removed by the vertical balance sheet?*

3   Are there any sound arguments for regular revaluation of assets, so that the balance sheet can more truly reflect the worth of the business?

4   Would asset revaluation in fact take us much nearer to a calculation of business worth?

Accumulate profit

	1967		Capital and reserves	1968	
	£	£		£	£
			Authorised capital		
	10,000		10,000 6% pref. shares of £1 each		10,000
	50,000		50,000 ordinary shares of £1 each		50,000
		60,000			60,000
			Issued capital		
	10,000		10,000 6% pref. shares of £1 each		10,000
	50,000		50,000 ordinary shares of £1 each		50,000
		60,000			60,000
			Reserves		
35,000			General reserve	45,000	
11,534			Profit and loss account	16,613	
	46,534				61,613
	106,534				121,613
	10,800		*Future tax liability*		13,500
	30,000		*Loan capital:* Electrical trades	30,000	
			Finance company (5%)		
			ICFC (7%)	10,000	
					40,000
	147,334				175,113

Represented by:

	£	£	Original cost £	Accum. depn. £	WDV £
Fixed assets					
Plant and machinery			78,599	40,718	37,881
Motor vehicles			4,151	1,818	2,333
Fixtures and fittings			4,050	6,594	2,694	3,900
		37,068	89,344	45,230	44,114
Current assets					
Stocks	89,427		125,515		
Debtors	81,643		90,600		
Bank balance and cash	2,092		116		
	173,162		216,231		
Less: current liabilities					
Creditors	47,146		52,143		
Bank overdraft			16,689		
Dividends due	3,290		3,290		
Current taxation	12,460		13,110		
	62,896		85,232		
Net current assets		110,266			130,999
		147,334			175,113

Fig. 2.3 Hardy Heating Co Ltd – balance sheet as at 30 September 1968 (vertical)

Case study no. 6 – 'the strength of the company lies in its plans'

After a visit from representatives of a large firm of wholesalers to whom the company sold many of its products, the managing director decided to talk to John Marsh about planning. Perhaps this was inspired by the fact that the wholesalers had been very keen to get some assurances from Hardy about the existing range of products and possible additions to it, and they had been extolling the virtues of long-range planning in business affairs. Hardy wanted to make sure that Marsh understood that he was a great believer in planning, though John felt that the examples which he gave were not very much to do with long-range planning in the sense that their visitors had been talking about. Hardy was a systematic man, and seemed to think that if one measured up the dining-room before papering it, and made sure that one obtained the right number of rolls of paper, then this was planning at its best. Nevertheless, to be fair, John was getting a good impression of his managing director and felt that an extension of the systematic management approach into some sensible planning, including financial planning, was on the cards.

'That's what I dislike a little about the financial statements which you accountants prepare. From what I've seen, they're entirely historical, and history, apart from the fact that it never repeats itself, is not planning. I feel that one of the strengths of this little business of ours is that we have grown

46

in a methodical manner based on sensible plans. Sam is a very practical chap, and may not appear to be too systematic, but he shares my view on planning. Your balance sheet hasn't really got any place in planning, has it?' asked Hardy. John Marsh explained that the balance sheet not only accounted for historical facts, but it could be used as a framework for planning. 'The way I look at it, a business has two financial objectives. It must be profitable, making an adequate return on the money which is invested in it, and it must be liquid, in other words, it must be in a position to pay its way. The balance sheet not only gives an indication as to the liquid position of a business, but it also indicates quite clearly the various factors which have to be controlled if liquidity is to be kept in balance. And apart from that, the balance sheet indicates the amount of capital which is employed, and this is the basis for determining what profit return is required.'

'Perhaps you could tell me a little more about using the balance sheet as a framework for planning,' said Hardy. Marsh explained that classification of the items in the balance sheet gave some clues to planning requirements, and he instanced the fact that it was necessary to look carefully at the sources of capital, in order to keep a balance between the various funds items. 'The gearing of capital in the business and debt capacity is something which needs to be looked at before the need for extra capital arises, and in the very long term as well,' John said. He explained that there is also a considerable problem of deciding where the funds of the business should be invested, whether in fixed assets or in the working capital area. Again, he suggested, this should be the subject of proper planning and control.

Required

1   Is John Marsh exaggerating the role of the balance sheet in planning?
2   At the beginning of a trading period, is it possible to plan the balance sheet as it will be at the end of the trading period? If so, what work would have to be done to take out such a balance sheet?
3   John Marsh said that the balance sheet indicates the amount of capital which is employed. Which figure is he referring to?

3

The profit and loss account

Definition of profit

In Chapter 2 it was stressed that one major source of capital is the profit retained within the company. Students are often confused when they see the item 'retained profits' shown under the heading of 'liabilities', but a simple example should help to clear the issue.

Assume that a firm sells goods which cost £500 for £600 cash. It is useful to separate the two elements in this transaction. If we examine the £600 sale in isolation, this results in an increase in owners' claims of £600 and an inflow of assets (cash) of £600. This dual movement is necessary if we are to observe guideline 3 (claims = assets). An increase in owners' claims from current operations like this is known as revenue.

But the firm no longer owns goods costing £500, and if this fact is treated in isolation, there is a decrease in owners' claims of £500, and an outflow of assets of £500. Such a decrease in owners' claims arising from current operations is known as expense. The relationship can be expressed in an equation as follows:

$$\text{Profit} = \text{increase in owners'claims} = \text{revenue} - \text{expenses}$$
$$= \text{increase in net assets.}$$

If expenses are greater than revenue, a loss has occurred, and the claims of the owners of the business have been reduced accordingly.

Now assume that the company sells goods which cost £500 for £600 on credit. The two elements can be distinguished:

(Revenue) increase in owners' claims   £600: increase in assets (debtors) £600
Less
(Expenses) decrease in owners' claims £500: decrease in assets (stock)   £500
Equals

Profit: increase in owners' claims   £100: increase in assets   £100

The profit and loss account gives details of revenue and expenses and can be regarded as a convenient way of summarising temporary charges to owners' claims. This helps to explain the presence of retained profits under the heading of liabilities.

The owners, as a result of profitable operations, now have an additional claim against the company. This claim is a general one against total assets, and not a preferred one against cash, or against any other single asset.

Profit need not be held in cash. Profit is an increase in net assets, and therefore may be reflected in an increase in assets generally, or a decrease in liabilities. The cash balance will be altered by transactions quite apart from those affecting revenue and expense.

This concept of profit has important implications in planning the progress of a company. A company might well be profitable and yet have a serious shortage of cash. On the other hand, surplus cash may exist in a company which is running at a loss, particularly if the company is unable to find a profitable use for the cash.

Two guidelines help to measure profit; the first deals with the problem of revenue, and the second deals with the measurement of expenses.

Guideline 6   revenue is realised on delivery

A number of events take place before a sale is actually achieved. Assuming that the fixed assets and raw material stocks are already in existence, a typical list of these events would be:

1 On 1 January an order for finished goods is received.
2 Material is drawn from stores, and is worked upon by labour. The work is now in progress.
3 The work in progress is now complete; the goods are finished.
4 The finished goods are delivered to the customer.
5 The customer pays cash for the goods.

Revenue is realised when the goods or services are delivered, i.e. at step 4.

Revenue is not realised at step 1, when the order is received, even though the company can be reasonably certain of achieving the sale. Nor is it realised at step 5, when the customer pays cash for the goods. Since profit is the difference between revenue and expenses, and since revenue is not necessarily realised when the cash is received, profit is not necessarily held in cash.

There are, however, two exceptions to this.

First, when a firm is working on long-term contracts covering several accounting periods, revenue is realised by spreading the income over the period of the contract in proportion to the work completed. This method of measurement is often used in shipbuilding or construction projects.

Second, when a firm is selling by long-term instalment contracts, and the customer may not complete the payments, revenue is often realised only when instalment payments are actually received.

In the first case, revenue is realised earlier than is usual in guideline 6, and in the second case revenue is realised later.

There is no necessary connection between the realisation of revenue for profit computation and the receipt of cash. Revenue may be realised before, during, or after the period in which the associated cash is received.

Guideline 7 _expenses must be matched with revenue_

In guideline 6 we dealt with the problem of realising revenue. The last guideline, 7, is concerned with the fact that expenses recognised in an accounting period are matched against the revenue realised under guideline 6.

Once one has selected an accounting period, which might cover one day or twelve months, one problem is how to determine the revenue and expenses that belong to that period. Guideline 6 shows how to determine the revenue that belongs to an accounting period. In following guideline 7, the accountant assigns costs to periods of time on the basis of association with revenue.

If the accountant realises revenue of £100,000 in an accounting period, the profit and loss account should include all expenses associated with that revenue irrespective of whether the costs occurred in past years, in the present year, or will occur in cash in the future years. The expense of raw materials or finished goods during an accounting period is not related to goods purchased or paid for during that period. The expense is related to the outflow of assets involved in earning the revenue which has been realised.

Goods which have not yet been used to earn revenue are treated as an asset and are shown as such on the balance sheet. Assets can therefore be viewed as stored-up costs; during the accounting period some of these stored-up costs will be released as expenses. Expenses can be defined as used up assets.

Timing the release of assets as expenses is a fundamental accounting problem. Whilst guideline 7 can be expressed simply in principle, difficult problems must be faced in practice.

For instance, the cost of buildings or equipment to be charged in an accounting period as depreciation must be decided. The aim of depreciation is to allocate the cost of the fixed asset to the particular periods or products that benefit from its use.

The two main methods in use are the straight-line method and the reducing balance method. The first involves allocating the original cost of the asset (less its estimated scrap value, if any) in equal instalments over the periods of the asset's expected use. The second involves allocating as an expense in each period a fixed percentage of the asset's residual book value, so as to reduce the asset to its estimated salvage value at the end of its life. This latter method provides higher charges in earlier years and lower charges in later years, while the straight-line method provides equal charges in each year.

Charging depreciation as an expense against profits does not automatically create a fund of cash out of which spent assets can be replaced. However, it does result in retaining assets within the company which might otherwise have been distributed. These assets may be held in several different forms and management must ensure that a proper balance between assets is held so that fixed assets can be replaced without undue difficulty.

Another problem is that some costs are extremely difficult to allocate to specific years. Advertising costs incurred in one year for instance may well benefit future years, but since we cannot be sure of the benefit, we cannot with complete accuracy allocate the advertising costs to specific years. The accountant usually adopts a conservative attitude and follows the maxim 'if in doubt, write it off'. Research and development costs often create similar problems.

It is usual conservative practice in accounting to anticipate losses but not to anticipate profits. For instance, if the anticipated net realisable value of stock is less than the original cost, it is customary to anticipate this loss, and to value the stock at net realisable value. Similarly if the estimated current market replacement cost is less than the original cost the lower value is used. The result is that stock is valued at the lowest of (a) cost (b) realisable value, and (c) replacement price.

Limitations of the profit and loss account

As in the case of the balance sheet, it is possible to be mislead by the apparent accuracy of the profit and loss account. The measurement of both revenue and expenses requires estimates, and in making such estimates, differences of opinion will exist between accountants. The true profit can only be shown when the assets of the enterprise have been finally and completely liquidated. Accounting statements are collections not only of historical facts, but of opinions and estimates. To minimise the possible dangers of their opinions, accountants simply ensure that profits are not overstated nor losses understated.

This leads to a major inconsistency in the treatment of revenues and expenses. Revenues are recorded only when realised, but impending losses are usually recognised and included. It also leads to an understatement of asset values, and the creation of secret reserves.

The distinction between fixed and current assets must be a matter of opinion in practice, and thus the computation of profit may be affected by the objectives of the firm. A machine tool in one engineering company may be regarded as fixed capital, but in another company the machine tool may be classed as part of the circulating capital.

Measuring in money terms, the accountant assumes that the pound is an unchanging yardstick. Changes in the value of money are ignored, and so the concept of profit is not expressed in real terms. Accountants' desire for objectivity to some extent distorts accounting statements in times of inflation or deflation.

The profit and loss account is principally a report to outsiders. Certainly as far as management is concerned, the profit and loss account has severe limitations, both of time and detail. To run a business efficiently, management needs much more information about revenue and expenses, and this information must be available more frequently. From a management point of view, it is necessary to think of an accounting period of one month, or one week, or even one day, rather than one year. The global figures given in the profit and loss account must be analysed to produce information about the detailed activities of the company. And the emphasis in management information must be on the future rather than on the past.

The funds statement

Students and managers often are perplexed as to what has happened to the profits earned during an accounting period, and a statement showing changes in assets and claims can be a most useful link between the two essential financial statements—the profit and loss account and the balance sheet. The funds statement shows how the profit earned has been reflected by changes in assets and other balance sheet items.

Let us compare the balance sheet at 1 January 19X1 with the balance sheet at 31 December 19X2.

	1 January 19X1 £	31 December 19X2 £	Change £
Assets	10,000	14,000	+ 4,000
Less liabilities	6,000	8,500	+ 2,500
Owners' claims	4,000	5,500	+ 1,500

Assuming no introductions or withdrawals of capital by the owners, the claims have increased by the profit earned, £1,500. This profit of £1,500, is reflected in an increase in assets of £4,000 less an increase in liabilities of £2,500. We can express the changes in the two balance sheets as follows.

Funds statement for the period 1 January to 31 December, 19X1   £

Funds provided

Increase in owners' claims arising from profit on operations	1,500
Increase in liabilities	2,500
	4,000

Funds applied

Increase in assets	4,000

Details of changes in individual items of assets and claims are not given here, but clearly some assets may have increased while other assets have decreased. Similarly during the accounting period some liabilities may have increased while others have decreased. It is useful to distinguish between these items in compiling a more detailed statement which should include the following:

A Sources of funds
1 Profits from operations before charging depreciation.
2 Capital contributions by owners.
3 Increases in long-term liabilities.
4 Increases in short-term liabilities.
5 Reductions in short-term financial assets.
6 Reductions in long-term financial assets.
7 Proceeds from the sale of fixed assets.
B Uses of funds
1 Withdrawals of profits or capital by owners.
2 Reductions in long-term liabilities.
3 Reductions in short-term liabilities.
4 Increases in short-term financial assets.
5 Increases in long-term financial assets.
6 Expenditure on fixed assets.

Since the charge for depreciation does not involve any actual outflow of funds, it is necessary to use the figure of profits before depreciation as the funds earned from current profitable operations.

Total sources of funds in any period must equal total uses of funds (guideline 3). In addition to historical statements, forward plans need to be developed to cover the sources of funds and their use. This planning cannot be carried out by the accountant alone, since other managers are responsible for the management of resources. Decisions by other managers affect the source and use of funds, and participation and co-ordination in planning the decision is essential.

Case study no. 7 – the profit and loss account

John Marsh felt that his conversations with Jean Wilkins on technical accounting matters were paying off. She was even more interested than ever to tie up all the routine accounting in order that she could devote more time to consider and improve the less routine matters. Their discussion on the balance sheet had been useful, and John felt it was time for a similar session on the other financial statement. He invited Jean into his office and asked her what she thought about the profit and loss account. (See Figures 3.1 and 3.2.)

'You sound just like my technical college teacher all over again, but at least while I am here I have the opportunity of relating it to practical examples, so here goes. To me, the profit and loss account has two main characteristics. Firstly, it acts as a bridge between the balance sheets, and secondly it is a statement of sales income less costs, to show whether the business has made a profit or not.'

John Marsh agreed with her definition and asked why she felt there was a distinction between gross profit and net profit in the account. 'It's even more than that', replied Jean. 'We classify the costs of the business in the profit and loss account in such a way that we can arrive firstly at the cost of production, then the cost of finished production, then the production cost of sales. These are important classifications. I suppose that they should tie up with costing activities in the firm somehow, though they don't here. But I haven't answered your question. I suppose we distinguish between gross profit and net profit merely to emphasise that some of the costs which we deduct from sales turnover are the indirect costs of production, administration, selling and distribution.

Again John Marsh agreed, pointing out that while the relationship between net profit and sales income could be important, the relationship between gross profit and sales income might be even more significant, though the trends of both were worth observing. 'What would you say are our particular problems in preparing the profit and loss account?' he asked. Jean explained that there were not many routine problems. She suggested that the problems were specific year-end problems of valuing stocks and work-in-progress, calculating the provision for depreciation and dealing with accruals and prepayments. 'I have always imagined that these were the standard problems in any business.'

'What rules have you followed in dealing with them?' asked Marsh. Jean explained that the rules had been handed down to her as far as stock valuation and depreciation were concerned, since in both cases the procedures were standard. Raw material stocks were always valued at cost or market value, whichever was lower, though a few problems were thrown up by the changes in non-ferrous metal prices. The valuation of work-in-progress was handed to her in summary form by Tom Rose and she knew that it was a prime cost valuation, with a 100 per cent on direct labour added to cover some part of the overhead expenses. The finished stock valuation was 'a piece of cake', she said, because all the quantities of finished products in stock were priced at their average selling prices, less 30 per cent to cover profit and some part of the overhead expenses. As for depreciation, she kept a fairly detailed plant register with separate sections for the three main headings of fixed assets, (see Figure 3.3), and there were only three separate rates of depreciation, all based on original cost. She had had no reason to challenge the procedures which had been handed over to her. On the subject of accruals and prepayments, she followed what she hoped was a commonsense approach, merely carrying forward payments made in respect of the costs of the ensuing period, and reserving for costs of the current period those which were not yet paid for.

'We'll obviously want to take a look at the way we do many of these things, but I'm sure that your commonsense approach will prove right when we do,' said John Marsh.

Required
1 *Comment on the impressions which uninformed people have of the profit and loss account.*
2 *Appraise the value of comparative figures in the profit and loss account.*
3 *How are the accounting 'rules' of stock valuation and depreciation provisions made?*

— Estimate for a cost when you have no bill.

— Raw Material Cost. + 100% Added. on the labour

Case study no. 8 – where has all the profit gone?

It was a bit of a shock one day when John Marsh's managing director said casually, 'We had a good year last year from a profit point of view. The figure was near enough £35,000. Where did it all go? I know that you accountants can explain it in lots of ways, and as a layman, I think I understand. But it might be revealing to both of us for you to carry out the exercise.' 'That's a job I can do quite quickly in overall financial terms,' said John. 'Good', replied the managing director, 'perhaps you'd bear in mind when preparing your figures that, in spite of the profit, we've been hard up for cash for some time. You might explain why.' *Stock & Investment*

John was in his office only a very short time preparing this statement (see Figure 3.4).

'I don't know whether this is exactly what you had in mind, Mr Hardy,' said John. 'It's a very simple overall statement, showing what additional capital became available to us during the year, and how we've used it, either by design or by accident. You'll see right away that most of our additional capital came from profit, and that we've used most of it to finance increases in current assets.'

'What can you use this for?' queried the managing director. 'I must say I've never seen anything quite like it before.'

'It's got several uses. It lets you keep an eye on cash flows in the business, what funds are becoming available and how they are being used. You can watch key points, the current gearing of the capital intake, for example, or the current allocation of capital between fixed and working capital areas. Then, as far as working capital is concerned, you can check how much extra money is tied up in stocks, for example. In this case, stocks have gone up from last year by £36,000, that's 40 per cent, while the increase in sales has been only 12 per cent. Then there are debtors, another area in which the capital tied up could be critical. This figure has increased by £9,000 during the year, 11 per cent, against a sales increase of 12 per cent.

Hardy replied that it might be useful to look at this sort of statement over a longer period of years to get a picture of trends, and John Marsh agreed, adding that it could be useful for budgeting ahead as well.

Required

1 Why did John Marsh make the point that this statement was only in 'overall financial terms'?

2 What is the merit in preparing interim statements of this type?

3 Explain Marsh's 'by design or by accident' comment.

Manufacturing, Production and Trading Account

Debit side

	1967 £	1967 £	1967 £	1967 £
Stock of raw materials and components at beginning of year	20,472		29,946	
Purchases	117,542		158,402	
	138,014		188,348	
Stock of raw materials and components at end of year	29,946		44,696	
Raw Materials Consumed		108,068		143,652
Direct Wages		55,189		59,837
		163,257		203,489
Work-in-Progress at beginning of year	16,182		14,562	
Cost of Production b/down	163,257		203,489	
	179,439		218,051	
Work-in-Progress at end of year	14,562		26,940	
Cost of Finished Production		164,877		191,111
		164,877		191,111
Stock of finished goods at beginning of year	47,282		44,919	
Cost of finished production b/down	164,877		191,111	
	212,159		236,030	
Stock of finished goods at end of year	44,919		53,879	

Credit side

	£	£	1967 £
Cost of production c/down		203,489	163,257
		203,489	163,257
Cost of finished production c/down		191,111	164,877
		191,111	164,877
Sales	364,021		
Less Returns	8,179	355,842	317,019

167,240	*182,151*	*Cost of Sales*			
149,779	*173,691*	Gross profit c/down			
317,019	*355,842*			*355,842*	*317,019*
			Gross Profit b/down	173,691	149,779
41,882	45,312	Indirect wages			
18,583	19,672	Salaries			
6,585	6,845	National Health Insurance			
1,107	1,384	Graduated Pensions			
15,863	19,327	Tools and consumables			
5,894	7,270	Repairs and renewals			
6,427	7,891	Fuel, gas and electricity			
2,976	3,012	Rent and rates			
1,209	1,120	Insurances			
—	1,200	H.P. interest			
278	1,847	Bank charges			
2,318	2,886	Selling expenses			
1,642	2,253	Miscellaneous expenses			
7,349	9,218	Depreciation			
600	625	Audit fee			
7,150	7,650	Directors' remuneration			
1,000	2,000	Interest on loan capital			
28,916	34,179	Net profit for year			
149,779	173,691			173,691	*149,779*

Fig. 3.1   Hardy Heating Co Ltd – Detailed Manufacturing, Trading and Profit and Loss Statement for the year ended 30 September 1968

		£	*1967* *£*
Profit on trading		34,179	*28,916*

after deducting	£	£
DEPRECIATION	9,218	*7,349*
AUDIT FEE	625	*600*
DIRECTORS' REMUNERATION	7,650	*7,150*
	17,493	*15,099*

Corporation Tax		13,500	*10,800*
Profit after tax		20,679	*18,116*
Dividends payable on pref. shares net	353		
Income Tax	247	600	*600*
10% on ordinary shares net	2,937		
Income Tax	2,063	5,000	*5,000*
		5,600	*5,600*
Profit after tax and dividends		15,079	*12,516*
Transfer to General Reserve		10,000	*10,000*
Addition to opening balance on			
Profit and loss account		5,079	*2,516*
Opening Balance on			
Profit and loss account		11,534	*9,018*
Balance carried forward		16,613	*11,534*

Fig. 3.2 Hardy Heating Co Ltd – Profit Statement for the year ended 30 September 1968. It gives minimum information in accordance with the Companies Acts.

PLANT AND MACHINERY

	Original Cost £	Accum. Depn. £	WDV £
Balance, 30 September 1967	64,226	34,578	29,648
Additions	15,274	—	15,274
	79,500	34,578	44,922
Sales and scrappings	(901)	(901)	—
Depreciation provision	—	7,041	(7,041)
Balance, 30 September 1968	78,599	40,718	37,881

MOTOR VEHICLES

	Original Cost £	Accum. Depn. £	WDV £
Balance, 30 September 1967	4,151	781	3,370
Depreciation provision	—	1,037	(1,037)
Balance, 30 September 1968	4,151	1,818	2,333

FIXTURES AND FITTINGS

	Original Cost £	Accum. Depn. £	WDV £
Balance, 30 September 1967	6,329	2,279	4,050
Additions	1,624	—	1,624
	7,953	2,279	5,674
Sales and Scrappings	(1,359)	(725)	(634)
Depreciation provision	—	1,140	(1,140)
Balance, 30 September 1968	6,594	2,694	3,900

Fig. 3.3 Hardy Heating Co Ltd – Schedule of Fixed Assets as at 30 September 1968

	£	£	£
Sources of additional capital			
Trading profit	34,179		
Add back depreciation	9,218		
		43,397	
Loan capital		10,000	
Available from creditors		4,997	
			58,394
Dispositions of that capital			
Fixed assets, additions less disposals:			
Plant and machinery	15,274		
Fixtures and fittings	990		
		16,264	
Increased stocks	36,088		
Increased debtors	8,957		
		45,045	
Payments:			
Dividends	3,290		
Tax	12,460		
		15,750	
			77,059
Deterioration in cash position through the year			18,665

Source of Application of funds (handwritten annotation)

Fig. 3.4   A 'Where got, where gone' statement for the year ended 30 September 1968

Case study no. 9 – 'more detail, more often, please'

John Marsh made the point that the annual profit and loss account had limitations. He had already admitted to many people around the business that accounting in general, with all its man-made rules, had its limitations. Remarks like these are bound to make for extra work, and they did on this occasion, too. The managing director sent for John and said, 'I'd like to take you up on one of the points we discussed in connection with the annual profit and loss account. You said that it was ludicrous for a business of any size to be waiting until the end of the year before getting precise details on profitability. Well, in spite of all that certain business friends of mine say about keeping tabs on the business by watching the sales figures, the cash levels and so on, I agree with you. When can we have monthly accounts?'

John Marsh took a deep breath, swallowed hard and said 'Well, I'm bound to run into a few problems, material consumption, stocks and so on. But I reckon I can let you have the first set of monthly accounts in a few days time. Stock is always a bogey for interim accounting, but if you're prepared to accept some figures for stocks which are assessments rather than accurate valuations, then we can get started. We haven't got all the various mechanisms required to deal properly with accruals and prepayments, but these are matters of accounting routine, and I can lay these on quickly, particularly since we have such an excellent bookkeeper in Mrs Wilkins.'

In fact, the first monthly accounts were a valiant attempt. John was able to produce two previous months for comparison, and this is what he presented to his managing director (Figure 3.5).

Sam Howell turned up to talk over the accounts with Jack Hardy and John Marsh. John found it difficult to get Sam to treat the accounts seriously. The annual profit and loss account was always a bit of a joke to Sam, but in the end he viewed it seriously because it had the final stamp of the auditors on it. But interim accounts, to Sam, were statements that were 'written on the back of a fag packet', although, in fact, John Marsh had been very careful to have them typed on the electric machine and on the best paper. Much of the discussion, inevitably, centred on the variability of the profits shown by the statement, and on the problems connected with getting and valuing stock figures. John said it was going to be extremely difficult proceeding with costing arrange-

Mat.
% of Sales

	September £	October £	November £
Sales	22,846 *32%*	27,448 *34.8%*	31,988 *38.7%*
Prime costs:			
Direct matls.	7,369	9,542	12,393
Direct wages	4,009	4,563	5,402
	11,378	14,105	17,795
Gross profit	11,468	13,343	14,193
Overheads:			
Indirect wages	3,802	3,647	3,719
Salaries	1,650	1,662	1,667
Tool and cons.	1,703	1,683	1,205
Depreciation	800	800	800
All other overheads	5,807	5,783	5,750
	13,762	13,530	13,141
Margins	2,294 (loss)	187 (loss)	1,052 (profit)

Fig. 3.5   Monthly accounts 1968

Wages have gone up. (Bonus Payment)
materials have gone up (

ments in the factory until better stock control procedures were in use.

Sam Howell jumped in at this point. 'I take it that from now on we shall be having monthly trading statements. This is an improvement, particularly if we can get some guarantees that the figures in them are accurate. From what you are saying, I gather that we might have to have a closer look at stock control. Well, let's do that together. It isn't an area for an accountant to look at on his own. We don't have stock control just to produce accounts.' 'I couldn't agree more,' replied John, 'I'd be delighted to join you any time for a thorough look at the procedures.'

But Sam Howell was in again, 'Before we all start getting very happy about the improvement in our accounting, can we be clear between ourselves that much more detail is really required than is shown on these trading statements. I've got Tom Rose doing a lot of work on costs of production, analysing costs to departments in particular. Shouldn't his work be tied up with these trading statements in some way?' 'Yes, it should, and I'd like to discuss with you ways of integrating the work of the accounting department and the costing work,' replied John. 'I hope I won't be too unpopular if I suggest that Tom Rose really ought to work for me.'

'As I see it, we all want information which will help us in doing our jobs,' retorted Howell. 'Apart from wanting to know how the business as a whole is faring, and on a regular monthly basis, I want a lot of information about departmental costs and efficiencies, and about product costs and profitabilities. Apart from that, I've no doubt that Mr Hardy wants a lot of facts and figures to do with costs, and Wilf Appleby must have some requirements as well. Why don't we all give you our ideas on the sort of information we think we need. I don't know how to go on after that, but it will probably be pretty clear to you.'

'Perhaps we could then talk about how all these information services should be laid on,' added Jack Hardy. All three submitted lists.

Jack Hardy

1 Annual and monthly financial statements, balance sheet and profit and loss account.

2 Periodic statements showing the profitability of individual products, and the separate channels of distribution.
3 Some measures of overall company performance and, if
possible, the performance of individual departments.
4 Regular statements illustrating the liquidity position.
5. *Forecasts.*

Sam Howell   Production Manager

1 Product costs and product prices compared.
2 Comparisons of overhead expenses, works in particular,
with direct material and direct labour.
3 Some departmental figures on cost, to give clues about
where significant spending occurs.
4 Occasional exercises to show the comparative costs of
different methods, for example, machine moulding as
compared with plastic moulding.

Wilf Appleby   Sales Manager

1 Comparisons of product selling prices with their costs.
2 Information on the income and costs of wholesale, retail
and industrial channels of distribution.
3 Schedule of selling costs compared with sales achieved.
4. Competition.

Required

*1   Comment on and interpret John Marsh's monthly
accounts.*
*2   How far are annual accounting, interim accounting and
cost accounting linked?*
*3   Are these lists of information requirements appropriate
to the managers' responsibilities?*
4   To whom should Tom Rose report?

4

Accounting ratios

Liquidity versus profitability

In Chapter 3 it was emphasised that the profit earned by the company need not necessarily be held in cash. The management of a company is therefore faced with problems of liquidity and profitability. Often a business will find that these two basic aims are in conflict, and that a compromise has to be made. For instance, when cash is tight the maintenance of liquidity may be more important than increased profits. In this situation, freedom of action in the operating functions of the company (e.g. marketing, production, purchasing) may be severely restricted by the need to conserve cash. Indeed, the ability of the company to obtain additional funds often depends to some extent on the liquid position. This interdependence reinforces the need for planning at the corporate level.

The basic aim of profitability can be viewed in two ways. First, the management aims to spread its investment in assets and products so that the return produced is as great as possible, without sacrificing too much liquidity. The relationship between fixed assets and current assets is important, together with the composition of the current assets. The profit obtained needs to be viewed in relation to the fixed assets and current assets employed in the business. Second, the management aims to use those sources of funds which will provide a return to the shareholders, as great as possible, without undertaking risks which might adversely affect future liquidity and/or profitability. This is a problem of financial gearing.

Management Decision, Whether new markets, or keep cash.

ratio of shareholders money Profit of business with outside capital (loans).

73

The company obtains gearing when it uses funds from sources other than the equity or owners' interest in the business. The attraction of such funds into the company requires the payment of a fixed return, and management must decide the extent to which gearing should be used. The balance between the sources of funds is important to the company since the 'after corporation tax' cost of borrowing is less than 5 per cent, whereas the comparable dividend returns on ordinary capital is at least 7½ per cent. Indeed, if the required cover of retained profits to dividends is taken into account, the cost of ordinary dividends is probably near 12½ per cent. These figures seem to recommend obtaining additional funds from borrowing at fixed interest rates. But over-gearing may adversely affect the liqudity of the company, and also produce undesirable fluctuations in the rate of return on owners' investment.

Preliminary steps in the analysis of financial statements

Management information on liquidity and profitability calls for detailed study of the relationships underlying the items in the profit and loss account and balance sheet. A useful first step in this study is to arrange the data of the financial statements in columnar or vertical form. This allows easy comparison of items within each accounting report, and also comparisons of items between them. If financial statements for a number of periods are available, successive vertical listings will make the study of the trend of the relationships between component items easier.

A further preliminary step is to arrange the classification of items within the financial statements so that significant relationships affecting liquidity and profitability can be easily calculated and interpreted. In analysing the profit and loss account it will probably be necessary to classify revenue items by product groups, and to classify and group expenses by type of expense, by products, and by operating departments. Items within the balance sheet will also need to be classified conveniently to facilitate the process of analysis and interpretation. Chapter 5 considers the classification of costs for management information purposes in greater detail.

The next basic step is to compute percentages from the listed vertical items. These calculations will show various convenient classifications of costs as a percentage of sales; individual assets as a percentage of total assets; and individual liabilities as a percentage of total liabilities. Even at this early stage in analysis, questions may be raised which may indicate ways of improving the overall efficiency of the business.

It should now be possible to look more closely at the relationships affecting liquidity and profitability. It is often useful to express relationships between items in the form of financial ratios.

Liquidity ratios

The best known indicator of short-term liquidity is the current ratio:

$$\frac{\text{current assets}}{\text{current liabilities}}$$

This ratio is a measure of the ability of the company to meet its current obligations. The underlying idea of this ratio is that in the short term current assets are converted into cash, which is used to meet current liabilities. A commonly quoted desirable current ratio is 2:1. However, as with all other generalisations on ratios, such rules of thumb must be regarded with some suspicion. The following figures for current assets and current liabilities give a current ratio of 3:1, which according to the rule of thumb is highly satisfactory.

Current assets	£	
Stocks of raw material	7,000	} *stock depends on sales.*
Stocks of work-in-progress	6,000	
Stocks of finished goods	1,000	
Debtors	3,000	] *very liquid*
Cash	1,000	
	18,000	

Current liabilities	
Trade creditors	5,000
Other creditors (tax)	1,000
	6,000

But close examination of the quality of the individual items making up the ratio indicates possible liquidity problems. If the trade creditors have been pressing hard for payment for some time, and if sales have only recently been made to debtors, the company has only £1,000 cash to meet immediate outstanding commitments of £6,000. The conversion of stocks at various stages of completion into debtors and then into cash may take place over such a long period of time that the company will be severely embarrassed by its inability to pay its creditors from immediate resources. Short-term creditors of the company will normally look for a substantial cushion of current assets to protect their claims. The bulk of current assets are often needed in business as a permanent feature and are therefore not available to meet current liabilities, unless the company is willing to reduce the size of the cushion. For this reason, and also because of the implications of unsold stocks in current assets, it is wise for the creditors and the management to examine the short-term relationship of cash inflows to cash outlays.

This relationship is expressed by the 'acid test ratio':

$$\frac{\text{cash + debtors}}{\text{current liabilities}}$$

In the example given, the ratio is $\dfrac{1,000 + 3,000}{6,000} = 0.6:1$

which is lower than the often quoted standard of 1:1. As we have seen, the low ratio in this example may give cause for concern, but it is quite possible for a company (buying on credit, selling for cash) to have an acid test ratio of less than 1, and have no immediate financial problems. The ratios must therefore be viewed against the economic background of the company, the terms of trade in the industry and markets in which it is operating, and the economic state of the national economy. Changes in ratios and their trends may be more significant than the absolute values and more useful than comparisons against doubtful rules of thumb. High liquidity ratios might well indicate financial strength to deal with short-term financing problems, but might also involve low profitability through poor utilisation of resources. It is necessary therefore to consider the relationships involved in profitability ratios.

Profitability ratios

The first approach is to consider the return realised on the investment in assets. Three basic factors affect this: capital employed; profit; and sales.

The return on capital employed can be expressed as an equation.

$$1\ \frac{\text{Profit}}{\text{Capital employed}} = 2\ \frac{\text{Sales}}{\text{Capital employed}} \times 3\ \frac{\text{Profit}}{\text{Sales}}$$

It is interesting to see that the return on capital employed (Ratio 1) is affected by the turnover of assets (Ratio 2) and also the profit margin (Ratio 3). Many companies put a great deal of effort into cost reduction techniques in an attempt to improve Ratio 3. Certainly this is a significant tactic, but often the most important single problem is the utilisation of assets; concentration on Ratio 2 may also produce an improvement in Ratio 1.

Both capital employed and profit can be defined in a number of different ways. From the investors' point of view, capital employed will consist of total assets minus all liabilities, or alternatively of paid-up share capital and reserves. From the managers' viewpoint, the long-term capital employed in the business can be defined either as total assets minus current liabilities, or as total assets only. In this latter case, however, fluctuations in the level of current assets (without deduction of current liabilities) may invalidate comparisons. In order to make comparisons between companies and divisions, it will be necessary to adopt a uniform approach to the bases adopted for valuation of assets and liabilities, and also to the treatment of obsolete and intangible assets. It may be necessary to use average figures for some items rather than absolute figures which may be unrepresentative. Similarly in defining profit, it is necessary to agree upon uniform treatment of such items as taxation, financing costs, non-recurring items, depreciation and amortisation.

Figure 4.1 shows how the equation can be extended to show other relationships.

The second approach to profitability ratios is to examine earnings in relation to the risk involved in borrowing from outside sources at fixed rates of interest. In its simplest form this relationship might be expressed in the ratio:

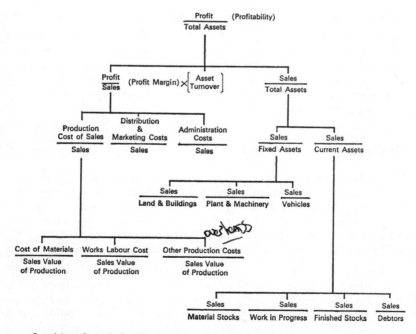

Fig. 4.1   Extension of return on capital employed equation

Earnings before taxes and interest
Annual interest charges on debt capital

[handwritten: Profit with Annual interest on Debt capital Loan. + Tax.]

This ratio gives a rough indication of the margin of safety in the company's financial structure. In interpreting the ratio, reference must be made to fluctuations, experienced and expected, in earnings. The greater the fluctuations in earnings, the higher should be this 'coverage' ratio.

The financial structure of the company might also be appraised by calculating the relationship of debt to net worth, i.e.

Total borrowings other than share capital
Net worth

[handwritten: Equity loan Against Capital Employed.]

Once again the debt ratio needs to be considered against the pattern of fluctuations in earnings.

Some ratios, which are commonly used, reflect *both* liquidity and profitability. For instance the ratios of:

$$\frac{\text{Sales}}{\text{Stock}} \text{ and } \frac{\text{Sales}}{\text{Debtors}}$$

express relationships reflecting the utilisation of assets and therefore profitability. The two ratios also give an indication of the speed at which the stock and debtors are being converted into cash, which is directly related to the problem of liquidity. This emphasises the inter-relationship of factors, and the need to examine the trends of a number of ratios over a significant period.

The limitations of ratio analysis

Calculating financial ratios clarifies the financial behaviour of a business by enabling comparisons to be made with past performance within the company, and also with the performance of other companies. Such comparisons may assist in pinpointing areas where action could be taken to improve performance. But there are a number of limitations affecting financial ratios which need to be stressed.

1   Ratios are calculated from financial statements, which have limitations, as discussed in Chapters 2 and 3. It was stressed there that the financial statements contain arbitrary estimates and figures which are based on personal decisions. The interpretation and application of the accounting guidelines followed in the construction of the financial statements must also be thoroughly understood in attempting to interpret financial ratios.

2   The financial statements do not represent a complete picture of a

business, but merely a collection of those facts which can be expressed in monetary terms. The earning power of a business may well be affected by factors which have not been included in the financial statements, and which are consequently omitted from the financial ratios.

3 The accounting periods covered by the financial statements may not reflect representative financial positions, which are required in order to interpret the financial ratios satisfactorily.

4 Comparisons with other companies are only likely to produce valuable information if the firms involved are of similar size and are engaged in the same kind of work. Unless the ratios are calculated in a uniform manner from uniform data, comparisons can be very misleading.

5 The apparent accuracy of financial ratios often leads to their introduction into companies as measures of performance. For instance, the performance of divisional managers is sometimes assessed by the ratio of profit to capital employed. The weakness of this ratio, if used on its own, is that the manager may be motivated to improve the ratio rather than to improve the total profit. Concentration on this ratio alone may dampen the incentive to growth and expansion, to the detriment of the long-term interests of the company. The use of financial ratios as measures of performance must therefore form part of a complete scheme to establish the 'key result areas' of managers, rather than be the sole test of efficiency.

6 A ratio is a comparison of two figures, a numerator and a denominator. In comparing ratios it is often difficult to determine whether differences are due to changes in the numerator or in the denominator or in both. A great deal of analysis and investigation is often required in order to determine the root cause or causes of changes in ratios, and to propose remedial action. Ratios, therefore, only scratch the surface and offer clues; they do not provide an automatic means of controlling a company. Business problems usually involve complex inter-relationships of factors which cannot be wholly explained, analysed or solved by a few simple ratios.

Case study no. 10 – a first attempt at ratio analysis

John Marsh's contacts with his directors and Appleby were making him think seriously about ways of measuring the performance of this lively small business which he had joined. By now, he was feeling that basic accounting routines were being very capably handled by Jean Wilkins: she was going great guns, and John was pleased about that. He had always felt that, as information manager, one of his first tasks was to provide some overall measures of company performance, and he could not proceed with this exercise if he was bogged down with the routine tasks of accounting.

All sorts of questions were being thrown at him of late. Appleby had started it all with a few little digs at the accounts department, which had sparked John off. He pointed out how important it was to have, amongst other things, a clear picture of the trend of debtors on one hand, and the turnover of capital on the other. And he did not fail to emphasise that to some extent the responsibility for these particular trends would rest with Appleby. This brought some retorts from the sales manager about failures on the part of the production department, and what he considered to be adverse trends in production costs. 'Shouldn't these be looked at as well?' said Appleby. John agreed that they should, and this reinforced his feeling that it was about time that they got down to working out some appropriate measures.

He felt that he should speak to his managing director about this, and Jack Hardy showed an enthusiasm which was, by now, no surprise to John. Hardy wanted to get started right away, and pulled out his copy of the annual accounts. John was sure that Jack wanted him to get out his slide-rule and work out some ratios then and there, but he had to point out that the format of the accounts needed looking at before this was done. He said that it was usual to prepare ratio analyses in a particular way, and he felt that he ought to follow what was fairly standard practice.

John's first step was to recast the income statement, to make it into an operating statement specifically suited to ratio analysis. The emphasis was mainly upon breaking down the costs on a divisional basis, regarding production, distribution and marketing, and administration as separate functions within the business. This analysis was partly achieved within the profit and loss account, but some apportionment of expense items was necessary. John would have liked to do this more scientifically than was possible at the first attempt, but he felt that the bases which he used were reasonable enough. For example, he spread employer's national insurance and graduated pension contributions *pro rata* over direct and indirect wages and salaries, and he adopted various percentage bases for other overheads, such as rent and rates, repairs and renewals, depreciation, insurances and miscellaneous expenses. He treated the various interest charges as financial costs outside the range of normal operating costs in order to arrive at a figure for operating profit and a separate figure for net profit. The recast figures are on pages 82 and 83 (Figure 4.2).

Conscious of the need to relate some of the figures in the operating statement to suitable figures of capital employed, John turned his attention to the balance sheet. A figure for capital employed can be computed in many different ways, but John had always felt that all the capital in use should be included in such a figure, so that he was tempted to use the total assets figure in the 1968 balance sheet. On the other hand, there were arguments for using only the average figure of current assets in use throughout the year, so he finally

	Year ending 30 September 1968			Year ending 30 September 1967		
	£	£	£	£	£	£
Sales		355,842				317,019
Production costs						
Materials and components	143,652			108,068		
Direct wages (including NHI and GP)	63,951			59,035		
Opening stocks of work in progress and finished goods	59,481			63,464		
	267,084			230,567		
Less						
Closing stocks of work in progress and finished goods	80,819			59,481		
	186,265			171,086		
Production overheads						
Indirect wages and salaries (including NHI and GP)	50,653			46,894		
Tools and consumables	19,327			15,863		
Repairs and renewals	6,543			5,305		
Fuel, gas and electricity	7,342			5,930		
Rent and rates	2,711			2,678		
Depreciation	7,363			5,906		
Insurances	1,008			1,088		
Miscellaneous expenses	513			410		
	281,725			255,160		

Distribution and marketing costs				
Salaries (including NHI and GP)	8,198		7,741	
Selling expenses	2,886		2,318	
Depreciation on vehicles	1,037		787	
		12,121		10,846
General and administrative costs				
Salaries (including NHI and GP)	10,248		9,676	
Repairs and renewals	727		589	
Light and heat	549		497	
Rent and rates	301		298	
Depreciation	818		656	
Insurances	112		121	
Miscellaneous expenses	1,740		1,232	
Audit fee	625		600	
Directors' remuneration	7,650		7,150	
		22,770		20,819
Total operating costs		316,616		286,825
Operating profit		39,226		30,194
Financial costs				
Interest on loan capital	2,000		1,000	
HP interest	1,200		–	
Bank charges	1,847		278	
		5,047		1,278
Net profit		34,179		28,916

Fig. 4.2 Operating statement prepared for ratio analysis purposes

settled for a figure of capital employed of:

Fixed assets	£ 44,114
Current assets	£194,696
	£238,810

Armed with this information, John produced a schedule of ratios (Figure 4.3) for management information purposes, which he decided that his managing director should see, in the hope that he could persuade Jack Hardy to join him in interpreting them. He found Jack very keen to do this.

Required

1 *Appraise the bases which John has used in preparing this first ratio analysis.*
2 *Make your own interpretations of the trends shown on the ratio analysis statement.*
3 *How do you believe that financial ratios should be used within the business?*

Ratios				1968	1967
Ratio	1	Operating profit/operating assets	%	16.5	14.8
	2	Operating profit/sales	%	11.0	9.5
	3	Sales/operating assets	times	1.50	1.56
Ratio	4	Production cost of sales/sales	%	79.2	80.5
	5	Distribution and marketing costs/sales	%	3.4	3.4
	6	Administrative costs/sales	%	6.4	6.6
Ratio	7	Materials cost/sales value of production	%	37.5	34.6
	8	Works labour cost/sales value of production	%	16.7	18.9
	9	Production overheads/sales value of production	%	25.0	27.0
Ratio	3a	Operating assets per £1,000 of sales	£	668	643
	10	Current assets per £1,000 of sales	£	544	526
	11	Fixed assets per £1,000 of sales	£	124	117
Ratio	12	Materials stocks per £1,000 of sales	£	105	80
	13	Work in progress per £1,000 of sales	£	58	48
	14	Finished stocks per £1,000 of sales	£	139	145
	15	Debtors per £1,000 of sales	£	242	252
Ratio	16	Land and buildings per £1,000 of sales	£	—	—
	17	Plant and machinery per £1,000 of sales	£	117	106
	18	Vehicles per £1,000 of sales	£	7	11

Fig. 4.3   Schedule of ratios

Case study no. 11 – inter-firm comparison

John's meeting with Jack Hardy on the subject of the ratio analysis which he had carried out, sparked off useful enquiries into costs, stock levels and capital expenditure, amongst other things. Most important, the exercise had been useful, in John's opinion, because he found it possible to emphasise once again the need for measures for management, financial and otherwise. His managing director was, in addition, beginning to appreciate the value and limitations of ratio analysis. John was delighted when Hardy asked, 'We know what these ratios have been for the last two years, but what ought they to be?' John replied, 'It's always difficult to say. You might feel that it's possible to set standards against which these actual measures can be compared. On the other hand, many people would argue that a first requirement is to have some means of knowing whether our performance is good or bad compared with that of similar firms. Then again, for ratios like profit to capital employed, some people believe it reasonable to compare one's own performance with the performance of any other sort of organisation. After all, I suppose if profit returns in some other sort of business were better than in our own trade, we would be prepared to consider changing, wouldn't we?' Jack Hardy was a bit surprised. 'I don't know,' he said, 'after all, this is very much our trade, and we've made some money at it. You'd better try that comment on Sam some time, but get ready to duck when you do. What about this business of comparing our performance with that of other companies in the trade?'

John explained that the only way of doing this was by taking part in an inter-firm comparison. 'This is very popular nowadays', he said, 'particularly in groups of companies where the activity is administered by the parent company. Also it's popular within trade associations, where a special bureau set up by the association administers such schemes. The objective is to supply each company within the trade with information which might guide them in diagnosing their strengths and weaknesses. As a matter of fact, I've already had a look at this, but it seems as though we don't have such a facility in our trade. On the other hand, there is the Centre for Interfirm Comparison, which organises such studies for many industries. I've seen some of their literature, and the internal ratio exercise which we have already done, I modelled on the basic ratios of their comparisons.' John was left to pursue this one further.

John established contact with the Centre for Interfirm Comparison, and in order to participate in the exercise, he was asked to submit the figures for Hardy Heating to the Centre on the basis of standard definitions used in the IFC scheme to ensure that the data of all participating firms was comparable. To do this meant adjusting some of the figures which John had already calculated. The main adjustments were in the following areas:

1 Stocks had to be revalued at full cost, including production overheads.
2 Plant and machinery had to be valued at true current values, rather than balance sheet values.
3 Although Hardy Heating rents its premises, a value for land and buildings had to be included in assets employed. In addition, rent paid had to be deducted from the operating costs.

These adjustments took time, but were not unduly complicated: inevitably, the valuations of fixed assets at current prices were the most difficult. When the ratios were recalculated on this IFC basis, this is how they looked (Figure 4.4).

Ratios		1968
1 Operating profit/operating assets	%	12.6
2 Operating profit/sales	%	12.0
3 Sales/operating assets	times	1.05
4 Production cost of sales/sales	%	78.4
5 Distribution and marketing costs/sales	%	3.3
6 Administrative costs/sales	%	6.3
7 Materials cost/sales value of production	%	36.6
8 Works labour cost/sales value of production	%	29.2
9 Production overheads/sales value of production	%	12.6
3a Operating assets per £1,000 of sales	£	950
10 Current assets per £1,000 of sales	£	626
11 Fixed assets per £1,000 of sales	£	324
12 Materials stocks per £1,000 of sales	£	105
13 Work in progress per £1,000 of sales	£	71
14 Finished stocks per £1,000 of sales	£	208
15 Debtors per £1,000 of sales	£	242
16 Land and buildings per £1,000 of sales	£	141
17 Plant and machinery per £1,000 of sales	£	172
18 Vehicles per £1,000 of sales	£	12

Fig. 4.4 Ratio analysis for IFC purposes *Copyright © Centre for Interfirm Comparison Ltd. 1968.*

The Centre came back quite quickly with the inter-firm comparison table (Figure 4.5), together with a detailed report explaining how the ratios for Hardy Heating Ltd compared with those of the other firms. This again sparked off some searching enquiries in the company.

Required
1   What do you feel would be the main points of the detailed report which the Centre submitted?
2   Suggest what 'searching enquiries' might be prompted as a result of the table and report.
3   At the beginning of the case, John was emphasising the need for financial and other measures. Suggest what other measures he might have been referring to. Do they link in any way with the interfirm financial measures?

Ratios	Firms 1	2	3	4	5	6	7	8	9	Median
! Operating profit/operating assets (%)	20.2	17.9	14.3	13.3	12.6	11.3	7.9	7.4	3.9	12.6
2 Operating profit/sales (%)	18.2	14.9	13.1	11.9	12.0	10.9	6.1	7.6	3.1	11.9
3 Sales/operating assets (times)	1.11	1.20	1.09	1.12	1.05	1.04	1.30	0.98	1.25	1.11
Departmental costs (as % of sales)										
4 Production costs	71.3	77.1	77.4	79.6	78.4	79.4	84.2	82.5	89.5	79.4
5 Distribution and marketing costs	4.9	3.7	4.1	2.2	3.3	3.3	2.9	4.4	3.3	3.3
6 Administrative costs	5.6	4.3	5.4	6.3	6.3	6.4	6.8	5.7	4.1	5.7
Production costs (as % of sales value of production)										
7 Materials cost	31.9	38.0	36.0	35.8	36.6	41.2	40.3	41.3	41.5	38.0
8 Works labour cost	25.4	24.8	22.3	25.1	29.2	24.2	27.3	23.2	31.1	25.1
9 Production overheads	14.0	14.3	19.1	18.7	12.6	14.0	16.6	18.0	16.9	16.6
Asset utilisation (£'s per £1,000 of sales)										
3a Operating assets	899	833	918	893	950	960	770	1019	798	899
10 Current assets	528	584	600	551	626	579	604	789	623	600
11 Fixed assets	371	249	318	342	324	381	166	230	175	318
Current asset utilisation (£'s per £1,000 of sales)										
12 Materials stock	58	73	43	58	105	86	65	129	80	73
13 Work in progress	51	90	104	63	71	44	114	164	122	90
14 Finished stocks	166	194	223	163	208	218	177	247	160	194
15 Debtors	253	227	230	267	242	231	248	249	261	248
Fixed asset utilisation (£'s per £1,000 of sales)										
16 Land and buildings	240	87	102	143	141	156	88	47	73	102
17 Plant and machinery	116	143	207	189	172	213	67	163	89	163
18 Vehicles	15	19	9	10	12	12	11	20	13	12

Fig. 4.5 Inter-firm comparison. © *Centre for Interfirm Comparison Ltd. 1968.* The figures in this table are hypothetical but typical of figures in actual comparisons

Case study no. 12 – ratio analysis in planning

The CIFC exercise had been considered very worthwhile. Perhaps a particular ratio had merely suggested that the figures in support of the ratio should be examined in some detail: on occasions, the facts behind the figures had to be sought out. Often it was a matter of deciding at that point whether the ratio was good or bad according to policy or accident. In dealing with his managing director, John was keen to make the point that an adverse ratio might just happen, because of unfavourable circumstances, or because of managerial inefficiency. On the other hand, such a ratio might be planned. In other words, a decision might be taken which it was known would have an adverse effect on a financial analysis, but might be considered to be desirable or to have a long-term benefit.

In a conversation John repeated his previous point, that it might be reasonable to set target ratios. 'All right, where should we start?' asked Hardy. 'Obviously with the return on investment ratio. What sort of return do we need? What do we want to set as our objective?' asked Marsh. 'This depends upon so many things,' replied the managing director, 'on external factors such as what sorts of returns other people get, and upon economic circumstances, but also on internal factors, such as what our pricing policy is and what turnover of capital this brings in volume of sales. In any case, isn't the setting of a return on investment target a long-term issue? I've got a lot of other things to think about. If I do all these things in an efficient manner, won't the return on investment look after itself?'

Marsh explained that there was no pressing need to set target ratios, as long as it was appreciated that, from the examination of past events and from some knowledge of future operating conditions, it was possible to use ratio analysis as a guide in forward planning, to ensure that when things happened, they happened because this was the way in which it had been planned, not just because of accidents.

Required
1   *Your thoughts on the extent to which past events can be used as a guide in forward planning.*
2   *Your ideas on how target ratios might be used.*

5

Cost classifications and product costing

The limitations of financial accounts for management purposes

Financial accounts are constructed on generally accepted principles and deal with the financial affairs of the company in a global sense. Shareholders must now be given information on the principal activities of the company during the year, but the financial accounts do not usually supply sufficient details to allow management to operate effectively on a day-to-day basis. Much more detailed information is required not only on past activities but also on future plans. This information is also required more frequently than the annual financial accounts. Although the profit and loss account shows the main elements of cost, a great deal of classification and analysis is required for management to use this same information for the execution of the management functions of planning, controlling and co-ordinating the company's activities.

Cost information

The classification and analysis of cost information is necessary for three major purposes:

1 for product costing
2 for management control
3 for decision making.

This chapter concentrates on problems of product costing, while

Chapter 6 considers information needed for strategic planning and management control.

Management information

The basic data of financial accounting are essentially the basic data of costing, so that the analyses required for both purposes are complementary. But cost information is also integrated with information used in production planning and control and in work study. There is a measurement aspect to these functions which form part of the management infomation system. As far as possible information from various sources should be joined to constitute an integrated data processing system. Cost information forms part of the accounting system which is itself a sub-system of the management information system of a company.

Managers within a business are in charge of the departments where costs arise. The manager has a responsibility to control costs and to seek to reduce them. He should know what his costs are, which are the significant items, and where excesses are being incurred, so that he can accept the challenge of accountability. Since much basic cost information stems from the shop floor, the shop floor manager should have a real involvement in the production of cost information.

The classification of costs

For product cost and management control purposes, cost information will need to be classified and analysed in a number of different ways:

1 by type of expense (materials, wages and other expenses)
2 by location (division, department or cost centre, group of machines or items of process plant)
3 by product, job or order
4 by behaviour (its relationship to the level of activity).

For decision making, that is, in choosing between alternative courses of action, other classifications will be necessary. According to the particular decision, cost information relevant to that decision will be required, which may not be available from routine classifications. Consideration may even have to be given to opportunity costs, which reflect the earnings obtainable by using resources elsewhere.

1   Classification by type of expense. This classification can be divided into direct costs and indirect costs. The implication of the word 'direct' is that some items of cost are easily identified with the product, job or order, which is called the 'cost unit'. Any items of cost which cannot easily be identified with the ultimate cost unit are termed 'indirect costs'. The total costs of all indirect materials, indirect wages and indirect expenses are called the 'overheads' of the business. The total cost of the direct items are called the 'prime costs' of the business.

PRIME COSTS are the total costs of:

Direct Materials: those materials which form a part of the finished product and can be allocated directly to it (e.g. the cost of sheet metal for making a filing cabinet).
Direct labour: that labour which contributes to the conversion of the direct material, raw material or components into finished products (e.g. the labour cost of folding the steel sheet).
Direct expenses: those costs other than material or labour which can be charged direct to the product (e.g. the sub-contractor's cost for spraying the sheet).

OVERHEADS are the total costs of:

Indirect materials: such as the tools and consumables used in a production department.
Indirect labour: such as shop cleaners and sweepers, storekeepers, inspection and maintenance personnel.
Indirect expenses: such as rent and rates, depreciation of plant, insurance of premises and stock.

2   Classification by location. Another classification of expense is by the functions, departments and cost centres of the business, which are quite frequently centres of responsibility.

In analysing cost to functions, departments and cost centres, some items can be *allocated* without difficulty, that is, attributed directly to the departments in which the cost is incurred. Other has to be *apportioned,* since they cannot be attributed directly and have to be charged to departments on some arbitrary basis.

As an example of *allocation*, the tool costs of a department are normally identified with that department by reference to the requisitions on the general stores. On the other hand, the *apportionment* of local rates and other building occupation costs to departments will often be made on the basis of floor area or cubic capacity.

Costs which can be allocated to a department are normally under the control of the departmental manager, but apportioned costs are usually outside his control. This classification helps to establish the responsibility for costs and represents an important first step in cost control. The classification is also important since it builds up the total overhead cost of departments and cost centres, which is necessary in order to charge a fair proportion of the overheads to the products which pass through the cost centre.

3   Classification by product, job or order. In determining the cost of individual products, the work of calculating the direct material and direct labour costs is usually relatively easy. The material cost is calculated by ascertaining the quantities of material used in the product, making due allowance for material waste, and multiplying by the purchase price. The direct labour cost of the product is obtained by specifying the operations involved and the time taken on them, and then multiplying the time by the appropriate labour rates.

Two major difficulties arise in the computation of the overhead cost of products. First, the problem of how to charge to products a fair proportion of the total overhead of the department or cost centre which has been built up by the previous classification. Many overhead costs cannot be associated with and assigned to individual products or orders directly. Such overhead costs are charged by using some equitable base which is common to all products, and which reflects the products' use of the overhead items. The most common bases or measures of activity are:

1   Direct labour cost.
2   Direct labour hours.
3   Machine hours.
4   Units of product.

The choice of the most equitable base will reflect the conditions under which the product is being made. Many overhead items accrue on the basis of time, and therefore bases related to time rates are often preferred to those related to direct labour cost or even direct material cost. Operating time data is needed, and since it is required for production planning and control purposes, the need for an integrated information system is emphasised.

The second problem is concerned with the level of activity chosen for calculating overhead rates. If the actual level of activity for the period is used, then the overhead rate must be expected to vary from period to period with changes in the level of activity. In other words, the total product costs will vary from period to period, depending upon the level of activity. A difficult decision for a company is whether to choose:

(a)   the actual level of activity.
(b)   the average level of activity over a number of periods,
(c)   the expected actual capacity,
(d)   the theoretical maximum practical capacity.

The criterion used will affect the product cost and will also affect computation of profit and stock valuation. A predetermined overhead rate overcomes the problems of using the actual level of activity, but it requires management to plan the estimated volume of activity for the coming period, together with the associated estimated amount of overhead. Participation in planning at this level often strengthens the resolution of management to plan other activities within the company. In order to calculate estimated overhead rates, we must study the behaviour of costs in relation to changes in the level of activity.

4 *Classification of costs by behaviour.* Costs may be classified into three patterns of behaviour: variable, non-variable (fixed), and semi-variable.

A cost whose total varies proportionately with changes in the level of activity is known as a variable cost. Direct material is often an example of variable cost. In this case the variable cost per unit is constant, irrespective of changes in the level of activity.

A cost whose total remains unchanged regardless of changes in the level of activity is known as a non-variable or fixed cost. The most regular fixed cost items are rent and rates, management salaries, and depreciation of fixed assets. In these cases the fixed cost *per unit* will fall as output increases, and will rise as output decreases.

A cost whose total tends to vary proportionately with changes in the level of activity, but which is also fixed at certain levels of activity, is known as a semi-variable cost. The behaviour of semi-variable costs can be split into variable and non-variable elements by statistical techniques such as the high–low method or the least squares method. Cost behaviour must be studied at some length and in detail before decisions can be reached regarding variability, but such study is an integral part of planning within a company.

For practical purposes, the accountant usually assumes that the behaviour of costs may be represented graphically by straight lines, and therefore as linear equations. This assumption is backed by empirical evidence, but it is necessary to state the relevant range over which it is valid. It is extremely useful in break-even analysis and profit planning.

The effect on product costs

Total cost

If some costs are variable while others are fixed, then the total cost per unit of product is representative of only one level of activity. A change in the volume of output will affect the total unit cost, since the fixed costs will be spread over a larger or smaller number of units. Fluctuations in the total cost per unit of output due to changes in the level of activity may be reduced by calculating a predetermined rate based on a predetermined level of activity. But predetermined rates involve difficulties in estimating output level and in deciding the time period to be used. And this does not completely solve the overhead problem, because the predetermined output is not likely to tally exactly with the actual output. Overheads are then either under-absorbed or over-absorbed; total cost per unit will have been under or over stated. This problem of differing total unit costs at varying output levels depending on fixed costs can be critical to a business, both as regards its selling price policies and the level of profit it achieves. But fluctuations in the unit costs of products due to changes in output levels can be avoided by the use of a technique known as marginal costing.

Marginal cost

This technique recognises the variability of cost items, and differentiates throughout the costing system between the variable, or 'marginal' costs as they are called, and the fixed, or 'period' costs.

When calculating the marginal cost of a product, the total of prime cost and variable overheads is computed. The difference between the marginal cost of the product and the selling price is the marginal income, or *contribution*, which can be a better guide than the so-called net profit per unit of product in planning sales mix and establishing a pricing policy.

The main difficulty in calculating total cost and net profit per unit of product is essentially that of deciding on the level of activity at which the fixed or period costs should be absorbed. A second difficulty is determining equitable bases upon which some of the general fixed costs, such as management salaries, may be apportioned to individual cost centres, so that overhead absorption rates can be calculated. The use of marginal costing avoids these difficulties. If the marginal cost of the product is a truly variable cost, then it will be constant per unit of the product. If the fixed costs of the business are truly period costs, incurred on a monthly, quarterly or annual basis, then it can be argued that they are not costs of the products but costs of providing the basic facilities of the business. The natural extension of this argument is that a product does not make a net profit but makes a *contribution* to those fixed costs. When a sufficient number of the products have been made for the total contributions to exceed the period costs, then, and only then, does the business make a profit.

Marginal cost v total cost

Discussion of the relative merits of marginal and total costing is best limited to the use of these methods for specific purposes.

Marginal costing is more significant for short-run rather than long-run policies affecting planning, decision making and control. For planning purposes, marginal costing highlights the relationship between output, costs and profits, and brings out the significance of fixed costs on profits. With respect to decision making, in a highly competitive situation it may well be wise to take an order which covers marginal costs and makes some contribution towards fixed costs, rather than lose the order and the contribution by insisting upon a price above full cost. The marginal costs are also the most important when considering whether to make or buy a given part, and since they are often very close to incremental costs, they are highly relevant to equipment replacement decisions. In managerial control, marginal costs are often those which are controllable by departmental managers, and therefore need to be reported upon.

For long-run pricing purposes, it is important to have an understanding of the full cost of a product to the company, since in the long run the company must make sufficient contribution from all products to cover fixed costs and provide an adequate return on capital employed. It does not follow from this that in the long run all products should be priced individually above total cost, but even in the short run it is important to know the extent to which full costs are not being covered when prices are accepted below full cost. With regard to long-run control, it is important to judge how effectively the department, division, or product is using fixed costs and capital investment, since a decision to contract or expand will be based to some extent on the anticipated return on capital employed.

The real issue therefore is that the cost data must be relevant to the problem and time period under review. The accountant has a responsibility to advise management on the range of information which is applicable to particular business problems, and to arrange the classification of costs accordingly.

Case study no. 13 – the product costs

John Marsh was getting on well with Wilfred Appleby, the sales manager, socially as well as at work, sometimes over a cup of tea in the canteen, or a glass of beer around the corner at the local. Business matters inevitably came up at these tête-à-têtes, and John was learning fast about the products and the market. A summary of what John had learnt from Appleby, bearing in mind that Appleby was the sales manager, would be:

1 By and large, the company's products were wanted and were acceptable, but some were thought of as over-priced, and demand for these definitely suffered as a result.
2 There were instances where much bigger orders could have been obtained for products if special discounts could have been offered, but the managing director's inflexible rule was 'No discounts'.
3 Delivery on some products was poor, and in Appleby's opinion, finished warehouse stocks were not big enough.
4 No sales forecast was prepared. In fact, it was pretty clear that Appleby did not like anything that savoured of what he called 'scientific management'.

One day, Appleby arrived in the chief accountant's office

for a good business reason. 'I asked for the product costs from Tom Rose for these ten items days ago,' he said, 'and they've only just arrived! I don't know whether you've interested yourself in the product costs yet, but I'm sure you'll want to eventually. This is the way I always get product cost information; figures for materials, labour and overhead costs for each item, giving a total cost, then a comparison of that total cost with the selling price, to show the margin: profit or loss. There always seem to be some crazy results, items which one would think were very profitable showing up as unprofitable, and vice-versa. But I'd like your comments on this product costing business when you get an opportunity, particularly about the fact that we recover overheads at the rate of 235 per cent on direct labour.' John Marsh was content to listen at this stage, but when Appleby had gone, he got on to Tom Rose. Tom had originally been responsible to Sam Howell, but now he was under the accountant's wing.

Tom was the cost clerk, pleasant, getting on a bit, and with no formal costing training. He explained to his chief how he costed a product. He started off with the master route sheet for the product, which detailed quantities and types of material, and the allowable waste. It also detailed operations, the operation times and the piecework price currently paid. 'I work all this out at current prices,' said Tom, then I've got the prime cost, and I add overheads at 235 per cent on direct labour.' 'So your costs don't necessarily account for the actual material consumption?' questioned John Marsh. 'No, that's true, but they won't be far out, because I keep a close eye on that,' said Tom. 'And what about scrap, that is production rejects?' 'Well, I build that in, because we have records of production rejects weekly,' replied Tom.

'I find this overhead rate a bit odd. We are recovering all overheads, no matter where incurred, in this blanket rate?' asked John. 'Yes, but I've had nothing to do with the overhead rate,' said Tom, 'that's given to me each year by the auditors.'

'We've got a press shop, power presses and fly presses, an assembly department, a machine shop, plating and paint spraying, a manual moulding section and a machine moulding section. I wonder if one overhead rate gives accurate product costs?' thought John.

Required

1   *Comment on the costing procedures which are currently in practice in the company.*

Case study no. 14 – department overhead rates

John Marsh was a well-trained accountant. He had learned that you have to take a broad look at things before you make up your mind, that it pays to get all the facts before you make a decision. He was not happy with this blanket overhead rate, but he was going to get what evidence he could before condemning it.

One of his first moves was to take another look around the factory, and this time a really close look. He surveyed each department and got a picture of its size, the layout, the plant and the processes carried out in it. He noticed the labour force, tried to get a feel of the tempo, and the extent of manual and machine operations. He had a chat with the maintenance foreman about the services supplied to each department and about how much power was used. He questioned the foreman of the toolroom about the making, maintenance and use of tools. He talked to the work study engineer about the manning of each department of the business, and about work measurement.

After all this, John felt convinced that the blanket overhead rate was not right for the business. He had a chat with Tom Rose. 'You see, the real snag about using the blanket overhead rate is that you're charging every product with overhead cost on the same basis. Obviously there are expensive and inexpensive departments in a factory from an overhead point of view. Usually the machine departments are more expensive than the manual, and as a rule, the more expensive the machine, the higher the overhead rate. If you've got a wide range of products passing through all these different departments, the chances are that some spend more time in the more costly departments, and others less. In which case, the blanket rate leads to rather inaccurate product costs.' Tom made the point that there was, in fact, a very considerable divergence in the routes of products through the factory. John was obviously right, and Tom asked him, 'Do you want me to spend some time doing a departmental cost analysis?'

John agreed that it should be done soon. Tom said that he would welcome the job, would find it different and interesting, but that he could see some problems. He did not feel that the existing analysis of expenditure for accounting purposes went anything like far enough to enable the job to be done properly. For example, he could pick up the total company purchases of tools and consumables each month, but he had no idea how much should be allocated to the various factory departments. There must be a way of getting reasonable allocations of power consumption to departments, but it would certainly not be from meter readings. He finished on what John Marsh thought was the right note, an enthusiastic one. 'Perhaps I can go away and get started on it, and come back to you with any particular problems which arise.'

'Yes,' said John, 'that's fine. The only other matters which I would like you to consider are whether we should use actual figures for a previous period, say a quarter, or whether we should try to predetermine figures for a future period. Then do remember that, although our blanket overhead rate at the moment is expressed as a percentage of direct labour, there are other ways of calculating overhead rates.'

Required
1   Analyse the problems raised in this case study.

Case study no. 15 – a job well done?

Tom Rose was back to see John Marsh on several occasions for advice, and to get a more detailed breakdown than accounting figures provided. He was taking the last quarter, a thirteen-week period, as the basis for his analysis. Many of the questions which he asked John were about how particular items of cost could be apportioned to the departments of the business. He was obviously trying, he was enthusiastic, and he accepted that it was not necessary to be accurate to the penny. John was delighted that he did not have to make the point that there was no such thing as an accurate absolute cost of anything, even of running a department.

Eventually Tom came back with his work done. A copy of the historical cost analysis appears on pages 106 and 107 (Figure 5.1). He was quick to point out that the overhead rates he had worked out were very different from one department to another. Also, in those cases where figures of labour or machine hours were available, he had calculated the hourly rates as well as the percentage on direct labour rates.

He had two particular questions to ask his chief:

1 He had not included the costs of general administration or sales and distribution in his factory cost departmental rates. Should they be included? In what other ways could these costs be absorbed in product costs?

	Totals £	Production				
		Assembly shop	Hand press	Power press	Machine shop	Manual moulding
Direct wages	14,372	6,798	2,092	701	1,305	1,302
Net operating hours		24,250 labour hrs		1,382 machine hrs	4,773 machine hrs	
Overheads						
Indirect wages						
Supervision	975	675	200	100		
Toolsetting	400			400		
Maintenance	992					
Toolroom	2,604					
Inspection	2,518	1,682	105	77	163	163
General	4,075	430	150	110	152	82
Salaries	5,124					
Directors' remuneration	1,912					
National health insurance	1,802	673	148	76	91	85
Graduated pensions	433	117	32	18	22	20
Tools and consumables	2,562	95	134	283	417	72
Repairs and renewals (mat.)	2,075	189	24	18	388	205
Fuel, gas, power	1,012	20	47	78	158	119
Rent and rates	1,523	412	112	113	285	178
Insurances	296					
Discounts allowed	1,000					
Loan interest (approx.)	600					
Bank interest and charges (approx.)	482					
Carriage outwards	1,600					
Selling expenses	807					
Miscellaneous expenses	838					
Depreciation (approx.)	2,400	70	45	375	375	240
Audit fee	170					
	36,200	4,363	997	1,748	2,051	1,164
Apportionments of						
Toolroom (on work done)		133	241	907	473	552
Maintenance (on work done)		207	52	143	506	192
Stores and goods in (on direct wages)		397	119	40	74	74
Factory administration (on direct wages)		2,960	912	305	569	567
		8,060	2,321	3,143	3,673	2,549
Overhead rate						
% Direct labour		117%	111%	448%	282%	196%
Per hour		33p		227p	77p	

Fig. 5.1 Hardy Heating Co Ltd. Historical cost analysis for quarter

...lding	Plating	Paint spray	Tool room	Mainten-ance	Stores & goods in	Factory admin.	General admin.	Sales office	W'house & distrib.
						Service		Sales & Distrib	
6	892	806							
4									
hine									
			2,604	992					
63	93	72							
82	103	145	120	80	715	1,434	62		410
						3,061	1,340	723	
						912	1.000		
39	61	58	153	61	39	203	62	33	20
10	14	12	36	15	10	53	39	21	14
58	89	59	216	165	—	137	42	33	462
12	206	94	96	28	35	289	108		83
38	116	62	30	30	12	20	24	12	46
35	138	150							
							296		
								1,000	
							600		
							482		
									1,600
								807	
				189		71	300	205	73
80	115	85	220	50	15	80	50		
							170		
17	935	737	3,475	1,610	826	6,260	4,575	2,834	2,708
								5,542	
43	103	323	3,475						
63	189	58		1,610					
26	50	46			826				
07	389	351				6,260			
56	1,666	1,515	—	—	—	—			
%	188%	188%							

2 What he had prepared was a historical cost analysis. John Marsh had mentioned the possibility of predetermined figures for a future period. How would one do this? What would be the problems?

Required

1 *If you were John Marsh, how would you answer these questions?*
2 *What effect will these revised overhead rates have on product costs? What action do you recommend?*

Some of the product cost would reduce. Some of our product sales would increase. Departmental cost would be controlled better.

Case study no. 16 – a further classification required?

John Marsh was more than satisfied with Tom's efforts, and Tom had obviously enjoyed the task. They now had departmental overhead rates based more appropriately, they felt, upon time rather than direct labour. John expressed the opinion that these rates would be helpful in many ways, but in particular for product costing, and for estimating prices for any new products which might come along. But he was quick to point out to Tom that if a measure of the relative profitability of the individual products was required, they would have to analyse overheads into fixed and variable, so that they could then calculate departmental variable overhead cost rates as a prelude to working out the marginal costs of each product. Only by this means could they ascertain the contributions made by the products, which, he said, was a better measure of their profitability.

Tom took his cost analysis home with him one night, and he spent just half an hour looking through it with a view to deciding for himself which costs were fixed and which were variable.

He decided that it wasn't at all easy to classify the items.

Required
1   How would you classify them?

Case study no. 17 – cost–profit–volume relationships

The managing director called in John Marsh in the middle of the month while John was struggling to push out the figures for the previous month. As he had sorted out and improved the monthly trading statements quite a bit, John was keen to make further improvements all along the line, and one improvement he desperately wanted to make was to speed up preparation of the figures. He told Jack Hardy this when he was asked how things were going.

'Actually, I've taken several looks at the re-draft you did of the September to November figures,' said Jack. 'They make more sense to me now, but there are one or two things which I don't really understand. For example, turnover improves by £4,600 from September to October and the loss reduces by £2,100. Then between October and November the turnover improvement is another £4,500, and this time the profit improvement is only about £1,200. I don't really get that. Then the other thing which I don't really follow is this break-even point idea. Other business owners tell me that you can get a pretty good idea as to how the business is doing from the volume of sales. For instance, Fred Olson was telling me the other day that he knows that he's breaking even at about £10,000 a week and that at £12,000 a week, he'll clear net profit of about £40,000 a year. Can I read anything like this from our figures? They seem to be all over the place.'

110

John explained that it could well be possible in any business to get some idea of the break-even point, that was, he said, the point at which neither profit nor loss was made. But to express this in terms of a sales value figure might be dangerous; it might even be impossible where the company made and sold a considerable mix of products. The reason was that each product would not make the same percentage of contribution in relation to the sales price, and therefore an increase or decrease in sales would bring differing amounts of profit increase or decrease according to which products sold more or less.

There was another aspect which needed consideration: cost behaviour. It was now recognised that in any type of business activity, there were many different elements of cost, all of which had a behaviour pattern. Some costs tended to vary directly with output or sales, whereas some tended to remain relatively constant. Some items of cost were semi-fixed in nature, in that a part of the cost seemed to remain constant while another part seemed to vary with output. And there were some costs where it was very difficult to establish the behaviour as a clear pattern at all. 'And,' John went on to point out, 'whereas some costs are directly associated with a product, others are incurred just because one had a particular piece of plant.'

John told Jack Hardy that he would prepare a statement to express the September, October and November figures in these terms. He stressed that the statement which he produced would be a hypothetical one, but that it might at least indicate the possibilities of this sort of cost analysis.

Next day, he brought back the statement, as shown in Figure 5.2.

Required
1 *Relate these accounts to those shown in Chapter 3, Case 9, and see how you could explain their meaning fully to your managing director.*

	Sales value	Marginal costs	Contri-bution
SEPTEMBER 1968 (22 days)	£	£	£
Product group A—sockets, plugs	6,000	4,800	1,200
Product group B—other fittings	6,000	4,200	1,800
Product group C—proprietary products	10,846	6,992	3,854
	22,846	15,992	6,854
Fixed costs, or period costs			9,148
		Margin	−2,294
OCTOBER 1968 (21 days)			
Product group A	6,000	4,800	1,200
Product group B	6,000	4,200	1,800
Product group C	15,448	9,903	5,545
	27,448	18,903	8,545
Fixed costs			8,732
		Margin	−187
NOVEMBER 1968 (22 days)			
Product group A	5,000	4,000	1,000
Product group B	5,000	3,500	1,500
Product group C	21,988	14,288	7,700
	31,988	21,788	10,200
Fixed costs			9,148
		Margin	+1,052

Fig. 5.2   Statement demonstrating some aspects of cost—profit—volume relationships

6

Accounting in planning and control

The accountant and management

The accountant in business is often described in job advertisements as the 'management accountant'. Some discussion of the term 'management' is necessary in order to gain an understanding of the internal role of the accountant.

There are a number of schools of management which include:

The management process school sees management through the traditional functions of planning, organising, staffing, directing and controlling. The process involves getting things done by people operating in organised groups.

The human behaviour school concentrates on the inter-personal and inter-group relationship involved in getting things done; and studies the motivation of the individual and the group.

The social system school sees management as a system of cultural inter-relationships which involves mutual co-operation based on the needs of the individual to overcome physical, biological and social limitations of himself and his environment.

The decision theory school views management as a rational approach to decision making.

The mathematical school sees management as a logical process which can be expressed in mathematical terms and models.

In order to satisfy the title of 'management accountant', it is necessary to operate so that the complementary interests of these various schools are served. The management accountant is concerned with designing, planning and controlling an information system that serves management, as defined by all the various schools.

The management information system will reflect company objectives, and therefore the accounting and reporting system can have a significant influence on the attainment of company goals. Whilst profit and return on capital employed are usually regarded as basic objectives within a company, other goals such as product development, share of the market, personnel development or social service can also be important. The accountant has a design problem to ensure that the information system emphasises the overall aims of the company, and does not over-emphasise one facet of operations. Accountants must assess the effect of the accounting system on the motivation of managers. The goals of individual managers should match the overall objectives of the company, and the accounting system can have a vital influence on such goal congruence. The accountant must therefore be not only a student of economics but a student of all the social sciences, since his work is concerned with the behaviour of human beings as well as the behaviour of costs.

In addition to motivation, management is concerned with planning, controlling and co-ordinating activities in order to attain the basic objectives of the company. *Planning* implies setting up the organisation, breaking down the duties, devising the programme, and allocating the work. It calls for forecasts; it demands that managers look ahead and anticipate future events. *Controlling* implies that the plans which have been set will only be achieved if there is a means of ensuring satisfactory performance, checking performance against plans, and taking executive action. The first requirement of control is measurement. *Co-ordination* involves integrating and balancing individual plans so that the overall objectives are attained.

The accountant forms a vital link in this management process of making the best use of the limited resources available to the company.

Planning and control

It is useful to distinguish the various levels at which planning and control take place. *Strategic planning* is concerned with the objectives and policies of the enterprise. Decisions affecting the objectives, or changes in the objectives, must be made mainly on the basis of external information about the environment in which the business is operating. Such information will cover long future periods of time and the estimates made will involve a high degree of uncertainty. It is difficult to construct mathematical models to cover these decisions, but since the number of people involved in strategic planning will be small, the problems of internal communications are not likely to be significant. Such decisions do not necessarily represent a complete long-range plan for the company, covering say five years, but rather concentrate on specific proposals which will affect the character and direction of the company. The information and costs required to assess such problems will be in an unstructured form, and the specification of the data must depend upon the formulation of the strategic proposal. The area of strategic planning and decisions is that of the businessman and top management rather than the middle manager.

The middle manager occupies a key position at the level of *management planning and control*, which is concerned with obtaining and using resources effectively within the policies established by strategic decisions. The information required is more internal and covers shorter periods of time, and in consequence is more accurate. It is concerned with all the operations of the company rather than with one particular strategic decision, and is often expressed in total financial terms, in the form of a statement of future expected profits, a projected balance sheet, and a statement of future cash inflows and outflows. Unlike strategic decisions, which are basically economic assessments, the problems involved in management planning and control are both economic and psychological. The designer of a management planning and control system must take full account of inter-personal and inter-group relationships and motivations.

Operational control is concerned with the effective expedition of specific tasks within a framework of procedures established at the management control level. Information is required on specific jobs and units, and covers very short time periods. Indeed, if computers are available, information can be supplied to management on such operations as they take place. These activities are often capable of being expressed in mathematical terms and models, and the job of establishing standards of performance can be accomplished with a high degree of accuracy.

The measurement and evaluation of performance at various levels

Measurement is a vital factor in the process of control. Without measurement it is not possible to quantify plans, to measure actions, and to evaluate the actions in the light of the plans.

At the *operational level* it is often possible to postulate the efficient and acceptable relationship between inputs of resources and corresponding outputs. Work study techniques can be applied in this area with a high level of accuracy, and the results can be used in order to assess operating efficiency. These techniques and resulting data must be grafted into the management information system of the company.

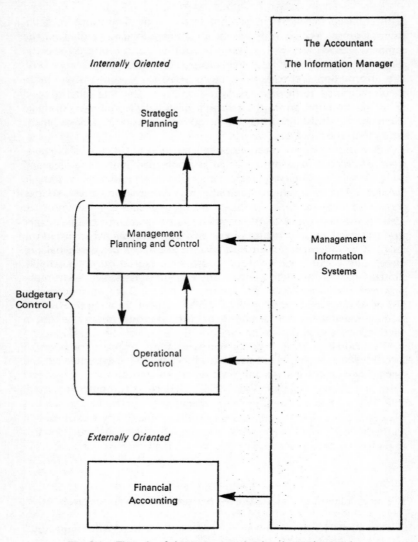

Fig. 6.1   The role of the accountant in planning and control

The problem of measuring and evaluating performance is much more difficult at the *strategic and management control levels.* It is not always possible here to state the optimum relationship between inputs and outputs in an objective manner. The relationship of output to input in some circumstances is a matter of subjective judgement. For instance: how much should a company spend on research and development?

There are areas of cost, where the levels are established at the discretion of management and where, in the absence of scientific standards, control is more difficult than at the operating level.

In operational control, the emphasis is on efficiency, that is, on operating at the optimum input–output relationship. At the management planning and control level the evaluation of performance must cover not only efficiency but also effectiveness, in the sense of achieving the objectives and policies of the company. Efficiency and effectiveness at this level cannot be evaluated by a single factor, but rather by a series of factors duly weighted in order to cover the many separate goals of the company. Profit and profitability represent one important goal, but there may well be other objectives which need to be reported upon and evaluated.

The psychological considerations of the area have been stressed, and such considerations are highly relevant when deciding how performance is to be measured and evaluated in a company. Individual managers should feel thoroughly involved in planning and controlling performance, cost and liquidity. This feeling is often encouraged by structuring the accounting system to report on expense centres, investment centres or profit centres. There is a strong connection between management organisation structure and the management information system; a budgetary control system will not solve the problems created by a confused organisation structure or inadequate information system. An effective budgetary control system depends upon a flexible information system which is geared to a co-ordinated organisation.

Budgetary control

The technique which is often used to assist in the management problems of planning, controlling, co-ordinating and motivating is called budgetary control. This term emphasises both the planning and control aspects: a budget, after all, is really a plan expressed in quantitative terms. The control is exercised by measuring actual performance against the performance standard, and taking corrective action where necessary.

It is useful to distinguish two main stages in budgetary control:

Stage 1 involves deciding upon the planning period, and then forecasting and planning activities for that future period. High, yet attainable, standards of performance will be the basis of plans.
Stage 2 involves taking action and evaluating performance in the light of the plans and standards developed in Stage 1. This second stage is dealt with in greater detail in Chapter 7.

Stage 1 can be reviewed under three main headings:

1 Operating budgets (expanded in Chapter 8)
2 Financial budgets (expanded in Chapter 9)
3 Capital expenditure budgets (expanded in Chapter 10)

Operating budgets

Two main questions need to be answered when planning operations:

1 What will be sold, in what volume, and at what price?
2 What therefore will need to be produced, and at what cost?

The sales budget deals with the first question, and is often the starting point and the kingpin of budgetary control procedures. When an organisation is making and selling relatively standard products through regular channels of distribution, it is often possible to forecast reasonably accurately sales demand. The problem becomes more difficult in the case of a jobbing organisation in the technical products field; yet it must be tackled since all other operating plans will normally be geared to the volume and mix of anticipated sales.

The production budget deals with the second question. The first requirement is an examination of plant capacity, and also the availability of other resources which are necessary to meet the sales requirement. Bottlenecks or limiting factors must be isolated and decisions taken about their treatment. Management decisions are also required regarding the stock levels of finished goods and raw material stocks. The production budget must be built up for individual departments, showing the numbers of different products to be made in individual control periods which together form the total budget period.

It is at this point that departmental cost budgeting needs to be undertaken. The budgeted cost of the department's production needs to be evaluated for each item of cost. The accountant should be able to help by supplying information on past performance and the behaviour of costs, but the responsibility for setting the budget rests primarily with the departmental manager and his superior. The performance of the manager will be assessed against his budget, and against the objectives which he sets himself.

Cost budgets will be required for all departments; production, service, administration, selling and distribution. The budgeting of costs can be extremely difficult, particularly when standards of performance need to be set for activities other than the relatively straightforward production operations.

Financial budgets

Management must be concerned with planning and controlling the liquidity aspects of business operations. The operating budget is prepared in terms of revenues and expenses, and the accountant must trans-

Sales & costs

late this budget into cash inflows and outflows. The object of the cash budget is to ensure that the right amount of cash is on hand to operate the business, yet at the same time to ensure that no cash is lying idle. It is also necessary to plan the inflow and outflow of cash from all other sources, and in this capacity the accountant operates not as a cashier, but as a funds flow manager. The total volume of funds required by the business must be planned, and arrangements made for its availability at the appropriate times. In addition, the accountant has a major responsibility for the effective use of funds and their velocity through the business, and in this role he inevitably becomes heavily involved in the plans and aspirations of other managers.

Capital expenditure budgets

In addition to planning activities which will take place in the near future, the management team must also plan expenditure which will yield benefits to the company over a long period of time. The problem here is the planning of expenditure on fixed assets, and it is double-edged. On the one hand, a decision has to be made about the type of fixed asset to be acquired. On the other hand, finance has to be made available for the purchase. The demands for this finance must be co-ordinated through the financial budgets with the demands for finance for activities covered in the operating budget (see Figure 6.2).

The advantages and limitations of budgeting

The discipline of expressing plans in quantitative and monetary form represents an invaluable exercise since management is forced to face the future. The managers within a business are responsible for the effective use of capital allocated to them, and budgeting implies that proper plans are developed which will secure this. Budgets act as a co-ordinating device and as a means of communication. Management becomes more aware of its various roles in the business, of overall and specific objectives. Perhaps more important than any of these points is the fact that standards of performance and cost have to be determined, and form the basis of planning.

However, there are a number of dangers which need to be recognised and avoided. Budgetary control is essentially a short-period technique which provides useful assistance in the areas of management control and operational control. Concentration on the annual budget cycle, however, may lead to a neglect of strategic planning, which could be to the long-term detriment of the company. Budgetary control is difficult to administer at times of rapid technological change and innovation, and there are dangers of inflexibility and constraints being imposed

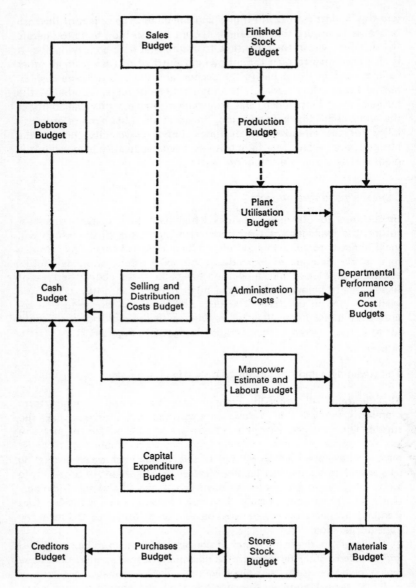

Fig. 6.2   The inter-relationship of various budgets

upon managerial action. Budgetary control can be a long, time-consuming and costly activity; consequently there may be pressure to take short cuts and avoid the difficult process of searching for the optimum usage of all resources.

Case study no. 18 – planning by objectives

John Marsh felt that he had at least contributed to the development of the company when his managing director sent for him and said, 'I've not forgotten some comments you made weeks ago about the need for planning ahead, and your role in such planning. How do you think we should start?' John made the point that there were many aspects to planning, amongst which was included sales forecasting based on a good knowledge of the markets for the various products, and identification and recognition of management skills within the organisation, but first of all what is needed is a clear picture of objectives. He continued, 'What many organisations are doing currently is to set target ratios as the fulcrum of a "management by objectives" programme. Look, I'll start the ball rolling by suggesting the key ratios which need setting as objectives.' Hardy agreed.

When John compiled his list of ratios, he concentrated on the prime ratios of profitability and liquidity.

Profitability
  1 Net profit before tax/sales.
  2 Sales/total assets employed.
  3 Net profit before tax/total assets employed.
Liquidity
  4 Current assets/current liabilities.
  5 Quick assets/current liabilities.

6 Stock/sales
7 Debtors/sales.

He suggested that the first decisions to be taken, obviously involving Wilfred Appleby and Sam Howell, were on matters of sales price, output volume and product profit margins, as these would affect the first three ratios. 'For example,' he said, 'if we are not satisfied with our turnover on capital, we could decide to reduce sales price marginally to increase turnover. If we could get a measure of the effect on sales volume and satisfy ourselves that we could cope from the point of view of plant capacity, we might well find that a sales price reduction, though causing a deterioration in the first ratio, would improve the other two, and most important, improve our ultimate return on investment.'

He went on to make the point that, stemming from these first decisions, it would involve planning, both in physical and monetary terms, sales, production, the stock levels to be carried, policies as regards terms of credit for customers and paying of creditors, and the costs which would arise in the various departments of the business in order to meet the production and sales budgets. 'In other words,' John said, 'we shall be starting the use of budgetary control, and we'll be initiating it properly, from a knowledge of our objectives.'

Hardy asked him where the accountant fitted in, and John pointed out that the accountant's role was a co-ordinating, information-supplying one, and that if one wanted planning to be effective, then one would have to accept the extent to which formal planning tends to cut across existing organisational lines. Hardy seemed a little worried by this comment, and asked whether John thought that a management meeting might be worthwhile, so that both he and John could discuss their ideas about future planning with the other managers.

Required

1 *Is it reasonable to express all company objectives in financial terms?*

2 *What ratios other than those on John Marsh's list do you consider to be important from an objectives point of view?*

3   What is John likely to have meant when he said that for-
    mal planning tends to cut across existing organisational
    lines? Structures   Management.

Case study no. 19 – budgeted ratios?

Hardy had sessions with Howell and Appleby on the subject of objectives reflected in the key ratios, and came back to John Marsh with a bit of paper which gave these details:

Target ratios			
	1	Profit/sales	12%
	2	Sales/assets	1.66 times
	3	Profit/assets	20%
	4	Current assets/current liabilities	2.57
	5	Quick assets/current liabilities	1.14
	6	Stocks/sales	13 weeks
	7	Debtors/sales	10 weeks

Marsh was pleasantly surprised to find that the unofficial management committee had put figures to all the items:

Profit £48,000 p.a. on sales of	£400,000 p.a.
using total assets of	£240,000
of which current assets would total	£180,000
comprising stocks	£100,000
and debtors	£80,000

John Marsh asked Jack Hardy one afternoon how far the figures and ratios which he had been given were 'last year's plus a bit'. Hardy could have been put out by this remark, but he remained calm. 'No, we have been through the points you made previously about pricing decisions, and the likely effect on volumes of sale of different items in our range pretty carefully, and we have set a sales budget. You can have this whenever you like, and you'll find that we have specified quantities and prices of all items, through each channel of distribution, home and export. We have, rightly or wrongly, set our debtor's target at 10 weeks sales, and having had a pretty thorough look at the matter of stocks of raw materials, work-in-progress and finished goods, we've set these at 13 weeks sales. Let me admit right away that, although we've stock quantities set, we haven't used any statistical O.R. techniques to do it, and you might be able to suggest some real improvements. But we've got off the ground.'

John Marsh was pleased. 'I think it's a marvellous start, but we must look very carefully at all the implications of your figures, and the inter-actions of the various detailed budgets which will have to stem from your key ratios. Let us take capital expenditure, for example. I can see from the figures you've supplied that you intend fixed assets to be of the order of £60,000, and since that is quite a bit larger than the present balance sheet figure, then you obviously have in mind some acquisitions. We shall need a detailed schedule of these to comprise the capital expenditure budget. Then, of course, there is the matter of what extra funds will be needed, both for the acquisitions and for the increase in output activity, and we'll need to plan the sources of such funds. What I'm really saying is that we're really getting into the teeth of budgetary control now, because we need all the detailed budgets. Take costs, for example. You've fixed them at £352,000 for next year because you've fixed the turnover figure and the profit figure. But can we achieve this? Can we produce and sell the volume and mix of products included in your sales budget for the cost figure I've just quoted? We'll want departmental cost budgets, and these depend upon what individual supervisors of departments are capable of, their own standards of performance.'

Required
1   *Schedule the detailed budgets which are required to make a comprehensive budget system.*
2   *What management decisions are still to be taken to implement the plan?*

Case study no. 20 – standards of performance

Sam Howell was impressed with the forward-looking attitude being demonstrated by John Marsh in all this new work of planning the operations of the business and expressing them in financial terms. But he was a little uneasy about one matter—the involvement of an accountant-trained man in all the budget-setting. He had always argued that the accountant was a mere recorder, but John obviously wanted to be more than that. On the other hand, Sam himself felt he was capable of bigger things.

But if one wanted budgets for all the various activities of the business, then one needed the grass roots, standards of performance, and it was his opinion that no accountant, however competent, could set these. He took his opportunity to discuss the matter with John. 'Oh, no,' said John, 'for goodness sake don't misunderstand me, Sam. I wasn't for one moment implying that I was going to set all the standards we need. That I would find quite impossible, and we would have defeated the object of the exercise immediately.' He went on to explain that his hope had been that he and Howell could get together and schedule the standards needed, and pinpoint the managerial personnel who would be expected to set them. For example, it was quite clear that, on the matter of production operation times, Bill Twist had done most of the

work required, but these standard times would need verific-
ation with the appropriate production department supervisors, and in addition, waiting time and efficiency standards
would be required. These should, he explained, be set by
the supervisors responsible. After all, it was a responsible
accounting approach which was needed.

'I'm not sure that I'm quite with you on waiting time standards and efficiency standards,' said Sam Howell. 'Well,' said
John, 'we have standard times for operations, but it is still
necessary to accept and budget for two important factors.
Firstly, that not all attendance time will be working time.
There will be delays and stoppages. Secondly, that we may
have a group of operators who are capable of better or worse
than the standard times. We want to budget for what we
believe will happen. On the other hand, we want to make our
budgets targets—attainable, but hard to attain.'

'I've got it,' said Howell, 'now, for what other things will
we need to set standards?'

Required

1   Can you produce a complete schedule of standards re-
     quired, bearing in mind all the activities in the business
     other than production?

7

Standards and flexible budgets for control

Weaknesses of historical cost accounting

Product costing on an actual historical cost basis was the main theme of Chapter 5. While this provides some useful information on the cost of goods manufactured and in process, such historical accounting has the following disadvantages from the viewpoint of cost control and managerial efficiency:

1 There is no indication of what the costs ought to be, given a reasonable level of efficiency.
2 Managers have only past results against which to compare performance, and this may not be a satisfactory basis.
3 Little information is given on the causes of changes in costs or variations in efficiency.
4 Information is provided after such a time lag that corrective action can be inhibited.

Further, in order to calculate overhead absorption rates, it was necessary to build up the total overhead costs that benefitted the cost centre. In arriving at the total overhead cost, apportionments of some costs were made. For management control purposes interest lies in those costs which originate from the cost centre, and over which it has control. The apportionment of costs often confuses the control of costs, and such items are best excluded from control reports.

Standard cost systems

Standard cost systems have been developed to overcome some of the weaknesses of historical cost accounting. The emphasis here is on 'what costs should be' rather than 'what costs have been'. The information is used to promote cost control and managerial efficiency. A comparison is made periodically between the standard cost and the actual cost to determine how and why they differ. This allows management to concentrate its attention on exceptions to the standard. Often a great deal of the information on standards which is required for this exercise is also needed in the planning and control of production operations.

It is necessary to cultivate this vital link between cost information and other information in the business, since management accounting is part of the total management information service of the business. For example, many of the basic documents of production planning and control systems will provide the basic framework of a standard cost system.

Setting the standards for direct labour and direct material

Standards should be set after a careful analysis of the job, the methods which are used, and the efficiency of performance. In practice detailed targets are often only established for the two major elements of cost, direct labour and direct materials. All other costs are usually controlled with the help of departmental overhead budgets.

Several managers may contribute to the establishment of a standard direct labour cost. In accordance with the design issued by the design engineer, the production engineer will specify the operational layout which will show the operations, the machines and the type of layout to be used. The work study engineer will specify the time to be taken when the job is performed according to the operational layout. The personnel manager will be responsible for wage administration. Each of these managers is establishing a standard of performance. The task of the accountant is to co-ordinate the standards established by a number of managers into one *standard labour cost,* which is standard hours multiplied by standard rates of pay.

Before the accountant is able to compute the *standard material cost*, other managers need to be involved to specify requirements and establish standards of performance. Production personnel will have specified the quantities of material to be used, and the buyer will have specified the prices which should be paid for the material. The accountant will then have the straightforward task of multiplying the standard quantity of each item of material by the standard price.

Flexible overhead budgets

Some companies regard their cost control system as complete when standards have been established for direct labour and direct material. Wherever possible, the basic principles of specification and work measurement should also be applied to overhead items.

The flexible budget approach compares the actual overhead to the budgeted overhead for the same level of activity. The accountant can help the departmental manager in the preparation of his budget by analysing the behaviour of costs as the level of activity changes. He will separate costs which are likely and those which are unlikely to vary with the level of activity. Cost studies will be required to assess the degree of variability at different levels of activity. This measure of cost variability of each item of overhead expenditure will then be used to calculate the flexible overhead budget.

The use of standards

Variance analysis is the term which is often used to describe the technique of analysing the difference between planned and actual costs. The primary objective of variance analysis is to provide information for control and so it is vital to identify the factors that caused the total variance. As a first step we can say that variances for labour, material and overhead will be either 'price' or 'quantity' variances.

It is useful to view the problem graphically. We can represent standard cost as a rectangle whose sides represent standard quantity and standard price, see Figure 7.1.

In the example both variances are adverse, and it could be argued that the upper right-hand area should be represented by a third variance, since it is caused by both excess hours and excess wages. However, many accountants would disregard this argument and treat it as part of the price variance. This point is made since the essential objective of variance analysis is to provide management control, which can only be exercised if the variances are properly understood in the context in which they are being used.

For control purposes, the quantity variance is likely to be more valuable than the price variance. However, it is essential to analyse this variance by the factors which have contributed to it, and this detailed analysis must be planned, and integrated into the information system. It can often form part of the wages booking and production planning systems of control.

Overhead variances

We need to distinguish between overhead costs which can be linked with a given level of activity with reasonable accuracy, and other items

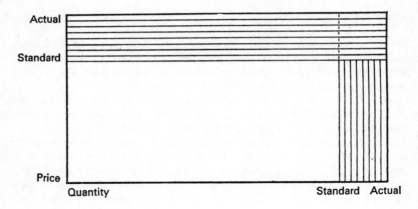

We can also superimpose actual costs, and variances are seen as shaded areas.

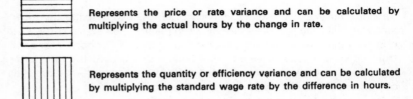

Fig. 7.1   Labour and material variances

of overhead expenditure which are at the discretion of the management. In the case of *discretionary* costs, such as marketing, training, research and development, there is no scientific way of deciding how much should be incurred at a particular level of activity. It does not follow that such expenditure is uncontrollable, since it may be possible to apply standards of performance after it has been decided what discretionary amount the company can afford. A saving on discretionary costs may not necessarily represent a benefit to the company. The aim regarding discretionary costs should be, first, not to exceed the budget without good reason, and also to employ the allocated resources in the most effective way.

Where it is possible to budget reasonably accurately the variable overhead cost which should be incurred at a given level of activity, then the objective is to spend as little as possible, consistent with safety and quality standards. As in the case of *direct labour and direct materials*, it is often useful to calculate quantity and price variances for such variable overheads.

In addition to efficiency and expenditure variances, it is possible in

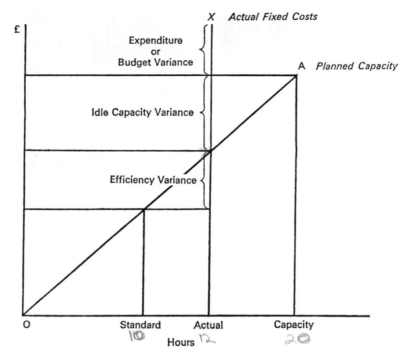

Fig. 7.2   Fixed overhead variances

the case of *fixed* overheads to compute a volume or idle capacity variance. This variance indicates the cost of working longer or shorter hours than originally planned. But this is only a starting point, since a number of factors may affect the volume of operations. Further examinations and analyses will be needed before significant information becomes available for management control purposes.

We can view the problem of fixed overhead variances as in Figure 7.2.

The line OA represents the amount of fixed costs that will be absorbed by production at different levels of activity expressed in hours. Point A represents the planned capacity and point X represents actual fixed costs. The difference between point A and point X represents the fixed overhead expenditure or budget variance. The idle capacity variance is the difference between actual hours and planned hours valued at the fixed overhead rate, and the efficiency variance is the difference between standard hours and actual hours valued at the fixed overhead rate. It is often useful for supervisory managers to know what the fixed overhead efficiency variance is costing the company, since this variance arises as a result of operators producing more or less than is expected of them in a given period. Departmental managers readily understand direct labour efficiency variances, but the effect of such variances on fixed overheads is not so obvious. Yet from the viewpoint of the company, managers are just as responsible for the effective use of fixed resources as for the use of direct materials and labour. The idle capacity variance may not fall so closely under the influence of departmental managers and may be the result of a variety of other factors. Further analysis will be required in order to point to possible corrective action to deal with the problem of over-capacity.

The variances which are shown by the accounting system should be thoroughly understood by all managers because essentially accountants are concerned with making comparisons which will help in planning and controlling activities.

Case study no. 21 – compiling the standard cost of a product

John Marsh was keen to show that costing operations had many prongs, that cost data could be used in many different ways. He particularly wanted to get managerial personnel more involved in cost control. Quite recently he had attended a discussion at the local branch of an accountancy body, which had stressed the need for managers to examine more closely the role of cost information—how such information could aid cost control, and how much more effective cost control activities could be if one developed the standard cost approach. So he was very keen to use the standard cost approach himself. To start with he decided to ask Jack Hardy if he could call a meeting of managers to discuss it.

'No, I have no objection at all to that,' said Hardy, 'though you'd better have a word with Mr Howell and get his reactions, too. I think the meeting will have to be played rather carefully. I'm not at all sure that some of the supervisors will see themselves terribly involved in this, and you'll have to find some appropriate way of introducing things, otherwise you'll never achieve your objectives. But I agree that we want them to be more cost-conscious. That would be very welcome.' Marsh checked with Sam Howell, whose reservations were inevitable, but mild, and then organised the meeting. It went well, though John had some difficulty keeping it on the rails now and again once discussion had started. Some of the foremen looked a little blank on financial matters in general, but John quickly got down to the consideration of departmental costs. He got over his point that if departmental costs were going to be controlled, then they had to be controlled at source, and that the foremen had a big role to play in this. It was quite clear that few of the foremen had any knowledge of what their costs were, although they warmed to the idea of having some information, and welcomed the idea that they might be expected to offer their experience, knowledge and ideas on the setting of standards as the basis for deciding what costs ought to be.

It was a good meeting, and John Marsh took the opportunity of closing on the note that the 'management accounting function, cost department, call it what you like' needed the active co-operation of everyone in management, if it was to provide timely, reliable and meaningful information. He added that he would need to call on their help fairly soon, because he wanted to get down to the preparation of some standard costs (e.g. Figure 7.3).

When John Marsh and Tom Rose started to work on compiling the first 25 standard product costs, the prime cost information came together very readily with the aid of the designer, the foremen, and Bill Twist, who had some of the basic work measurement standards of operator performance. It was essentially a matter of picking up existing information, verifying it wherever possible, and in many cases getting Sam Howell to act as a final arbiter, particularly when it involved levels of waste and production rejects. The crunch often came when Sam was left to decide what was an acceptable standard, a vital activity in management anyway, and one which John Marsh suggested to Tom Rose was often funked. 'But now we're forcing him to do it,' he added.

The information required for departmental overhead cost budgets was trickier. It was a long, painstaking job, deciding the levels of activity for each department on which overhead budgets would be based, and then getting decisions on the level of each item of overhead expense. But finally it was done. Sam Howell was a major contributor to this exercise as well. When the first standard product cost was completed, Tom Rose and John Marsh looked at it together. It covered

Product. *Pull switch PS 67*
Standard quantity. *144* ⚲
Drawing. *A. 362* Layout. *B 39*

Materials

Part no.	Specifica- tion	Standard quantity	Standard waste	Working quantity	Standard price	Amount £.p
EL 51	Cam	144	6	150	1p	1.50
EL 52	Cord	144	6	150	0.4p	60
EL 53	Screw	144	6	150	0.3p	45
EL 54	Indicator	144	6	150	2p	3.00
EL 55	Rivets	288	12	300	0.08p	24
EL 56	Fasteners	288	12	300	0.08p	24
RM 21	Powder	18.0 lb	1.0 lb	19.0 lb	8p per lb	1.52
RM 22	Copper	7.2 lb	0.8 lb	8.0 lb	13p per lb	1.04

material standard cost 8.59   **8.59**

Labour

Operat. no.	Operation	Standard mins	Standard rate	Amount
1	Power press	2	50p per hour	.02
2	Hand press	31	30p per hour	.16
3	Machining	60	40p per hour	.40
4	Manual moulding	—	5p per doz	.58
5	Plating	—	2p per gross	.02
6	Assembly	290	30p per hour	1.45

labour standard cost 2.63   **2.63**

Overheads

Operat. no	Operation	Standard rate	Amount
1	Power press	400% DL	.07
2	Hand press	100% DL	.16
3	Machining	75p per hour	.75
4	Manual moulding	200% DL	1.17
5	Plating	150% DL	.03
6	Assembly	100% DL	1.45

overhead standard cost 3.63   **3.63**

Total works standard cost £14.85
Standard cost per unit   10.3p

Fig. 7.3   Standard cost sheet

factory costs only, because they decided for initial simplicity
not to include administration, selling and distribution costs.

Required
1 How do you now see this standard product cost being used?
2 How would you propose to make it a total standard cost?
3 Do you feel that the computation of the standard cost has, of itself, been of value?

1(a) Material Cost high (buy ourself).
Ship waste

(b)

Case study no. 22 – flexible budgetary control and standard costing in operation

Since the assembly department was the biggest production department, employing the most personnel and massing the most cost, John Marsh decided to apply standard costing first to that department, but only as a pilot run. He explained to Tom Rose that the pilot run method was the best, because it gave one an opportunity to iron out some of the 'bugs' and sell the scheme to managerial personnel, before becoming too heavily involved all round the factory.

The first aspect of this pilot run was to be the preparation of the departmental budget, based on a flexible, not a fixed budget. John Marsh explained to Tom that some companies followed the fixed budget idea for all costs, but that it was obviously unrealistic. 'We know that some costs are fixed, and some are variable, so we know that to set a fixed cost budget for all items would be quite wrong. Some organisations set a level of activity and set cost budgets in relation to that. Then they proceed to compute actual costs which arise against the budgets, but they ignore the fact that the actual costs are for an actual output which is very different from the budgeted output. That won't do for us.' Tom was then given the job of agreeing the appropriate manning of both direct and indirect personnel with the senior foreman of the assembly department for the level of output finally decided upon by Sam Howell in the production budget.

Basically the manning of direct labour was determined by standard cost data, since the standard assembly times were available for products, but there was some thinking to be done about indirect labour, where inspection was the largest item. It wasn't just a matter of using the existing manning figures, but of deciding what labour would be required in the future to meet the programme. As Tom said to the foreman, 'This is budgeting, not just putting down current actual figures, plus 10 per cent for good measure. It's really thinking out our tactics for the future.'

Then there were overhead items to be budgeted for, the associated costs of labour—national health insurance and graduated pension contributions, costs of maintenance, use of tools and consumable materials, power, building occupation costs, depreciation of plant and equipment, and apportioned costs of services. When Tom was discussing these with the foreman, he said he appreciated that not all these costs were controllable within the department, but they were all incurred by or on behalf of the department, and so they had to come into the reckoning.

Budgeting was a new technique in the company, and no one, not even John Marsh, knew enough about the behaviour of costs to be very accurate with it. But as he said, 'We've got to lay the lines for our control procedures. I should think it will be a really old steam engine which will puff along for some time yet, but we'll improve it and quite soon it will be a modern locomotive, you'll see.' And at last the flexible budget was prepared (see Figure 7.4).

This budget was based on a budgeted production of 127 different items assembled, and it was now a matter of getting details of actual output. Since nearly all assembly was paid on a time piecework basis, actual output figures could be extracted on a daily basis, and then summarised weekly. Such figures could most easily be picked up from operator piecework tickets, and were, in fact picked up in a very rough and ready way at the moment by the production controller to give information on the extent to which the production programme had been achieved. The first information which John Marsh issued to the assembly department foreman was a daily document, like this:

ASSEMBLY DEPT. *Foreman: W. E. Thomas*
Operating statistics for: Thursday 2 March 1969
A   Recorded attendance hours   410
B   Booked waiting time hours   33
C   Direct productive hours   377
D   Standard hours produced   415
E   Budget in standard hours   450

Activity ratio	*Efficiency ratio*	*Productivity ratio*
D/E	D/C	D/A
92%	110%	101%

PERFORMANCE		*Budget*				
Standard hours produced		2,025	2,138	2,250	2,362	2,475
Activity %		90	95	100	105	110
COSTS						
Directly allocable:		£	£	£	£	£
Direct materials	V	to be based on direct material				
		standard costs of products				
Direct labour	V	608	641	675	709	743
Indirect labour						
–Supervision	F	52	52	52	52	52
–Inspection	F	130	130	130	130	130
–General	F	34	34	34	34	34
Tools and consumables	V	7	8	8	8	9
Power	V	2	2	2	2	2
Repair materials and labour	V	20	21	23	24	25
Depreciation of plant	F	6	6	6	6	6
Apportioned:						
Associated labour costs	SF	57	58	60	61	63
Rent and rates	F	33	33	33	33	33
Factory admin. and services	F	300	300	300	300	300

Fig. 7.4   Weekly budget for the assembly shop

He explained to Tom that he believed this was a logical first step in standard cost reporting, because it emphasised the physical side of production and should be understood by everyone in works management. 'Standard hours' had not been used in this way before as control measures, but they had been used for paying people.

John Marsh arranged with Sam Howell for the information to be gathered and the report to be prepared by the wages office, vetted by Tom, and then sent to Sam, to the foreman of the assembly department, and to the production controller. This eliminated the present record-keeping.

But this was a simple daily control, and John wanted a weekly operating statement prepared for the foreman, though he was ready to settle originally for a monthly operating statement. This meant picking up all the actual cost details, some weekly, like wages paid in the various classes, and some monthly, like repair costs, consumption of tools and shop supplies. It was not too difficult to lay these on, since a wages analysis of a reasonable sort already existed, requisitions for issues of indirect materials from stores were already made out, and the maintenance men did book their time to different departments. The ultimate idea was to give each departmental foreman a weekly operating statement in respect of his own department's performance and costs, and to give Sam Howell an appropriate summary for the whole works. The first departmental operating statement is presented in Figure 7.5.

Required

1 Criticise and appraise the two different operating statements.

2 How would you proceed to analyse the variances which have been thrown up?

3 What details from the operating statements would you include in a summary to Sam Howell?

MONTH March No. of weeks 4 No. of working days 20
PERFORMANCE Budget—Standard hours 9,000
                Actual—Standard hours 8,100 Activity ratio 90%

COSTS	Original budget	Adjusted budget	Actual costs recorded	Variances
	£	£	£	£
Direct materials	—	4,814	4,981	167 (unfav.)
Direct Labour	2,700	2,430	2,554	124 (fav.)
Variable overheads:				
Tools and consum-				
ables	32	28	18	10 (fav.)
Power	8	8	8	—
Repair matls and				
labour	92	82	148	66 (unfav.)
Fixed and semi-fixed overheads:				
Indirect labour				
–Supervision	208	208	208	—
–Inspection	520	520	578	58 (unfav.)
–General	136	136	107	29 (fav.)
Depreciation of plant	24	24	24	—
Apportioned costs	1,572	1,560	1,560	—
Totals (excluding matls)	5,292	4,996	5,205	209 (unfav.)

Fig. 7.5   Departmental operating statement, assembly department

Case study no. 23 – variance analysis

John explained that you do not throw an operating statement at a departmental manager or supervisor, but that you discuss it with him and interpret it as fully as may be necessary. So Tom had the job of seeing the foreman of the assembly department with it. Tom was not at all sure of himself at the best of times, and he did not radiate confidence yet on this new approach. He was a little diffident about seeing the foreman until he was quite sure of the implications of what appeared on the operating statement. The one point that occurred to him was that it told the foreman what the variances were in total, but there was no analysis of this, and in any case, Tom felt that a particular variance which wasn't even shown wanted highlighting. He took up the matter with his chief.

'Let's tackle the second bit first,' said John. 'Well,' said Tom, 'there are some overhead costs of the department which were fixed or semi-fixed when we drew up the budgets. Wouldn't it be fair to say that if the actual activity of the department is only 90 per cent of the budgeted activity, then we have in effect lost some of these costs, or put another way, we budgeted to recover them, and we haven't done so.' 'True,' replied John, 'that situation gives rise to what is often called a volume variance on fixed overheads, and you could

148

certainly argue that we should show this. On the other hand, from a control point of view, although this may be partly within the control of the supervisor of the department, it may not be wholly controllable by him.' 'How do you mean?' asked Tom. 'Well, the fact that activity is down may be due to a failure by the departmental supervisor to pull all the stops out and get the work done, control waiting time, and so on. But on the other hand it could be due to the fact that orders were down, and there was a shortage of work for the department to get on with. Perhaps you wouldn't mind giving a little thought to this and deciding how we should deal with it, and the extent to which we should show it on the operating statement. What was the other point?'

'About analysis of the variances which we are showing. Take the variance of £124 on direct labour cost, for example, which is unfavourable. We really ought to get down to explaining how this has arisen, and I've got the relevant figures on my pad. Could we have a look at them and decide how we analyse the variances?' 'Good idea,' replied John. Tom's pad had these figures on it:

	Original budget (20 working days)			Actuals	
	Hours	*Rate*	*Cost*	*Hours*	*Cost*
Attendance hours	10,000	7.5p hour	£750	9,640	£723
Waiting time hours	1,000	15p hour	£150	1,407	£211
Productive hours	9,000				
Standard hours produced	9,000	20p hour	£1,800	8,100	£1,620
			£2,700		£2,554

Required

1 Analyse the variance on direct labour cost from the information given.

2 Comment on the so-called 'volume variance on fixed costs' in this situation.

8

Planning for operations and profit

FIXED — Rent / Depr.

VARIABLE — MATERIAL.

over 50 make money.

New Product.
Sales
Production.

Exam Question

THE OBJECT of profit planning is to estimate the amount of profit which may be anticipated for a forthcoming period; and in order to achieve this it is necessary to estimate revenue and associated costs.

Estimating revenue

When overhead rates are predetermined, the amount of cost to be estimated depends upon the estimated volume of activity. For this reason it is usual as a first step to concentrate attention on estimating revenues, or as it is usually known, on sales forecasting, followed by the preparation of a sales budget. The sales budget is the common base underlying the entire budgeting system. The problems involved in its preparation should not be underestimated. Accurate sales forecasts may be very difficult to obtain, particularly if the national economy is unsettled. Information, not only on internal company operations, but also on conditions within the national economy, and the state of the industry within the economy must all be considered. In making a sales forecast consideration must be concentrated on external factors before estimating the portion of the industry's market that the firm will capture, and the distribution of sales, product by product, month by month. Some companies use very elaborate methods to estimate sales figures and to test the accuracy of the results.

Methods of forecasting sales can be classified in a number of ways:

1 *Industry forecast:* by estimating the company's share of the fore-
   casted sales of the industry.
2 *End use analysis:* by surveying the disclosed estimates of major
   consuming industries.
3 *Trend and cycle analysis:* by identifying and forecasting movements of basic factors underlying fluctuations in sales.
4 *Field sales force estimates:* by summarising the individual forecasts of salesmen.
5 *Jury of executive opinion:* by synthesising the views of executives.

One critical factor to be determined by the firm is the choice of the
time period. Sales forecasts may indicate long-term trends, extending
perhaps for twenty years. This kind of information is necessary for
strategic planning, but for management planning and control, information is required for much shorter time periods. The choice of the budget period will depend upon the accuracy with which forecasts can be
made, which might well be linked with the type of industry in which
the company is operating. The shorter-term period might therefore
cover three months to one year. In many companies an annual budgeting procedure is adopted, within which quarterly or monthly budgets
are prepared, and which is itself connected to longer-term strategic
planning.

Estimating costs

After the sales forecast is approved by the committee responsible for
short-term budgets, the various costs to be incurred in attaining these
sales are estimated.

It is useful to distinguish between three main types of costs—committed costs, variable costs, and managed costs.

Committed costs are the easiest to estimate since they represent the
after-effects of decisions taken in the past which cannot be reversed in
the budget period under review, e.g. lease payments.

Variable costs are closely related to the estimated volume of goods
to be sold or manufactured in the budget period. These costs are sometimes called 'engineered costs', since it is possible to calculate the right
and proper amount for a given level of activity.

Managed costs are incurred at the discretion of management, and
unlike variable costs, have no cause and effect relationship with volume.
Specific decisions on managed costs are required in each budget period,
and many managed costs, once incurred, become committed costs for
subsequent periods. The costs in this area are generally concerned with
order getting, advertising and sales promotion, research and development, and expenses to promote a more favourable corporate image.

Estimated costs of manufacturing goods

To estimate the cost of manufacturing goods, the first step is to establish the production level. Budgeted production will vary from the sales forecast by changes in the finished stock position and also by changes in the stock of work in progress. Decisions on these stock levels will involve not only the production manager interested in physical resources, but also the accountant viewing the cash position and the sales manager considering the interests of the customers. Their plans must be coordinated in some organised framework through which communications and decisions can take place. Separate production cost budgets are needed for each step in the productive processes, and in compiling the detailed operating budgets it is necessary to take into account past experience of cost–volume relationships. The operating budgets must reflect the anticipated external economic conditions, and also the required internal standards of efficiency. This problem will be greatly eased if the company has satisfactory experience of operating a standard costing system. The detailed operating budgets must be prepared with an eye to their eventual use as control statements, and this means that separate budgets must be prepared for different centres of managerial responsibility, with a clear distinction made between contollable and uncontrollable costs and revenues.

Estimated distribution costs

Distribution costs are often more difficult to estimate than manufacturing costs, because of the incidence of managed costs. It is useful to distinguish between order-getting costs and order-filling costs. *Order-getting costs*, which are managed costs, are incurred in order to obtain sales, rather than as a result of sales. The factors which are likely to affect the level of the managed cost element are general economic conditions, behaviour of competitors, market research, past experience, and the general level of profit required within the company. The cost effectiveness of managed costs must be kept under review.

Order-filling costs are incurred after sales have been obtained, and in consequence there is a definite relationship between the volume of sales and these costs. Work measurement can often be used in this area in order to determine standards of performance which cover the fields of warehousing, packing, shipping, invoicing and collection. The measurable unit may not be sales value but, for example, the number of orders or invoices processed.

Estimated administration costs

Similar problems exist in the field of administration, and work measurement techniques are being increasingly applied here. In common with other areas within the business, management must constantly attempt to move costs from the discretionary category to the variable cost category. In this transfer, it is necessary to establish suitable measuring sticks which will assist in the planning and control of operations. Unsuitable measuring sticks are often used. For example, the manning of wages booking clerks may be mistakenly calculated on the basis of the number of factory operatives, whereas work volume and content should be the main determinants.

Matching estimated revenue and estimated costs

Having estimated revenues and costs the next step is to prepare a preliminary operating budget by matching them. But further analysis will be needed in order to determine whether the resultant profit is reasonable and satisfactory. Cost–volume–profit analysis is frequently used in this analysis which must precede the decision on the final operating budget.

Cost–volume–profit analysis

The preliminary operating budget consists of four interacting factors: cost, revenue, volume and profit. Since the factors interact, the preliminary operating budget may not necessarily represent the most satisfactory inter-relationship. By changing one or more of the four factors, the equation can be altered and cost–volume–profit analysis be used to choose the most satisfactory inter-relationship. The factors can be shown as in Figure 8.1.

Profit may be increased by:

1 decreasing managed costs
2 decreasing variable cost per unit
3 increasing sales price per unit
4 increasing volume.

Committed costs are not being considered at this point, since by definition they are the after-effects of decisions which cannot be reversed in the budget period. A company with high committed costs is in a relatively inflexible position, and room to manoeuvre in profit planning is limited.

Figure 8.1 concentrates attention on the four key factors which

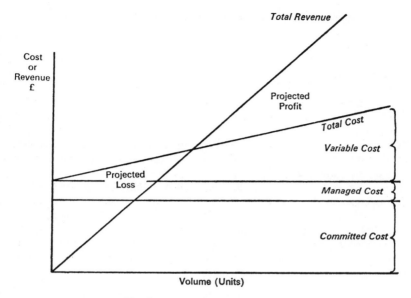

Fig. 8.1   Cost–volume–profit analysis

affect the level of operating profit, but it does contain limitations which must be clearly understood if it is to be used sensibly in profit planning.

1 The figure assumes that if one factor is altered all other factors remain unchanged. This is not necessarily so, and often factors may change in opposite directions. If this is the case, a detailed analysis of the net effect of the changes is required, and this cannot be achieved directly from the chart.

2 It is assumed that the product mix remains constant over all volumes. In a multi-product company, a change in the product mix will require a restatement of the chart at each affected volume.

3 The figure is drawn with straight lines at all levels of volume. This assumption is usually acceptable within a limited range of activity, but may not hold when the volume is extremely high or extremely low.

4 It is drawn on the assumption that sales and production are in balance and there are no changes in stock levels. The chart calculates profit on direct cost principles, and therefore the profit shown on the chart at a particular level of activity need not necessarily agree with the profit shown in the traditional profit

and loss account, in which a proportion of costs may be carried into stock.

Product break-even charts

Despite these limitations, break-even charts are useful in analysing different levels of operations; and individual product charts may represent their most significant application.

Consider a company which is hoping to introduce a new product. The following figure (8.2) represents the estimated situations for three products under discussion.

It is clear from the figure that Product A is likely at this stage to produce more profit than Products B or C. Product B will produce smaller profits even at very high volumes, and Product C will never produce profits until factors are changed, allowing the chart to be redrawn. These charts can act as useful indicators for managers when discussing new products and also when considering dropping existing products or determining the product mix.

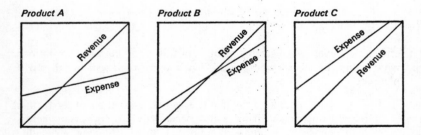

Fig. 8.2   Introduction of new products

The finalised operating budget

Two final steps need to be taken before the budget committee is in a position to agree upon a final operating budget.

First, it is vital to convert the operating aspects of profit planning into financial budgets in order to plan the financial resources which must support the operating plans. This involves planning for liquidity and funds management which are discussed further in Chapter 9.

Second, the concentration has been on profit and margins rather than on profitability. The budget committee must consider asset turnover and must also relate both margin and asset turnover together in an evaluation of rate of return on capital employed. The execution of the operating profit plans may involve the introduction of new products and additional plant facilities. It is not sufficient merely to concentrate on the resulting profits or savings in isolation, but to evaluate profits in relationship to capital employed. The problem of measuring the productivity of capital employed is examined in Chapter 10.

Finally, no planning and control system is complete without prompt and accurate feedback of operating results. Management at various levels must know how actual performance compares with budgeted performance, and analyses of the variances must be produced.

Case study no. 24 – break-even analysis

The basic tasks of setting budgets and standards made it clear to all concerned that a considerable proportion of total cost was fixed. John Marsh had had discussions with his managing director previously on the subject of fixed and variable costs, product contributions and the impact of volume and mix on profitability; now the subject was coming up again in relation to cost control. Much of the cost which one would ultimately want to charge to departments had to be located for responsibility accounting purposes in fixed cost budgets under the charge of the managing director, Howell, Marsh and Appleby, and as a result, the topic of cost variability and cost behaviour was getting very thoroughly aired.

Hardy broached it again one day when he said to Marsh, in Howell's presence, 'Once before, when I was concerned about the movements of profits and losses on the monthly trading statement, I mentioned my pal Olson and his talk about knowing the break-even point for sales in his business. We never really pursued that, did we?' John Marsh explained that a real knowledge of cost variability only came when one had some experience of the business and became actively involved in budgeting and standard-setting, so he had felt it reasonable to postpone any such exercise for a while. But he was, as usual, keen to show enthusiasm and suggested that the time was perhaps ripe now to pursue the matter further. Howell was interested, 'What do you propose to do then, lad?' he enquired. 'I thought that I'd produce a break-even chart on the basis of our agreed budget figures for the current year, and see where the break-even point lies. We'd then have a clear picture of our targets, because the chart would show the budget profits and losses at various levels of activity. If you like, I'll do a rough one right away.' John Marsh went back to the budget figures and took half-an-hour to produce his break-even chart.

When John rejoined his managing director and Howell, Wilf Appleby had arrived on the scene. 'On the basis of my figures, the break-even point is at approximately £286,000 sales, against our budget of £400,000,' said Marsh. 'In other words, we make our budgeted profit of £40,000 on turnover of £114,000 above the break-even point, so that the P/V ratio is near enough 35 per cent.' That required a little more explanation, which Marsh offered, before Howell and Appleby took up the cudgels. Howell said, 'Now hold on. You're not going to claim anything very wonderful for this, I hope, because it's got a lot of limitations. For one thing, the chart you've drawn only holds good provided that we stick to the mix of products which we budgeted for. And it makes no allowance for finished stock-holding of products—it assumes that all we make we sell, and vice-versa.' 'And there's worse to come,' said Appleby. 'Surely it's wrong to draw the chart with the fixed cost line running as a straight horizontal line across the chart, and the variable cost line as another straight line on top of it. Quite apart from the fact that we get alterations of prices of cost items at different levels of activity, our own flexible budgets recognise the existence of some variable costs which are not *directly* variable with output.'

John felt a little squashed, but the points made were fair and reasonable, and he admitted this. He suggested that the chart could be refined and improved and that he would look at it more closely with this in mind. His managing director said that he felt that this could be worthwhile, because a new product might be coming up for consideration, and he wondered how far break-even analysis could be useful in profit planning. John Marsh made the point that, as he saw it, it had two uses in profit planning; first, the revenue and costs of

any individual project could be illustrated in break-even
terms, so that the break-even point would be clear, and then
the effect of any project or projects on the total break-even
position could be determined. 'In other words,' he said, 'it
will answer the question whether a particular volume of output is viable or not as a profit plan.'

Required
1 Draw the break-even chart which John Marsh presented.
2 Criticise and appraise the chart stating its assumptions
   and limitations.
3 How do you see the role of break-even analysis in profit
   planning?

Case study no. 25 – the accountant and the economist discuss cost–revenue–output relationships

Kenneth Marshall was John's friend and an economist. He met John on the evening of the break-even chart debate. John suggested that they might discuss break-even analysis as it was seen by the economist on one hand and the accountant on the other.

Kenneth Marshall outlined the situation as it is usually presented in elementary economic text books. He emphasised that the economist was concerned with building a theory of the firm which shows how the businessman should make decisions involving pricing and the optimum level of output. The economist concludes that the firm will maximise its output by producing at the output where marginal cost equals marginal revenue. Output should be increased as long as the revenue from the next unit (marginal revenue) is greater than the costs of producing that unit (marginal cost). The relationships can be shown simply by graphs (see Figures 8.3 and 8.4).

It is assumed in these figures that it is usually necessary for prices to be reduced in order to increase the volume of sales. Thus the marginal revenue curve slopes downwards to the right, and is below the average revenue curve, indicating that the price of all previous units is lowered to make the additional sale.

The economist assumes that until point A is reached the

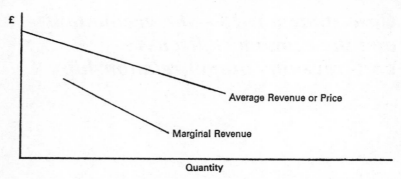

Fig. 8.3   Conventional economic analysis of revenue–output relationship

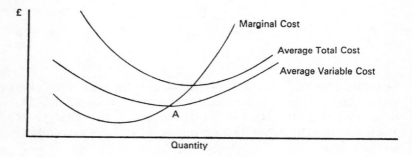

Fig. 8.4   Conventional economic analysis of cost–output relationship

economies of increased output apply to variable costs, as well as to fixed costs. Thus the average variable cost curve slopes downwards to the right reflecting increased efficiency, and then moves upwards as the quantity produced exceeds output at minimum average cost. This condition is often summarised as 'the law of diminishing returns' or 'the law of variable factor proportions.'

These two figures can be combined to demonstrate the cost–revenue–output relationships (Figure 8.5).

Kenneth Marshall showed that two break-even points were detailed on the figure, with a range of output between the two points which was profitable to the firm. The economist is concerned with showing the output which gives the maximum profit, and the optimum level of output is where marginal cost equals marginal revenue.

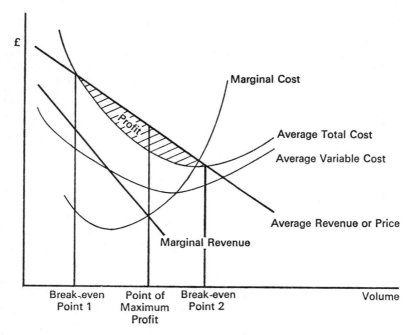

Fig. 8.5   Conventional economic analysis of cost–revenue–output relationships

John Marsh was grateful for this clear exposition of the attitudes of the economist. He pointed out that he was a pragmatist, and from a practical point of view there were a number of points which he would like to discuss arising from the economist's assumptions.

Referring to the revenue figure, John said that in practice firms tended to take the prices of their products as given, and to try to affect demand by other means such as advertising and sales campaigns. He was also rather unhappy about the cost figure. In his experience, which seemed to be confirmed by empirical cost studies, the average variable cost curve tends to fall slightly and unevenly over the whole range of output. The marginal cost curve thus tends to be constant or falling over a wide range of output. The 'U' curve, as shown in economic text books, does not seem to be substantiated in practice, since decreasing costs with size are almost universal, whereas sharply increasing costs with size are rarely encountered. Businessmen seem to anticipate the sharp upturn in the marginal cost curve, expand capacity, and move on to a different marginal cost curve.

John Marsh said that, in accounting text books, the profit graph or break-even chart usually assumed linear relationships between total costs and output, and between total revenue and output, as in Figure 8.6.

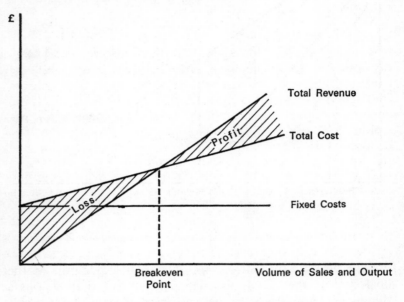

Fig. 8.6 Profit graph or break-even chart

The same figure can be expressed in average costs (Figure 8.7).

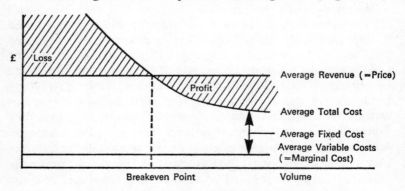

Fig. 8.7 Break-even chart expressed in average costs

John Marsh pointed out that the chart implies constant average revenue and constant average variable cost. Average variable cost is held to be equal to marginal cost at all levels of output, and both are constant. John said that, although the chart appeared to cover all production possibilities from zero to infinity, the accountant has in mind a given, though perhaps wide, range of activity. Within this relevant range of activity, the linear cost function is held to be a reasonable working approximation.

Kenneth Marshall thought that the accountant's assumption that average revenue (i.e. price) and marginal revenue are constant, existed only in conditions of perfect competition. The economist would suggest that markets for manufactured goods very rarely have conditions of perfect competition and would therefore justify a falling average revenue curve. The economist distinguished between the short-run situation and the long-run situation. It seemed from the break-even chart that while the accountant distinguished between fixed and variable costs, he might fail to distinguish between the short-run and long-run period.

John Marsh countered by querying whether it was possible in the multi-product firm to calculate accurately the economist's marginal costs of one unit of any one product. In practice the accountant usually has to satisfy himself by calculating the increase in revenues and costs arising from the additional sale of a 'block' of units. These 'differential' costs will equal the variable costs per unit times the number of units, plus any additional 'fixed costs' that arise from the increased production. The break-even chart can be used for profit planning within the firm, and differential cost analysis is extremely useful in analysing the financial aspects of business decisions.

Kenneth Marshall was concerned with the possible dangers of over-simplifying the problem of profit planning through the unskilled use of the break-even chart. He agreed that the break-even chart represented a convenient starting point, but the inbuilt assumptions and limitations should be clearly understood by the management of the company. But given this, they both agreed that within the individual firm it was extremely important to attempt to establish cost and revenue curves, both for the firm as a whole and for individual

products. This represented a field where the theory of
the economist and the pragmatism of the accountant could
be joined to further the economic planning and control of
the firm.

Required

1   On the economist's chart the 'point of maximum profit'
    represents an output less than that at minimum average
    total cost. Why?
2   What is meant by the law of variable factor proportions?
3   Detail how you would attempt to establish the cost and
    revenue curves for Hardy Heating Co. Ltd, and also for
    their individual products.

Case study no. 26 – a new product

Hardy Heating was not particularly adventurous in its product range, but now the suggestion scheme had come up with the idea of a plastic fan for automobiles, bigger than a metal fan, but much lighter in weight, and taking only a quarter of the power to drive. Naturally, such a fan would be flexible, and because the blades flatten out under pressure, engine resistance is cut also. Sam Howell was impressed, and a meeting with Jack Hardy, John Marsh and Appleby was quickly under way to consider the product itself and its viability, likely avenues of sale and methods by which market information might be obtained. Appleby got the job of pursuing the marketing aspects, starting first of all with visits to garages and shops, to try and form some picture of likely demand.

John Marsh accepted the responsibility for digging out cost information in respect of the new product, and was happy to lean on Sam Howell for much of the basic data. He had most of the information together in a rough and ready form when Appleby arrived in his office with a sales forecast. This was for the first year of the project, and based on sales to retail outlets (Figure 8.8).

The conversation between Marsh and Appleby was essentially a session in which John quizzed the sales manager about the method used to arrive at the figures and their

Forecast of sales quantities	Sales value each	Total sales value
150,000 and above	40p	£60,000
130,000	43p	£55,900
110,000	45p	£49,500
90,000	50p	£45,000
70,000	55p	£38,500
40,000	60p	£24,000
30,000	65p	£19,500
20,000	70p	£14,000

Fig. 8.8   Cost information on new product

accuracy. John believed that a project like this needed to be properly evaluated, and that a vital ingredient was reliable forecasts of sales.

But there was another vital ingredient, the one which John had been working on: cost information. John had prepared this for different levels of activity, based on some tentative ideas which the original discussion on the new product had thrown up. His statement was in two parts:

Part 1 Output and costs with present machinery

Output	Cost per unit	Total cost
30,000	35p	£10,500
40,000	30p	£12,000
50,000	25p	£12,500
60,000	25p	£15,000

Part 2 Output and costs with a new machine to supplement existing plant

Total output	Cost per unit	Total cost
70,000	43p	£30,100
90,000	35p	£31,500
110,000	30p	£33,000
130,000	25.5p	£33,150
150,000	23p	£33,750
170,000	21p	£36,125

John was pleased that the sales forecast and his own statement coincided near enough in the range of outputs. It was immediately apparent to him that some form of break-even analysis could be attempted if the two sets of figures were brought together. He felt that this would be a useful exercise. It did not evaluate a project, but at least it might aid the decision on price and volume to aim at. This would be useful.

Required
1   *What form of break-even analysis do you consider appropriate to this exercise? Prepare it.*
2   *Decide from this analysis the volume and price at which to aim.*
3   *Are there any qualifications you feel apply to the decision?*

Case study no. 27 – limiting factors

Things seemed to be getting very busy, since there was all the furore about getting into the field of plastic fans, the new look at planning the company's operations and thoughts about using any techniques which might help with profit planning. And in all these considerations, limiting factors were coming to the fore.

As Hardy himself put it, 'The bigger the business becomes, the wider its operations, the more limiting factors there are which can make themselves apparent at a moment's notice. Suddenly they're on you.' John Marsh did not entirely agree. He said, 'What we've got to try and do is to identify the current limiting factors and find ways to get round them. Also to anticipate, to plan for the limiting factors of the future, and to try to make appropriate plans for their solution.' Hardy asked, 'What are you including in your list of limiting factors?'

John Marsh pointed out the obvious restraints: shortage of space, plant capacity, labour, and particular things, such as the non-availability of an item of material, or a bottleneck on a particular piece of plant. 'But in addition there can be a limiting factor within management itself, a failure to develop or recruit the requisite managerial skills.' 'Well, that's not a crucial problem at the moment, as I see it,' retorted Sam

Howell. 'The fan project will bring most problems in the short term, and our planned upsurge of sales volume will bring a few more, mainly plant capacity and capital. It's clear that we will need to get involved in capital expenditure and our working capital requirements will be greater than up to now.'

Required

1 How significant are these 'limiting factors' in budgeting and planning for the operations of a business?
2 What techniques are available to solve the problems raised by limiting factors?
3 How might such limiting factors affect the pricing of products and be taken into account in determining product profitability?

9

Planning for funds

THE BUDGETS raised in planning for operations and profit in Chapter 8 are constructed on the same principles that were discussed in Chapter 3. Now the estimated revenues and costs must be converted into cash inflows and outflows, in order to produce the operating cash budget. This plan will allow management to begin to deal with the problems of liquidity and funds management, which are quite separate from those of profit or profitability. In addition to cash receipts and payments arising from internal current operations, all other inflows and outflows of cash have to be estimated including dividend and interest payments, taxation, long-term investments, and both short- and long-term finance raised outside the company. This second plan, which includes the surplus or deficit on the operating cash budget, is the finance budget.

The operating cash budget

In computing profit, a significant accounting problem is concerned with the point in time at which it is reasonable to conclude that revenues have been earned and costs have been incurred. In planning for funds, time is still an essential part of the problem, but in this case the critical factor is the point at which cash actually flows into and out of the company. The operating cash budget will differ from the operating budgets from period to period as a result of the following factors:

1 Revenue items, involving sales on credit, result in the first in-

stance in the creation of debts, with a time lag before the debt is converted into cash.

2 Costs included in operating budgets will often represent materials used or services performed before the actual cash is paid out. In some instances, the reverse situation applies, and cash is paid out prior to the inclusion of the expense in the operating budgets.

3 Certain items included in the operating budgets involve no outflow of cash, and are therefore omitted from the operating cash budget.

The expense of depreciation falls into this latter category. It is reasonable in computing profits to charge depreciation representing the use and obsolescence of the fixed assets. However, the actual cash outlay on the fixed assets has no connection with the charge for depreciation shown in the profit and loss account. The intention of the depreciation charge is to spread the cost of fixed assets to the particular periods or products that benefit from their use, so that the capital of the company remains intact. No cash outflow is involved in the depreciation charge, and so the item is not included in the operating cash budget. Provisions for repairs at the end of a lease, and for other long-term commitments involve no actual cash outlay and are similarly excluded. Other items—bad debts and cash discounts which represent reductions in the value of assets—are properly included as costs in operating budgets, but they involve no outflow of cash, and so are not included in the operating cash budget.

The periods covered by the operating cash budget may not necessarily be identical with those covered by the operating budgets. It may be necessary to plan for seasonal fluctuations, which will probably involve monthly budget periods, and perhaps even daily periods, if this detail is required.

It is quite possible that an operating budget which shows a profit has a matching operating cash budget (figure 9.1) which shows a deficit. The reverse positions may also occur. This emphasises the need to plan liquidity and funds as a separate management function from planning for profit, despite the fact that the two plans are obviously interconnected.

The finance budget (Figure 9.2)

The operating cash budget shows an estimated surplus or deficit of cash arising from current operations, but the company will not yet be in a position to consider the action required by such information. Other items affecting the operating cash surplus or deficit must now be considered.

Budgeted receipts	Jan.	Feb.	....	Dec.	TOTAL
Cash sales					
Receipts from debtors	____	____		____	____
	____	____		____	____
Budgeted payments					
Materials: cash purchases					
Payments to creditors					
Factory payroll					
Other production outlays					
(excluding depreciation, etc.)					
Selling outlays					
Administrative outlays					
Total payments					
Operating cash surplus	____	____		____	____
	____	____		____	____

Fig. 9.1.   Operating cash budget

Receipts	Jan.	Feb.	....	Dec.	TOTAL
Opening cash balance					
Operating cash surplus					
Investment income					
Total receipts	____	____		____	____
	____	____		____	____
Payments					
Taxation					
Preference dividends (net)					
Ordinary dividends (net)					
Interest payments (net)					
Bank interest					
Capital expenditure					
Total payments	____	____		____	____
Surplus finance or deficit to be financed					
Sale or purchase of investments					
Closing cash balance	____	____		____	____

Fig. 9.2   Finance budget

Taxation

A time lag exists in payment of taxation on a year's profits. The cash payment for taxation in any year will normally be based on the profits of the preceding year. The taxation payment based on the budgeted operating profit will be subject to a time lag averaging about one year. However, tax deducted from dividends must be paid in cash to the revenue authorities within one month of the payment of dividends.

Dividends and Interest

The amount to be included in the finance budget for these items will be net of income tax. Bank interest is an exception since the full amount is paid, and subsequently allowed as a charge in the computation of taxable profits. Payment of dividends on preference shares depends upon the adequacy of profits and liquid resources. Normally the directors will plan to pay the preference dividend, since to do otherwise might affect the credit rating of the company, and also may give voting rights to preference shareholders which in turn may affect the balance of control within the company.

Dividends on ordinary shares depend upon the type of company. A public company will be influenced by the level of past dividends and also by the expectations of the stock market in similar companies. Normally such companies will not distribute more than one-half or two-thirds of the profits available for dividend. A private company does not have these same considerations, and since the wishes of the shareholders can more easily be sounded, enjoys greater flexibility in dividend policy. But the requirements of the Inland Revenue regarding minimum distributions must be observed and in both types of company the dividend policy of the firm must be set against the background of the government's prices and incomes policy for the economy as a whole.

Capital expenditure cash budget

It is necessary to plan cash outlays on capital expenditure projects. The nature of the problem is such that once having committed the cash outlay, it is very difficult to retract without loss. Usually large sums of cash are involved in the expectation of worthwhile future returns, which will in turn be reflected in future operating budgets. Such projects may cover the replacement of fixed assets or expansion programmes, involving additional fixed assets and current assets, such as stocks and debtors. The volume and the timing of this expenditure are critical factors contributing to the future profitability of the company, and have in addition both an immediate and future impact on the finance budget. Such plans need to be very carefully integrated into the overall strategy of the company, and the immediate effects distinguished from the long term.

Having taken these points into account, the company now has an indication of the size of the financing problem. The resulting balances may represent a surplus or a deficit, and this raises the following management problems:

1 A surplus balance on the finance budget may involve further considerations of investment opportunities.
2 A deficit balance may indicate a need for short-term or for long-term finance.
3 In either case it may be necessary to make changes to the operating budgets and capital expenditure budgets in order to re-arrange the flows in the finance budget.

It is sometimes useful to produce an estimated statement similar to the funds statement shown in Chapter 3. In such a statement, the time lags involved in converting revenues and expenses into cash inflows and outflows are regarded as changes in working capital funds. Such changes will normally represent cash inflows or outflows after a short delay.

An example showing the residual financing problem is given in Figure 9.3.

Sources of funds	(£000)	(£000)
Internal from operations		
Profit before taxation for the year	50	
Funds retained equal to depreciation provision	10	
Funds retained equal to repairs provision	2	
		62
Uses of funds		
Taxation	20	
Dividends (net)	10	
Replacement of fixed assets	20	
Expansion programme—additional fixed assets	20	
Expansion programme—additional stocks and debtors	7	
		77
Deficit to be financed		15

Fig. 9.3 Estimated statement of sources and uses of funds for the year 19X1

This statement assumes that no changes are planned in the cash balance. Periodic fluctuations in the cash balance arising from time lags in converting the revenues and expenses into cash inflows and outflows can be examined in the operating cash budget.

The accountant—the funds flow manager

To regard the accountant as a manager primarily concerned with cash balances is to take an altogether too narrow view of the modern management accountant. Just as other managers are concerned with planning and controlling physical resources, the accountant has responsibility for managing money, not in the narrow sense of cash, but in the systems concept of funds. Funds flow through all the assets of a business, and the accountant has a critical part to play in deciding upon and managing the volume of funds and the speed they travel through the system. Since funds flow through the capital structure of the company, the plans of other managers will affect this flow, and thus in his role as 'funds flow manager' the accountant will be operating at both the strategic and operational level. Essentially, he co-ordinates managerial actions affecting the flow of funds. Except when the accountant's resource is actual cash, he controls funds circulating through other resources, which in their physical form represent the primary responsibility of other managers. These primary responsibilities in limited areas need to be co-ordinated in a total funds flow through the whole company; this is the job of the funds flow manager.

It is useful to separate the planning and control activities of the funds flow manager into planning the provision of funds, and into planning and controlling their use. Planning their use concerns the management of the capital expenditure programme and this is taken up in Chapter 10.

The provision of funds

The main type of funds outlined in Chapter 2 were:

1   retained profits or internal funds;
2   long-term external funds in the form of loan and share capital;
3   short-term funds in the form of bank credit, trade credit, including hire-purchase.

The funds flow manager must decide on the balance between long-term and short-term capital and on the balance between loan capital and share capital in the total capital requirements of the company.

Total capital requirements

The funds flow manager is responsible for planning the total volume of funds which is adequate for the business. The total capital requirement depends on factors relating to the nature of the enterprise, the operating characteristics of the industry, the size of the physical plant, the length of the production cycle, methods of stocking and distribution, terms of sales, patterns of growth, and the stability of the industry. It also depends on management decisions about the degree of risk to be assumed, about the extent to which property will be purchased rather than leased, and also the scale of operations which will be attempted.

In some respects it is easier to judge whether the total capital available is adequate for a given level of operations than it is to firmly decide upon the level of operations.

Symptoms of inadequate total capital are:

1   inability to cope with minor changes in business activity;
2   inability to seize profitable opportunities as they appear;
3   inability to maintain a satisfactory working capital position—i.e. stocks too low for activity levels, inability to take cash discounts, difficulty in granting normal terms of credit;
4   inability to make necessary capital expenditure outlays at the appropriate time.

Symptoms of excessive total capital are:

1   excessive stocks and loose credit policies;
2   investment in projects giving inadequate returns;
3   poor management control systems;
4   reductions in the rate of return on capital employed.

In most businesses the major problem is more likely to be one of inadequate total capital rather than excessive total capital. For small and medium sized businesses, a period of rapid expansion can bring with it considerable financial problems. Rapid growth may well involve a need to finance increased stocks, increased level of debtors, and increased fixed assets, which exceeds the profit generated by the increased activity. Liquid capital required in large quantities at relatively short notice can produce severe problems for the funds flow manager. In such circumstances it is quite possible for a company which is producing and selling efficiently, with a full order book, to be pushed out of business through its inability to make adequate financial arrangements. It is possible to stretch the existing capital base and re-arrange the timing of the funds flow by:

1   factoring debts
2   obtaining extended credit terms;
3   obtaining advances on sales;
4   leasing and renting rather than purchasing.

But each of these involves some cost to the business and must be viewed against the ability of the company to attract additional capital, either in a permanent or short-term form.

Long-term versus short-term finance

A well-known business maxim is that long-term capital should finance all fixed assets and permanent working capital, and that short-term sources of capital should be used to finance short-term requirements. Excessive reliance on short-term capital may produce critical problems if the source is suddenly reduced or withdrawn; and this is a particular danger in times of rapid expansion. The small or medium sized company has a particular problem to plan its finances to deal with seasonal patterns, uneven corporate growth, and intermittent capital investment requirements. In such companies, long-term finance is often costly and difficult to arrange, and thus the company is faced with relying on short-term credit, and patiently building up its permanent finance from retained profits. In other companies the danger may be the reverse, i.e. long-term finance is surplus to current requirements. This may occur if a company is contracting, or if large seasonal changes take place.

Debt capacity

Since loan capital is generally cheaper than share capital, the balance of advantage would seem to lie with taking on further additions of loan capital. However, the limit to this strategy is imposed by the risk that earnings may be insufficient to cover the contractual debt of interest payments. The extent of the risk will depend upon the relationship of interest to earnings and also upon the degree of fluctuations in earnings. Generally speaking, the greater the degree of fluctuations in earnings, the lower should be the gearing of the company. The debt capacity of a business represents a resource which needs to be managed, and its use is just as important as that of more obvious physical resources. If the resource of debt capacity is ignored, or not used to proper limits, the effects on the company could be very similar to those stemming from the under-utilisation of physical resources.

A major task of the funds flow manager is to maintain financial flexibility to meet both current and future capital requirements in order to take advantage of investment opportunities at a reasonable capital cost without undertaking undue financial risks.

Case study no. 28 – depreciation: a source of funds?

John Marsh was discussing the question of obtaining new plant with Sam Howell. To some extent the conversation had been sparked off by the plastic fan project. The chief accountant pointed out that two separate problems were involved: the first concerned the choice amongst competing projects and alternative pieces of plant; the second covered the methods by which the capital expenditure was to be financed.

Sam agreed that he always had difficulty in choosing between alternative capital expenditure plans, and would welcome ideas on methods the company could use to evaluate and control capital expenditure. He said that the financing of the capital expenditure should be no problem. The company had been building up depreciation reserves for many years, and in his opinion it was about time that some of these were used. Further, there were other reserves in the form of retained profits.

Required

1   Advise Sam Howell on the use of depreciation reserves and retained profits.

Case study no. 29 – preliminary analysis of finance planning

'With the advent of a new project, which is obviously going to have capital requirements, do we need to plan for any additional finance in the future?' said Hardy to John Marsh over lunch one day. John said that he would need a little time before he could answer the problem, but hurried back to his office.

His first thought was that Hardy and Howell must be telepathic, or trying him out. Here was Howell talking about the use of depreciation reserves and almost at the same time the managing director asking about requirements for additional funds. On the other hand, it was significant stuff, and he thought hard about it.

John concluded that two separate problems were involved. First, he had to determine the size of the capital requirement, if any. To do this he must take a look at the estimated cash inflows and outflows in detail for the next 12 months, and in outline for a longer period. And second, if his estimates showed that the activities of the company required additional finance in the future, he had to determine the nature of the requirement. He also had to specify whether it was a long-term or a short-term requirement and which sources of additional capital should be used. On the other hand, if his estimates showed that surplus funds were anticipated, he had to prepare plans for their proper investment.

In dealing with the first problem he realised that he would need to seek information about future activities from Howell and Appleby. This information would have to be co-ordinated, and policy decisions agreed on: the size of stock levels, the use of factory capacity, the use of overtime and weekend working, and the timing of sales drives.

John Marsh sighed when he realised that his job would have been much easier if the company had fully developed its system of budgetary control. In the present circumstances he had to be prepared to remedy this situation. He was able to build up estimates of outflows of cash for running costs, but he needed to refer to Jack Hardy for more detail on capital expenditure.

John Marsh considered that he now knew how to approach the first problem, and decided that in tackling the second, it would be useful to have a clear picture of the sources of long-term and short-term finance.

He therefore produced a diagram (Figure 9.4) of each of these which he anticipated would be useful in explaining his reasoning to Jack Hardy.

John Marsh felt that he had now finished his preliminary analysis of the problem, and was now in a position to build up detailed statements.

Required
1 Anticipate the difficulties which are likely to arise in estimating cash inflows and outflows.
2 What would John Marsh's detailed statements comprise?
3 Assuming that finance is required, decide how you would determine whether a long-term or short-term source should be used.
4 Outline the considerations involved in making a choice between the alternatives of fixed return and residual return terms.

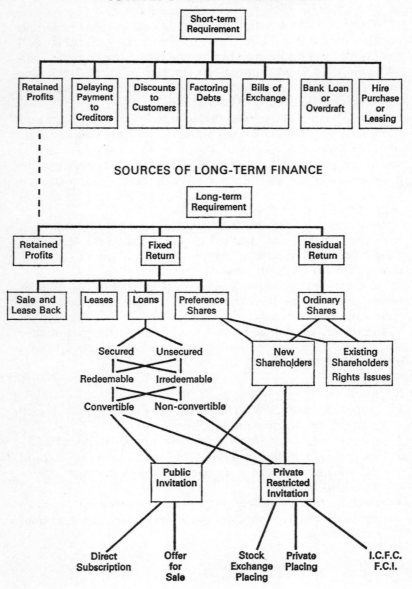

Fig. 9.4   Sources of finance

Case study no. 30 – finance and the new product

It was quite clear to John that additional capital would be required to finance the plastic fan project, and he decided that the assessment of this was a matter in which he could interest Jean Wilkins and call upon her assistance. It looked as though production was going to be projected at the rate of 80,000 for the first year and 130,000 for the second year, and he gave Jean this information together with the sales forecast and his own output and cost statement.

She produced two documents, the first of which outlined the likely capital cost of the new plant, when this was purchased.

Capital cost of new plant

	£
One R.H. Swindon injection moulding machine	20,000
2 Dies (One for existing machine)	6,000
Re-granulator	3,000
	29,000

Investment grant at the rate of 25% on this capital cost will be payable within 18 months of the date of purchase	£7,250

If purchased on H.P. over 5 years with an interest rate of 8% non-diminishing, in other words an effective 16%

Interest	£2,320 p.a.
Capital repayments £29,000 over 5 years	5,800 p.a.
	£8,120

This would mean a cash outflow of £677 per month.

John was interested to know why Jean had assumed that the plant would be bought on H.P. She said that it was nothing more than a guess, but she believed that her second document gave some clues.

ESTIMATE OF ADDITIONAL CASH OUT-FLOWS ARISING FROM FAN PRODUCTION

(a) Projected production: year 1   80,000
                               year 2   130,000

(b) If one assumes an average of 2 months' credit and 1 month's production, the estimated additional cash requirement would be for 3 months' production.

So in the first year, the average additional load
$$= 20,000 \times 35p \quad = \quad £7,000$$
While in the second year, it is $32,500 \times 25.5p =$ £8,287

(c) On the other hand, estimates of seasonal fluctuations show

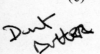

January, February and March	25% above average
April, May and June	25% below average
August and September	10% above average
November and December	10% below average
July and October	Average

(d) This implies that during the first year of the project, the maximum additional load would be (in January to March 1970)

       (£7,000 plus 25%) plus H.P. £677 = £9,427

And that during the second year, the maximum addition would be

       (£8,287 plus 25%) plus H.P. £677 = £11,036

(e) Since bank balances throughout the year are currently between £10,000 favourable and £10,000 overdraft (the present limit), the bank might support the additional working capital requirement, but this would leave the source of funds for the fixed assets undecided.

John was delighted with Jean's efforts. 'You've made a good start,' he said, 'but we'll need to go further. You see, you've been absolutely correct with your assessment of the capital costs and of the additional load of working capital requirements, but there is a need to get a month-to-month picture of the overall effect which this project will have on our liquidity position. Your statements really ought to be brought together into a cash budget, which properly accounts for the inflows as well as the outflows.'

Required

1 What are the limitations of the cash flow assessment which Jean has made?
2 Draft your own cash budget for the first two years of this project, making whatever assumptions are required.
3 Appraise the results of your cash budget, and specify the problems which it implies for Hardy Heating.

10

The planning and control of capital expenditure

The importance of capital expenditure decisions

Capital expenditure decisions are some of the most formidable that have to be made by management. When a decision has to be made to invest in long-lived *FIXED* assets, the company is usually committing itself to operating those assets for some time, and a reversal of the decision will probably mean selling the assets at a loss. These decisions shape the bed on which the company must lie in the future, and thus are mutually important to the shareholder, the employee, the consumer and the economy as a whole.

The shareholder is interested since capital expenditure decisions affect earning power and growth. The employee is affected since the investment may result in an improvement in profits and productivity, from which he may expect increased earnings. The consumer hopes to benefit from an increase in productivity by an improvement in quality or reduction in price. The economy as a whole is affected by the total volume of the investment, together with its timing and quality.

We can consider the total investment in a company as a series of projects or investment decisions.

In the traditional accounting statements emphasis is placed on the vertical rectangle (see Figure 10.1) which represents a cross-section of projects during a one-year period, whereas in capital expenditure decisions the concentration is on projects such as A, which covers a number of years.

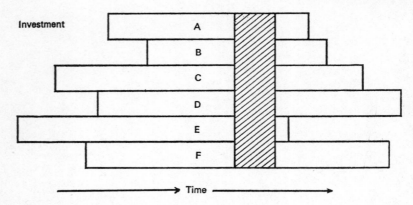

Fig. 10.1   Cross-section of projects over one-year period

The essential problem in capital investment appraisal

Figure 10.2 shows the pattern of cash inflows and outflows which might be involved in a capital expenditure decision.

The essential problem is to determine whether the cash outflow involved in the investment is justified by the cash inflows which will be created over its life.

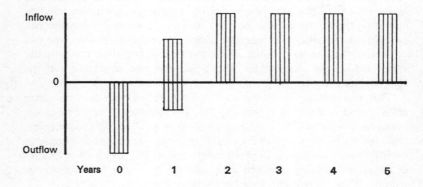

Fig. 10.2   Pattern of cash inflows and outflows

The factors which need to be evaluated are illustrated in Figure 10.2. They are:

1 the initial cost of the project;
2 the phasing of the expenditure over the project;
3 the estimated life of the investment;
4 the amount and timing of the resulting income.

The outflow of funds needed to acquire a capital asset is called 'the investment'. In the case of a renewal project, the investment will be not the cost of the asset, but the amount of funds needed to cover the difference between the cost of the new asset and the trade-in value of the old.

The inflows represent funds generated by the investment and can be called 'returns'. The returns on a project are represented by the excess of added revenue over added costs (other than depreciation, since in capital expenditure decisions depreciation over the life of the asset is represented by the investment). *[handwritten: NO depreciation]*

The comparison of returns with investment

Capital expenditure decisions involve comparing the two streams of funds, and if *returns* less *investment* is positive, a favourable decision may be indicated. However, the two flow at different times. In many projects returns from an initial investment outlay are yielded over a long period of time. It is necessary to make some adjustment for this time difference for two main reasons. First, we must wait for returns to materialise and such waiting implies uncertainty due to the inherent difficulty of long-term forecasting. Second, the waiting involves the sacrifice of present consumption or other investment opportunities. *[handwritten: Money in bank]* The process of adjustment for the time differential which takes into account uncertainty and sacrifice of alternative uses of funds, is known as discounting. The effect of discounting is to express the two streams of investment and returns in present value equivalents. The discount rate must be selected with care and represents a most important management decision. The discount rate is related to the cost of capital to the company, and is often expressed as the required earnings rate. The incidence of taxation has a significant effect on the timing of the streams of investment and returns. If the term:

> Total present values of returns   —   Total present value of
> after tax charges   investment after tax relief

results in a positive figure, then a capital expenditure project appears successful.

The capital expenditure management programme

There are distinct dangers in concentrating too heavily on the evaluation aspects of capital expenditure projects budgeting. In order to place the evaluation techniques in proper perspective, the main components of a capital expenditure management programme should be looked at.

The search for profitable opportunities

As the speed of technological change increases and the life cycle of products and processes becomes shorter, the search for new and more profitable activities becomes more intense. Management must organise to ensure a constant flow of investment opportunities for appraisal, and this involves the combination of a number of activities: market research, economic forecasting, cost estimating, profitability analysis, simulation. Management must look into the future, and try to measure economic attractiveness. An important part of the problem for the accountant is to recognise the assumptions and also identify the intangibles which require management judgement.

The identification of relevant alternatives

There is rarely only one way of carrying out a project, and a careful evaluation of alternatives is essential. When considering machinery to carry out specified tasks, there are frequently several new machines which will perform satisfactorily, but each might involve a different investment and a different flow of returns. Often the existing machine need not be replaced this year, and therefore the timing of the replacement needs to be considered. A satisfactory decision must begin with a consideration of the best alternatives.

The determination of costs and revenues

The costs and revenues which are relevant to the capital expenditure decision are those arising from the decision to invest. The emphasis is on future incremental cash flows and not on traditional historical cost accumulation. It is cash flows and not book values that are important in the long-run assessment and not the short-run statement. The information used for evaluation may, therefore, be different from that shown in accounting statements.

The screening and ranking of projects

The next step is to determine whether the project offers satisfactory returns. A minimum satisfactory rate of return must be determined, and the firm's cost of capital is one factor in this. Assuming that satisfactory projects have now been short-listed, the next problem is to rank the projects in order of attractiveness. To do this, we must be able to measure the benefits of projects, and express the results in measures that can be used for comparison. Both before and after this stage of evaluation, management must exercise judgement on issues of overall company strategy. These factors which weigh with them may not necessarily all be included in the return on investment computation.

The administrative control system

Procedures must be developed to cover applications for the authorisation of expenditure. Once the expenditure is authorised, controls are needed to ensure that expenditure conforms to specification and is within the authorised amount. Periodic statements will be required to assess progress and outstanding commitments. An audit of such statements will help to ensure the accuracy of future estimates, and also allow the benefits of experience to be applied to future projects. Finally procedures must be devised to cover the disposal of assets when the market value of the asset exceeds the value of its future earnings.

Case study no. 31 – a capital expenditure decision (1)

Sam Howell had been considering the problem of replacement of one of the automatic moulding machines, and had had some discussions with John Marsh about it. Apparently there were three possible alternative machines which could be purchased: a Tri-Rod machine, near enough the same as the present machine, and from the same British supplier; a Poli-dot machine from France; and an American Plastidex machine.

In discussion John stressed the need for proper evaluation of the alternatives and made the point that the first step was to estimate accurately the cash flows for each of the alternatives. Howell and Jean Wilkins had done this and produced the figures shown in Figure 10.3.

Sam stressed that the figures were approximate, but that no one was likely to be able to prepare better estimates.

John, eager to show Sam that he was familiar with some of the latest management techniques, decided to point out the weaknesses as well as the strengths of the various ways of looking at capital expenditure decisions. He prepared his case carefully and at a meeting with Sam he outlined three methods of evaluating capital expenditure decisions:

	The Tri-Rod Machine (A)	The Polidot Machine (B)	The Plastidex Machine (C)
	£	£	£
Initial outlay (approx.)	10,000	10,000	10,000
Cash inflows			
Year 1	1,000	4,000	3,000
2	2,000	3,000	3,000
3	3,000	3,000	3,000
4	3,000	1,000	3,000
5	3,000	500	2,000
6	3,400	500	1,000
	15,400	12,000	15,000

Fig. 10.3   Cash flows for each alternative

1   payback
2   unadjusted rate of return
3   discounted cash flow.

Payback

John said that the object of this method was to calculate the length of time which must elapse before the cash inflow from the project equals the total initial cash outflow. This method gave the following results:

	Machine A	Machine B	Machine C
Payback method	$4\frac{1}{3}$ years	3 years	$3\frac{1}{3}$ years

Sam Howell reflected carefully, 'I can see that this method tells us when we will get our money back, and in fact suggests that we should invest in Machine B. But you keep on telling us that we should be interested in rate of return on capital employed, and this method tells us nothing about the return we are making after we have covered the initial outlay.'

John Marsh nodded, and said that another major weakness was that the payback method ignores the timing of cash flows.

Unadjusted rate of return

John said that the object of this method was to calculate the average annual profit as a percentage of the original cash outlay.

	Machine A £	Machine B £	Machine C £
Total profit covering six years	5,400	2,000	5,000
Average annual profit	900	330	830
Initial cash outlay	10,000	10,000	10,000
Unadjusted rate of return	9%	3.3%	8.3%

Sam was interested to see the calculation of a rate of return on capital employed, but said that it now seemed that he should purchase Machine A, which was the least favoured machine under the payback method. John Marsh explained that the unadjusted rate of return method again did not take into account the timing of cash flows, and there were obvious dangers in working on an average basis of the whole life of the projects.

Sam asked whether there was a method which dealt with the difficult problem of the timing of cash flows. He pointed out that the £1,000 receivable at the end of year 1 in the case of Machine A was given the same weight under this second method as the £1,000 receivable at the end of year 6 in the case of Machine C. Sam preferred money today rather than money tomorrow, and in his opinion any sensible method of evaluating capital projects should take this simple preference into account.

Discounted cash flow

John said that the discounted cash flow method covered satisfactorily Sam's objections to the first two methods. The basic problem was that Sam was faced with an immediate cash outflow to purchase the machine, from which would arise future cash inflows. As Sam rightly said, he preferred to calculate in present values; in other words he wished to express future cash inflows in present values. Sam winced at what he regarded as 'jargon', but agreed that £1,000 receivable in one year's time was worth less than £1,000 receivable now. John asked him to state the value of £1,000 receivable in one year's time. Sam thought for a moment and replied that the answer depended upon the rate of interest which was used, but using a 10 per cent rate of interest the £1,000 receivable in one year's time was worth £909 now. John agreed. The £909 could be invested at 10 per cent, which would represent a total of £1,000 in one year's time.

Just at that point, the foreman of the machine shop entered hurriedly. 'You'll have to make up your mind about the replacement of that old machine, because we've got another breakdown on our hands.' Sam frowned and told John to produce some figures which gave him some real advice. At the moment he was confused by the ranking of the machines under the first two methods.

	Payback	Unadjusted rate of return
Ranking 1	Machine B	Machine A
2	Machine C	Machine C
3	Machine A	Machine B

'The first shall be last and the last shall be first. Accountants! I expect that you'll tell me next that the discounted cash flow method will give yet another ranking.' John Marsh backed out, saying he would return when Sam had settled his engineering problems.

Required

1 Using a 10 per cent discount rate complete the following table representing the present value of £1000 receivable at the end of a number of years.

(present day)	YEAR 0	£1,000
	YEAR 1	£909
	YEAR 2	
	YEAR 3	
	YEAR 4	

2 Evaluate the capital expenditure decision, using the discounted cash flow method.

Case study no. 32 – a capital expenditure decision (2)

John Marsh took up the problem of the three machines once again. 'I know you are anxious to make a decision, but the very essence of capital expenditure decisions is that we shall be committing resources for a long period of time. It is worthwhile taking a long look at the problem, because once we have committed the resources, it will not be easy to retract.'

Sam Howell agreed, but pointed out that meanwhile his old machine was breaking down regularly. 'This,' said John, 'reflects the need to regard the planning of capital expenditure as a major management problem, and so the company should be organised to deal with the planning and control of such expenditure.'

He quickly went on to the discounted cash flow method of evaluating capital expenditure decisions. Two main ways of using the discounted cash flow technique, he said, were the *net present value method* and *the yield or internal rate of return method*.

Net present value method

In this method, as Figure 10.4 shows, a minimum required earnings rate is assumed, and the present value of a project is

		10% dis- count rate	MACHINE A		MACHINE B		MACHINE C	
				present value		present value		present value
Year	CASH OUTFLOW							
0	Initial outlay	£1	10,000	10,000	10,000	10,000	10,000	10,000
	CASH INFLOW							
1		£0.909	1,000	909	4,000	3,636	3,000	2,727
2		0.826	2,000	1,652	3,000	2,478	3,000	2,478
3		0.751	3,000	2,253	3,000	2,253	3,000	2,253
4		0.683	3,000	2,049	1,000	683	3,000	2,049
5		0.621	3,000	1,863	500	310	2,000	1,242
6		0.564	3,400	1,918	500	282	1,000	564
			15,400	10,644	12,000	9,642	15,000	11,313
	PROFITABILITY INDEX			$\frac{10,644}{10,000}$ = 1.06		$\frac{9,642}{10,000}$ = 0.96		$\frac{11,313}{10,000}$ = 1.13

Fig. 10.4   Calculation of the net present value method

calculated by discounting all future cash flows at the required earnings rate. If the sum of these exceeds the initial outflow, then the project is giving a return greater than the required earnings rate.

To compare two or more projects, the accountant can compute the profitability index of each project by dividing the net present value of returns by the net present value of outlays. The project with the highest profitability index is the one to prefer.

John asked Sam to examine the table and pointed out that, assuming a required earnings rate of 10 per cent, Machines A and C would give a return greater than 10 per cent. Machine B, however, failed to meet the required earnings rate of 10 per cent.

In comparing Machines A and C, the profitability index of C is greater than the profitability index of A. Machine C best meets the required earnings rate and is the one to prefer.

Although Sam felt that working in present values was right, he wondered whether it was possible to state the return to be obtained from each project separately. John Marsh replied that this was the objective of the yield or internal rate of return method.

Yield or internal rate of return method

All future cash flows from a project are discounted at a variety of discount rates until by trial and error the rate is found at which the present value of outlays and returns are equal. John said that he had calculated the yield of each project as follows:

	Machine A	Machine B	Machine C
Yield or internal rate of return	12%	8%	15%

He showed that this rate of return could be shown in the form of a repayment statement from a bank or building society, a form with which Sam Howell was familiar (Figure 10.5).

Year	Net investment at start of year £	Interest at 15% £	Cash inflow £	Reduction of investment £
1	10,000	1,500	3,000	1,500
2	8,500	1,275	3,000	1,725
3	6,775	1,016	3,000	1,984
4	4,791	719	3,000	2,281
5	2,510	376	2,000	1,624
6	886	114 (adjusted)	1,000	886
		5,000	15,000	10,000

Fig. 10.5   Repayment statement—Machine C

One point that Sam made was that it might not be possible to re-invest the earnings from Machine C at 15 per cent.

John Marsh agreed that this was a problem, and added that there is not always a unique rate of return. There may be more than one rate of return for the same project. He mentioned also the difficulty in estimating the life of the project, and pointed out that the internal rates of return would have been different if they had assumed a seven-year life instead of a six-year life for the machine.

In the net present value method an obvious difficulty lies in deciding what interest rate should be used for discounting. Should the minimum required earnings rate be the borrowing rate of the company or the lending rate? John also argued that allowance should be made for the period in which the receipts are received, since money received in the third year of a project may be worth more, due to a shortage of cash, than an equivalent amount of money received in the second year.

John thought that despite these problems, there was real benefit in evaluating the project on a discounted cash flow basis. Now he wanted to demonstrate to Sam the significant effects of taxation on investment decisions, and would return to take up the discussion, when he had reworked the examples on an after-tax basis.

Required

1 Compare the net present value method with the yield method, considering their application to differing projects with differing capital sums to be invested.
2 What should be the minimum required earnings rate of projects for the company?

Case study no. 33 – a capital expenditure decision (3)

John returned again, this time to deal with the taxation and grant aspects of investment appraisal. He presented Sam Howell with a sheet on which he had listed the main factors regarding tax, taxation allowances and investment grants and went through these with him.

Sam appreciated all these points, but seemed grateful to have them summed up in this way. John continued, 'Well, those are the facts which we must take into account. I have computed the after-tax position for the three machines on a discounted cash flow basis and Machine C is still to be preferred. However, the position of Machine B is most interesting.' (See Figure 10.6.)

These figures surprised Sam Howell. 'On a pre-tax basis, Machine B did not meet the required earnings rate of 10 per cent. Yet on a post-tax basis, the project is making more than 10 per cent.

John Marsh said that the explanation lay in the investment grant and the timing of the tax payments. Nevertheless he agreed that from a management point of view it was most important to appreciate that Machine B had a greater earnings rate on an after-tax basis than on a before-tax evaluation. This meant that unless valuations were made on an after-tax basis many potentially satisfactory projects might be turned down.

NET CASH INVESTMENT   Initial outlay   10,000
Less cash grant   2,500 × 0.909   2,272
                                         ─────
                                         7,728

	1	2	3	4	5	6	7
Year	Increased profits	Tax on increased profits at 40%	Annual allow-ances	Tax saved by allow-ances	Cash flow 1 − 2 + 4	Present value factor 10%	Present value
	£	£	£	£	£	£	£
1	4,000	—	1,875	750	4,750	0.909	4,318
2	3,000	1,600	1,406	562	1,962	0.826	1,621
3	3,000	1,200	1,055	422	2,222	0.751	1,669
4	1,000	1,200	791	317	117	0.683	80
5	500	400	593	237	337	0.621	209
6	500	200	1,780	712	1,012	0.564	571
7	—	200	—	—	(−200)	0.513	(−103)
	12,000	4,800	7,500	3,000	10,200		8,365

Profitability index: $\dfrac{8,365}{7,728}$ = 1.08

Fig. 10.6   Discounted cash flow—net present value method after tax: Machine B

Sam Howell confirmed that in the future he would like to examine the post-tax evaluations. He could see that this was particularly important if he had to make a choice between projects in which the incidence of expenditure, sales and profits expected, and working capital needs differed widely.

Sam thanked John for his efforts, which had been very useful in analysing this difficult management problem. Sam remarked that non-monetary factors would still be most important in the capital expenditure decision—but at least he now had a better understanding of the financial aspects of the problem.

Required

1 *Compute the* net present value *after tax of Machines A and C.*
2 *Compute the* yield and internal rate of return, *after tax of the three machines.*
3 *What are the non-monetary factors in capital expenditure decisions to which Sam was referring?*

Case study no. 34 – the cost of capital

John Marsh had recently involved the senior management in the various ways of evaluating capital investment projects. In these exercises, a 10 per cent required earnings rate had been used. Sam Howell, the works director, had been particularly interested in these studies and had written a memorandum on the problems of calculating the required earnings rate. Extracts from the memorandum are given below:

'I have been giving some thought to the problem of the earning rates which we require from investment projects. I have based my observations on the following most recent statement of capital structure and earnings.' (See Figures 10.7 and 10.8.)

'It seems possible to justify a number of required earnings rates for capital investment projects, for instance:

1 the return on the equity capital, including retained profits, was 18.2 per cent after tax. It seems unreasonable for the two working directors, who are the majority shareholders, to involve themselves in investments which offer a return less than that which has been obtained in the past;

2 on the other hand, the after-tax return on the net assets of £160,000 amounted to 12.5 per cent;

3 however, the company has debt capacity which can be

			£000	£000
%	Loans	Electrical trades		
		Finance company (5%)	30	
		ICFC　　　　　(7%)	10	
25.0				40
6.25	Preference	10,000 6% preference		
		shares of £1 each		10
	Equity	50,000 ordinary shares		
		of £1 each	50	
		Retained profits	60	
68.75				110
100.00				160

Fig. 10.7　Capital structure at 30 September 1968

	£000
Profit before interest and tax	36.1
Interest	2.0
Earnings before tax	34.1
Corporation tax	13.5
	20.6
Preference dividend (including tax)	0.6
Earnings available to ordinary shareholders	20.0
Dividends on ordinary shares	5.0
Retained profits	15.0

Fig. 10.8　Earnings for year ended 30 September 1968

used to finance part of the capital expenditure programme. The cost of this loan capital would probably be 8 per cent per annum before tax, i.e. 4.8 per cent after tax;

4 further, the majority of the programme will be financed from retained profits and depreciation provisions. Corporation tax will have been paid on these funds and, therefore, the cost of this capital is nil.

An authoritative statement is required from you detailing the appropriate rate to be used in the future.'

John Marsh reflected on this latest problem. At the moment, Hardy Heating was a close company but hoped to become a public company with widespread shareholdings in two to three years.

Required

1 *Reply to the points raised in the memorandum and pre-pare a statement of the earnings rate required by Hardy Heating from capital projects.*

A meeting was arranged to discuss the recommendations of · the chief accountant. John started by saying that he had iso-lated the factors which needed to be considered, but some judgement would need to be applied by top management before a cut-off rate could be started. 'For instance, do you want me to calculate the cut-off rate for a close company, as we are at the moment, where the interests of yourself and Jack Hardy are paramount? Or shall I calculate it for Hardy Heating as a public company, which we are planning to become within the next three years? The taxation and personal aspects are so different in the two situations that the cut-off rates might well be different.'

John explained that he had made a number of assump-tions, which he had listed, and had produced four tables showing different methods of calculating the cost of capital. He justified the concentration on the cost of capital, rather than on the historical earning power of the assets, by referring to the marginal analysis approach of the economist. He argued that it was reasonable to accept projects only if they showed promise of a rate of return in excess of the cost of financing.

If this approach was accepted, the next step was to calcu-late the cost of capital. One basic problem, here, was whether to concentrate on the cost of:

1 the sources of capital which had been used in the past;
2 the particular source of finance which was to be tapped in the immediate short term to finance capital expen-diture;
3 the weighted average of capital which represented a de-sirable financial structure for the company in the medium-term future.

John Marsh then drew attention to the four tables which he had prepared. Figures 10.9 and 10.10 were both based on the historical rates of interest and yields on equity. In Figure 10.9 the cost of equity was based on the historical dividend rate and, in Figure 10.10, the cost of equity was based on the historical earnings rate.

John pointed out that the historical rates were not necessarily a guide to what was expected or what was desirable in the future. He also emphasised that complete reliance on the dividend rate might seriously underestimate the cost of equity capital, particularly in the case of growth companies which often had a very low dividend yield.

Sam agreed that historical rates of return were not the answer, but made the point that the company expected to

| Equity based on historical dividend rate | | | |
	Capital structure	After-tax rate %	Cost
Loans 18.75		3.0	0.56
6.25		4.2	0.26
	25.0		
Preference	6.25	6.0	0.37
Equity	68.75	4.5	3.09
	100.00%		4.28

Fig. 10.9 Weighted historical cost

| Equity based on historical earnings rate | | | |
	Capital structure	After-tax rate %	Cost
Loans 18.75		3.0	0.56
6.25		4.2	0.26
	25.0		
Preference	6.25	6.0	0.37
Equity	68.75	18.2	12.50
	100.00%		13.69

Fig. 10.10   Weighted historical cost

finance the majority of its capital expenditure from depreciation provisions and net retained profits. Since tax had been paid, the cost of this capital was, presumably nil. John could not agree and referred to the opportunity cost of the retained profit; that is, the return which could be obtained from the alternative employment in similar equity investment. He pointed out that on distribution of retained profits, a leakage of income tax occurred and, thus, the company could always obtain a higher 'net of all taxes' return on investments than could the shareholders themselves. John argued that the cost of retained profits should, therefore, be based on the return obtainable by the company in investing in the equity of other companies. In other words, the retention of profits was justified only if the anticipated yield was equal to that from comparable external equity issues. For these reasons, no distinction had been made in the tables between the cost of retained profits and the cost of external equity issues.

John defended the weighted average approach by saying that any particular form of financing should be regarded as part of a process of managing a balanced capital structure. In the long term, low cost debt and high cost equity were inseparable, their proportions being determined by the gearing policy of the company. Figures 10.9 and 10.10 concentrated on the sources of capital used while Hardy Heating has been a close company. John Marsh argued that, since it was the objective of directors to convert Hardy Heating into a public company in the next two to three years, the calculations of the required earnings rate should take this into account. In Figures 10.11 and 10.12 a number of assumptions had been made as follows:

1 Hardy Heating is a public company;
2 plough-back ratio reduced from 75 per cent to 50 per cent, i.e. dividend distribution ratio increased from 25 per cent to 50 per cent.
3 corporation tax at 40 per cent;
4 price/earnings ratio 12.5, earnings yield 8 per cent;
5 current yield on loan stocks 9 per cent;
6 preference stock replaced by debentures.

Figure 10.11 attempted to move away from historical rates

and was based on the estimated capital costs of Hardy Heating as a public company. The cost of equity was based on the estimated price/earnings ratio or, in other words, the rate of earnings per share to the estimated current market price per share. Sam thought that this could be misleading if the market price per share fluctuated. John agreed and also suggested that since the market price often reflected growth of earnings it was highly likely that the cost of this capital would be understated by this method.

Equity based on price/earning ratio
Loans at current rates

	Capital structure	After-tax rate %	Cost
Loans	31.25	5.4	1.69
Equity	68.75	8.0	5.50
	100.00%		7.19

Fig. 10.11   Weighted current cost

John then suggested that they examine Figure 10.12 which was based on estimated future costs. The debt/equity proportions had been reviewed and were acceptable, assuming that the preference capital had been converted into debentures. The net of corporation tax rate of 14 per cent on equity was based on the return to be earned by the company assuming that the shareholders expected 10 per cent (net of all taxes) and that a profit plough-back rate of 50 per cent would be maintained. John reminded Sam that it was now assumed that Hardy Heating was a public company with

Equity based on investors' expectations of a return of 10%
(net of all taxes)
Loans at current rates

	Capital structure	After-tax rate%	Cost
Loans	31.25	5.4	1.69
Equity	68.75	14.0	9.62
	100.00%		11.31

Fig. 10.12   Weighted estimated future costs

widespread shareholders who were expecting from their investment a stream of dividends and also some appreciation in value which, in total, gave them a ten per cent DCF return, net of all taxes including capital gains tax.

Recent research, he said, suggested that the expected return to shareholders of ten per cent, net of all taxes, was a reasonable assumption. The calculation that the company must earn 14 per cent net of corporation tax, in order to provide a ten per cent net of all taxes return to shareholders, contained a number of assumptions, including:

1 that the company had a constant plough-back ratio of 50 per cent;
2 that the company was able and willing to invest a constant proportion of its profits at the DCF rate of 14 per cent;
3 that earnings, dividends and share prices grew at a constant rate and, consequently, that a pound of retained profits added an equivalent amount to the value of the company's shares.

Sam frowned at this last assumption and pointed out that he had made a number of investments in companies which had high plough-back ratios but whose share prices had not increased at the same rate. John agreed that the empirical evidence did not entirely support the model, presumably because of the implication of the second assumption above and, possibly, as a result of very low dividend policies leading to adverse effects on share valuations.

John concluded that Figure 10.12 represented the most appropriate calculation of the basic cost of funds. However, he felt that it was necessary to take into account expenditure which would not produce measurable returns, and also expenditures which could not be allocated to individual projects. Using the same basic approach as in Figure 10.12 he calculated that these two factors required a return of approximately 2 per cent.

He therefore recommended that, if his assumption were accepted, the company should require a 13 per cent net of tax minimum return on normal risk projects in the future.

Required
1 *Do you agree with the conclusions of John Marsh?*

Case study no. 35 – a complete evaluation of the new fan project

All the work which John Marsh had done in explaining the determination of a proper financial analysis for capital expenditure decisions had been worthwhile, he felt, when his managing director and Sam Howell came to see him one day for a further discussion on the plastic fan project. Jack Hardy opened the proceedings with the question, 'Can we apply this discounted cash flow method or any other method of evaluation to the fan in order to estimate more accurately than we have so far its overall profitability?' 'Before you answer that,' added Sam Howell, 'it seems to me that we've established pretty clearly the profits or losses which are likely to arise at different levels of activity on the fan, and you've tackled the question of what capital we shall need, but I don't know that we've got a real measure as yet of the profitability. You've sold us the idea of measuring profitability on a return on capital basis, and we've got the hang of this discounted cash flow business. Now what about the fan?'

John went on to explain that an additional exercise was now needed to spell out as accurately as possible the cash flows on the new fan project for whatever was considered to be the life of the project. This sparked off a discussion between the two directors, from which several facts emerged which John noted down, and which he explained were basic data for the evaluation exercise. This is how John enumerated the items:

1 The Swindon injection moulding machine, dies and regranulator would probably have lives of about seven years, after which they would be likely to fetch no more than scrap value.

2 It would be unwise, at this stage, to think of the project having a life greater than the life of the initial equipment required to get it off the ground.

3 One could not hope to be any more accurate with the forecasting of sales at this stage than to say that the first year should produce a turnover of 80,000 units and subsequent years of 130,000 units.

4 Although all three parties to the discussions recognised the cost increases which were likely to take place over a seven-year period, and the effect that this would be likely to have on product selling prices, no one felt that such increases could be estimated, and it was resolved that whatever increases occurred, attempts would be made to keep the margin between cost and selling price constant throughout the period of the project.

'If on the basis of that little lot, you're going to evaluate this project, and give us some idea of its profitability, it could be very wide of the mark,' said Sam. 'Just consider all the things which could alter during the life of the project. We could be miles out.' John Marsh agreed, but went on to suggest that any evaluation was better than no evaluation at all, and said that it was possible if one adopted the cash flow approach, to see the extent to which changes in any factor built into the exercise might change the ultimate profitability of the project.

'Well, I am always open to be convinced,' retorted Sam, with a hefty suck on his pipe.

Required

1   *Armed with all the data which is now available on the new fan project, carry out your own financial evaluation. Do you require any additional information?*

2   *Appraise John Marsh's comment that the cash flow approach enables one to assess the sensitivity of the likely profitability of the project to changes in 'factors'.*

PART II

HARDY DEVELOPMENTS LTD

From Hardy Heating to Hardy Developments

Stage 1 — Re-organisation in 1969

At the end of Chapter 10, and in the year 1968, Hardy Heating was a typical Bolton Committee small firm attempting to survive and prosper by increasing the sales of its existing products, mainly plugs, switches, and electric fires, and by introducing new products such as the plastic fan. From this time forward the company was involved in many changes, and in particular a period of rapid growth provided the opportunity to obtain a public quotation in 1973.

The process of rapid growth occurred in three main areas:

1 by expanding its existing and traditional lines of business;
2 by extending into the field of heating, ventilating and air conditioning;
3 by identifying and exploiting development possibilities in the distribution and packaging of electronic components.

The catalyst for this period of rapid growth was a school friend of John Marsh, Derek Moore, who had studied science at university and had obtained valuable operating experience with US-based electronic companies. Moore had also studied in the USA at Harvard, and while he was there two significant events occurred; first, he met Hugh Younger, a specialist in finance, and second, his observations on the development of the electronics industry in the USA led him to conclude that significant opportunities for development in the UK existed in the distribution and packaging of electronic components. Moore and Younger, fired with enthusiasm from their studies of venture capital investment at Harvard, decided to build up a company which would provide venture capital and assistance in commercial and financial management for small companies in technologically based industries. Venture finance of £100,000 was obtained from friends and acquaintances, and the scene was set for developments.

At the same time, over Christmas 1968, Sam Howell realised that a fall which he had suffered earlier in the year was a symptom of a more serious condition, and over the holiday shut-down, he and Jack Hardy held many discussions to decide what to do. A number of alternatives were considered, including selling the business outright to a third party, or Jack Hardy buying out Sam and continuing to operate with the help of John Marsh. What was clear was that Sam Howell could not continue to work full-time indefinitely and, therefore, needed to realise at least part of his capital in order to provide an income. Jack Hardy was younger at 50, and certainly did not wish to retire. On the other hand, the ill-health of Sam Howell had made him think about his own position and he concluded that, ideally, he would like to realise part of his capital but wished to continue running his own activities, which would provide both an income and an interest.

When the factory re-opened after the New Year festivities in January 1969, John Marsh was called in to discuss the matter. By coincidence he also had been thinking about his own future because over Christmas he had met Derek Moore and had become enthusiastic about the possibilities of development which Moore was planning to start. Moore had explained that his studies at Harvard of successful entrepreneurs had led him to identify a number of dominant personal characteristics. He was, therefore, searching for individuals with established businesses with some growth potential who were willing to give their business top priority in time, emotion and loyalty. This would involve total immersion and commitment; in addition, the individual must have a succesful track-record, demonstrating innovation and creativity. Finally, he must have personal values, together with integrity and reliability, which would enable him to attract, motivate and build a high quality entrepreneurial team. Moore explained that Younger, his financial specialist friend, had many other business interests and did not wish to be involved in the venture capital business full-time. Since he considered that John Marsh had many of the personal characteristics he was looking for, he asked if John was interested in joining him as financial director and also in developing his own business within the venture capital firm.

John Marsh was very interested since he had been wondering what the future held for him at Hardy Heating. He had reorganised and developed the management accounting system and now wished to be involved in developing the business. On the other hand, all the shares in the business were held by Jack Hardy and Sam Howell and, therefore, unless matters changed, there was no opportunity for John to participate in the capital growth which he might create.

After Jack and Sam had detailed their personal positions, John Marsh outlined the offer which he had received. At first there was utter consternation, but after much discussion it was decided to approach Derek Moore with the objective of offering Hardy Heating as the first investment by the venture capital firm.

A meeting was arranged and Jack Hardy started by explaining the development of the firm to date and also his plans for the future, which were unlikely to be implemented due to shortage of capital. He outlined the personal problems of Sam Howell which would probably mean the loss of the whole or part of Sam's capital in the business. For his own part he was not desperate to realise his own capital at the moment, but certainly planned to do so within the next five to ten years. He appreciated John Marsh's interest in capital growth but he knew that John could not afford to take over the whole or even part of the business.

After a prolonged series of meetings at which the long-term plans and short-term budgets of Hardy Heating were discussed together with details of product development, Derek Moore made the following proposition. The shares of Hardy Heating Ltd held by Sam Howell and Jack Hardy would be transferred to the individual venture capitalists in exchange for packages of convertible preference shares, a consultancy contract for Sam Howell and service contracts for Jack Hardy and John Marsh.

Sam and Jack would receive the dividend on the preference shares and also would have the option of converting them into ordinary shares in five years time. The consultancy contract would allow Sam Howell to retire yet still retain an interest in the business. The service contracts, offered to Jack Hardy and John Marsh, included both a salary and a share option scheme which allowed them to benefit from future capital growth.

From the viewpoint of Derek Moore, he would obtain the full-time services of Jack Hardy and John Marsh who both possessed in different forms many of the personal characteristics of successful entrepreneurs. The experience of Sam Howell would also be available on a part-time basis. No cash was involved and, therefore, the original venture capital was intact, to be used for other investments. The relatively assured stream of earnings of Hardy Heating would provide a cushion for the possible initial losses on 'start-up' operations. Derek Moore disclosed that he had planned to float a public quotation for the company within five years and this would require three separate developments. First, Jack Hardy would be expected to concentrate on the existing range of products and develop these, if necessary, by using some of the venture capital. He would be expected to operate this division of activities just as if he were running his own business, subject to some minimum overview from the centre. Second, John Marsh was to direct the financial affairs of the group, and also was to be responsible for developing a division concerned with heating, ventilating and air conditioning. Third, Derek Moore would act as managing director and initially would be responsible for developing a division concerned with the distribution and packaging of electronic components. The whole deal was discussed thoroughly by the individuals and their advisors and was finally accepted and implemented with effect from 1 April 1969. At this point an organisation chart was envisaged as follows (Part II Intro., Figure 1).

At this stage, two of the three divisions represented hopes and expectations rather than realities and operating businesses. Nevertheless, the course was set and soon detailed development plans were being discussed.

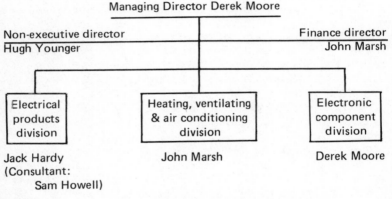

Part II Intro., Fig. 1   Organisation chart for Hardy Heating Ltd, 1969

Stage 2 — rapid growth 1969–73 to public quotation

The rapid development of the company can be reviewed through the three divisions which were operating during this period. Two of these can be regarded as 'new ventures' whereas the third, electrical products, represented the development of the existing business.

Electrical products division

The management accounting techniques introduced by John Marsh were particularly helpful in this period in directing attention to profit-

earning activities, and in highlighting loss-making products or those providing an unsatisfactory return. This approach led to a much keener
marketing analysis and resulted in a commitment to increase overseas
sales and overseas connections. A marketing director was appointed
with specific responsibility for exports and this side of the business was
making a significant contribution to profits in 1972 and 1973.

The plastic fan did well and the company began to build on this
expertise in plastics by taking in sub-contract work and also by beginning to design a range of plastic products for the car spares and garden
supplies markets. These were an established feature of business by
1973, and product managers were responsible for the two principal
lines of business; i.e. electrical products; car spares and garden supplies.
The profits before tax figures showed a healthy increase and further
growth was forecast in 1974 (see Part II Intro., Figure 2).

Year ending	£
31.3.70	45,000
31.3.71	55,000
31.3.72	65,000
31.3.73	80,000
31.3.74	100,000 (Forecast)

Part II Intro., Fig. 2   Profit before tax in electrical products division

Heating, Ventilating and air conditioning division

When the plastic fan was being investigated, advice was obtained from
many sources. Indeed, one of the outstanding features of Hardy and
Marsh was their ability to ferret out information, and to draw in other
people to provide different perspectives and experiences. One of those
consulted about the technical design of the plastic fan was Donald
Crosswell, a specialist in heating and ventilating, employed by a local
firm of architects. John Marsh had been impressed by the enthusiasm of
Crosswell for the technical details of fans of all types and knew that he
would welcome an opportunity to set up on his own account. Before
joining Hardy Heating Ltd, John had built up experience with a number
of large firms, including a construction company. He had formed the
impression that there was a gap in the provision of specialist technical
services which were not always well covered by architects. After much
testing of this basic idea, John decided together with Derek Moore that
they should set themselves the objective of designing, manufacturing
and marketing equipment for improving environmental conditions in
industrial and commercial buildings. This general objective was trans-

lated into a particular goal in the first twelve months to establish a design and consultancy service and then in subsequent years to begin the manufacture of units of their own design, also supplying an installation service, where necessary.

Donald Crosswell decided to join in this enterprise and was included in the share option scheme. His first job was to establish a team of consultants and designers and to deploy their time profitably. Fortunately the construction industry was buoyant in 1970 and 1971 and this initial step proved to be relatively straightforward. However, the next step of designing and manufacturing a house product proved to be much more difficult and although the investment in facilities was limited by buying in parts for assembly, losses were incurred in 1970 and 1971 (see Part II Intro., Figure 3). By 1972 the division was able to manufacture three types of extract ventilation of its own design as well as supplying a complete design and consultancy service for the whole area of heating, ventilating and air conditioning. By 1973 the division was reasonably well established although on a small scale and considerable problems were anticipated in the projected plans of extending the range of manufactured units. To this point the division had not made a feature of its installation service, since it did not regard itself as a contractor.

Year ending		£
31.3.70	Loss	10,000
31.3.71	Loss	5,000
31.3.72	Profit	20,000
31.3.73	Profit	45,000
31.3.74	Profit	60,000 (Forecast)

Part II Intro., Fig. 3   Profit before tax in heating, ventilating and air conditioning division

Electronic components division

The development of this division was the specific responsibility of Derek Moore and he now had the opportunity to realise his dreams at Harvard. He judged from his previous experience that it was necessary to get a toe-hold in manufacturing, packaging and distribution, although he was convinced that the greatest scope lay in distribution.

Electronic components (manufacturing)

The opportunity to enter manufacturing came through a conglomerate Falco Ltd in 1969 who wished to rid themselves of a loss-making small company Merrydale Ltd. Derek Moore and John Marsh visited this company and whilst Moore was reasonably impressed by the level of skill and the product range, John Marsh was appalled by the management accounting and marketing set-up. On balance they agreed that the company had potential, but that they must expect to make losses during the first year while the company was being reorganised. Falco Ltd was prevailed upon not to insist on a cash transaction and the majority of the purchase price was covered by debentures and convertible preference shares. As predicted, losses were incurred in the first year but in the second year the product range had been sorted out and the company was concentrating attention on the high contribution earners (see Part II Intro., Figure 4). Further work on the development and refinement of the product range continued thereafter and by 1973 the company had convincingly turned the corner and steady, increasing profits were forecast.

Year ending		£	
31.3.70	Loss	5,000	
31.3.71	Profit	10,000	
31.3.72	Profit	30,000	
31.3.73	Profit	40,000	
31.3.74	Profit	60,000	(Forecast)

Part II Intro., Fig. 4   Profits before tax in electronics components (manufacturing)

Electronics components (packaging)

From his contacts in the electronics industry, Derek Moore was familiar with the output of K. S. Hunter Ltd, a small firm producing, amongst others, a range of standard products in metalwork for the housing and packaging of electric components. This range had been well received at a recent electronics exhibition but the company was struggling to produce satisfactory financial results. To add to the worries of Paul Hunter, the managing director, he became ill in December 1970, which led to a long convalescence and rest. Paul Hunter and his wife agreed that whatever activities he might wish to follow later the immediate step should be to sell the business. Derek Moore carefully appraised the company's assets and its products and concluded that there was potential but there were problems on the production side which required urgent attention. Paul Hunter agreed to sell and to take his purchase price partly in cash, partly in convertible preference shares and a consultancy agreement. The old war horse, Sam Howell, was asked to take charge of the production side whilst a thorough appraisal of the business was undertaken by Derek Moore and John Marsh. A new general manager was recruited together with a works manager and both were included in the share option scheme. Since this was already a well established business, even though it was experiencing difficulties, the main problems were quickly identified and addressed. The company continued to make profits and the remedial actions augured well for the future (see Part II Intro., Figure 5).

Year ending	£
31.3.71	2,000
31.3.72	20.000
31.3.73	35,000
31.3.74	50,000 (Forecast)

Part II Intro., Fig. 5   Profits before tax in K. S. Hunter Ltd

Electronic components (distribution)

From Derek Moore's experience in the UK industry and his knowledge of US industry, he was convinced that there was tremendous scope in the distribution of electronic components. At this time, a fairly large number of manufacturers held their own stocks and the number of distributors holding a range of manufacturers products was limited. Moore was determined to fill this gap. This required the creation of a distribution network and the associated confidence of manufacturers to have their products handled on favourable terms. John Marsh took over the responsibility for finding premises and developing administrative proccedures whilst Derek Moore concentrated on the product range and relationships with manufacturers. This initial start-up operation involved a delicate balance between the growth of these two aspects of the problem. The manufacturers proved somewhat more difficult to handle than the suppliers of building and services and for the first two years, losses were incurred; however from the third year onwards profits were achieved (see Part II Intro., Figure 6). By 1973 the company, Disco,

Year ending		£
31.3.70	Loss	10,000
31.3.71	Loss	3,000
31.3.72	Profit	20,000
31.3.73	Profit	40,000
31.3.74	Profit	80,000 (Forecast)

Part II Intro., Fig. 6   Profit before tax in Disco

was distributor for 20 manufacturers and the leading lines were transis-
tors, integrated circuits and other semi-conductor products. Favourable
terms of credit were now obtained and the great majority of stock was
covered by agreements with suppliers which provided protection against
reduced selling prices.

A summary of the company profits 1969–73 is shown in Part II
Intro., Figure 7.

Profit before tax year ending		£ 31.3.70		£ 31.3.71	£ 31.3.72	£ 31.3.73	£ 31.3.74 (Forecast)
Electrical products division (J. Hardy)			45,000	55,000	65,000	80,000	100,000
HVA (division) (J. Marsh)	Loss	10,000	Loss	5,000	20,000	45,000	60,000
Electrical components division (D. Moore) Manufacturing (Merrydale)	Loss	5,000		10,000	30,000	40,000	60,000
Packaging (K. S. Hunter)				2,000	20,000	35,000	50,000
Distribution (Disco)	Loss	10,000	Loss	3,000	20,000	40,000	80,000
Total		20,000		59,000	155,000	240,000	350,000

Part II Intro Fig. 7   Hardy Heating Ltd — profits 1969–73

Stage 3 — The public quotation of the shares of the company

When the results of the year ending 31 March 1972 were known,
the budgets for 1973 were very carefully scrutinised and it was agreed
that a public quotation should be sought in the early summer of 1974.
By Christmas 1972, it was clear that the profits before tax for 1973
would exceed £200,000 and the forecast profits for 1974 would exceed
£300,000. On this basis, it was feasible to undertake detailed planning
of the public quotation of shares.

Through the expertise of Hugh Younger, the initial capital of
£100,000 was placed and taken up by people who knew Moore and
Younger. Not all the funds were required immediately and the total
sum was not called up until early 1971. In 1971 an additional £400,000
was raised to finance the purchase of K. S. Hunter and to cover the

increasing working capital requirements of the other businesses which were now on stream and rapidly expanding. This sum was raised in both ordinary and convertible preference shares, and was taken up by outside investors and institutions. Finally, just before introduction to the London Stock Exchange in July 1973, the company raised £300,000 by placing further convertible preference shares with several institutions. Permission to deal in and for quotation for the issued ordinary shares of the company was granted and brisk trading in the shares established a high price/earnings ratio which was one of the objectives of the exercise. The opportunity was taken to change the name of the company to Hardy Developments Ltd; a name which reflected the objectives stressed in the prospectus.

The main reason for seeking a stock market quotation was to facilitate the acquisition of new businesses by paying the purchase price in marketable securities. The high price/earnings ratio of Hardy Development shares placed the company in a relatively strong position when bidding for another company. However, it was now very important to maintain and, if possible, drive up the price/earnings ratio; and in these circumstances, any more 'start-up' situations involving initial losses were to be avoided. Takeover interest was now concentrated on established companies with an existing stream of earnings which had the potential for increase.

Stage 4 — the expansion of the publicly quoted company from 1973

The expansion from July 1973 involved four main features:

1 Soon after quotation Jack Hardy decided to retire to enjoy the considerable fortune which he had built up and which he was now able to realise as he wished. He continued to act as a consultant to the group which still bore his name and he was very proud of this and of its public success. His retirement gave the opportunity to reorganise and this was also necessary since Derek Moore and John Marsh had decided it would be in the best interests of the continued development of the group if they withdrew from the day-to-day management of their divisions and acted as chairmen for the reconstituted divisions from the centre.

   The electrical products division was, therefore, merged with the electrical components division and was re-named Star Components. A new managing director was appointed and Derek Moore acted as his chairman.

2 John Marsh also withdrew from the detailed management of the HVA division. A new managing director was appointed with

specific terms of reference to develop a civil engineering division, and as a first step James & Breasley Ltd, a company engaged in heavy constructional engineering production, was taken over in 1974. John Marsh acted as chairman of this division.

3 The directors had been considering their business strategy and had concluded that the increased involvement in manufacturing necessitated greater control over material processes. Accordingly, it was decided to establish a materials processing division and an appointment was made to lead the group into this area. Three takeovers quickly followed in 1974. Cresta was taken over, together with R. B. Ling (Aluminium Diecasting) and Kent Aluminium Castings Ltd. Derek Moore acted as chairman of this division.

At the end of March 1975 the organisation chart was as shown in Part II Intro., Figure 8.

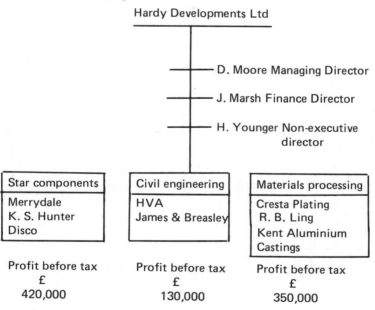

Hardy Developments Ltd

D. Moore Managing Director

J. Marsh Finance Director

H. Younger Non-executive director

Star components	Civil engineering	Materials processing
Merrydale K. S. Hunter Disco	HVA James & Breasley	Cresta Plating R. B. Ling Kent Aluminium Castings

Profit before tax
£
420,000

Profit before tax
£
130,000

Profit before tax
£
350,000

Part II Intro., Fig. 8   Organisation chart for Hardy Developments Ltd, 1975

4 Since 1975, whilst no further takeovers have been made, the group has prospered through the consolidation and development of its three divisions. Two major problems affected companies in the UK during this latter phase: financial liquidity and the financial effects of inflation, and Hardy Developments needed to adapt quickly in order to overcome some difficulties. The organ-

isation structure and the management accounting systems helped considerably in this process and whilst many companies were declining or even going out of business, Hardy Developments continued to grow. At the time of writing, the group has undertaken a thorough review of future prospects as part of its corporate planning process. The main conclusions are that the high interest rates of 1979 and 1980 will continue, and also there will be no recovery from recession until at least 1982–83. Prospects for profitable investment in the UK are therefore limited and a decision has been made that all three divisions will expand international operations in a number of different ways. The main developments for the Hardy group of companies will, in the future, be overseas.

11

The design and development of management accounting systems

THE FOLLOWING is an interview by a leading financial journal of the two key personalities in the public company Hardy Developments Ltd, which has attracted such attention since its flotation in 1973.

Question *The purpose of this interview is to explore the problems of financial control which faced Hardy Heating Co. Ltd in its dramatic rise from a small firm making electrical products to a diversified public company. Now you, Derek Moore, have been the principal architect of this rapid growth; what are the special characteristics of the present position?*

Derek Moore At this point in time, in 1981, we are operating with three main divisions, constituting eight separate companies. Each company is regarded as a separate business and the managing director of each company is expected to produce an efficient and progressive return on capital employed. For each company, therefore, there is an agreed model balance sheet in which key items are related to sales, and also each company produces annually a pro forma profit statement for the next year, together with an outline of the next few years. Actual performance is monitored against these models and is discussed with the divisional managing director at the monthly board meeting.

John Marsh and I act as non-executive chairmen of these companies and in this way, we believe that we keep a very close eye on all matters. Incidentally, our head office staff consists of John Marsh and myself and four secretaries. With this organisation structure and style of management we believe that we can continue to get the benefits of entrepreneurs working in small companies even though we are now quite a sizeable public company.

Question *Now, John Marsh, you were the first qualified accountant to be appointed by Hardy Heating Co. Ltd when it was a small company, and now you are the financial director as well as non-executive chairman of a number of its subsidiary companies. How important has the development of financial control systems been to the successful growth of the company?*

John Marsh Well I am, no doubt, biased, but I would say that the development of appropriate financial control systems has been a key factor in sustaining our rapid growth. I can think of many companies, which have started small, have grown rapidly and then have gone bust. One of the principal reasons for their failure has been their inability to design and implement appropriate management information systems. We have avoided that danger so far.

Question *Now you say, 'appropriate' and 'so far'; do you mean to say that your present financial control system might not be relevant in the future?*

John Marsh What I am saying is that as circumstances change so our financial control system must adapt.

Question *What circumstances have you in mind?*

John Marsh Well, let me share with you the model which I have in mind when I am thinking about financial control systems, and this will identify the key variables which affect and are affected by the financial control system.

Question *Yes, but first, will you define what you mean by a financial control system?*

John Marsh Well, I hold to the definition which I have heard Derek Moore use and which he probably picked up at Harvard Business School. The financial control system exists to ensure that the economic resources of the enterprise are used effectively and efficiently in the pursuit of agreed objectives. It is an information system which has a *structure* of, possibly, expense centres, product centres, profit centres or investment centres and a *process* or set of procedures which govern the planning and control of resources. A key job for a financial director is to ensure that an appropriate structure and process exists. We use the term 'financial control systems' now; other people say 'management accounting systems'; there is no difference; sitting at the centre we like the sound of the word 'control', that's all.

Question *So if we have a number of companies, as is the case with*

Hardy Developments, each company will need a different financial control sytem. Is this correct?

John Marsh   Yes, if their circumstances are different, but in addition the holding company must also have a financial control sytem which integrates matters for the whole group.

Question   *Well, what are these circumstances, and do you agree, Derek Moore, with this approach?*

Derek Moore   Yes, I do agree but I would look at the problem rather more broadly as you might expect the chairman and chief executive to do. John has restricted his comments to financial control systems, I am also anxious to ensure that we have appropriate operational control systems, manpower control systems and marketing control systems. In other words, I see the financial control system as a part of administrative control systems. As in this diagram (Figure 11.1):

Fig. 11.1   Administrative control systems

The four quadrants taken together constitute a complete management information system and it is important that the four are consistent or compatible with each other; otherwise we might have costly duplication or confusion.

Question   *Now, what are these circumstances or variables which you have hinted at and which affect or are affected by the financial control system?*

Derek Moore   From my Harvard days I have found it useful to distinguish between the variables contained in the goals system and those in the organisation system. So far as the goals system is concerned, I have this diagram in my mind (Figure 11.2):

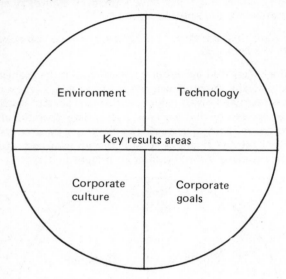

Fig. 11.2   Goals system

This diagram can help to explain matters relating to a subsidiary company like Cresta Plating and also it can be used for the holding company Hardy Developments Ltd. What it says to me is that as the *technology* of plating in Cresta Plating is different from that of component distribution in Disco, I would expect the financial control system to be different. The same is true of the other variables; the industrial *environment* faced by the Star components division is quite different to that faced by the civil engineering division. The *key result areas* and *corporate goals* are quite different for Merrydale Ltd compared with James & Breasley.Finally, the *corporate culture*, that is the generally accepted way of doing things is quite different in the West Country, James & Breasley, compared with London, Cresta Plating Ltd. In my opinion all these factors affect the design and operation of the financial control system. This does not mean that we should not have some common accounting and planning procedures — indeed this is a requirement of the holding company to ensure that at the centre we have a financial control system which is appropriate to the particular environment we face, which includes the Stock Exchange and the financial institutions. It follows from this that I see a close connection between the corporate planning procedures organised from the centre and the financial control systems of the group and subsidiary companies.

Question *You also mention the organisation system. What is this and how does it affect the financial control system?*

John Marsh The point here is that the *structure* of the organisation, or the ways in which activities and responsibilities are grouped, together with the behaviour of individual and groups (sometimes called the *process* of organisation) affects and is affected by the financial control system. For example, as we have already said, we have grouped similar activities into separate companies and treat them as profit centres. This decision on organisation structure should directly affect the design of the structure of the financial control system. Sometimes, however, managers forget these relationships and inappropriate financial control systems are used which irritate individuals and adversely affect their behaviour.

Question *How would you summarise your experience regarding the development of financial control systems in Hardy Developments Ltd?*

Derek Moore I would say that first of all we have used the following framework (Figure 11.3):

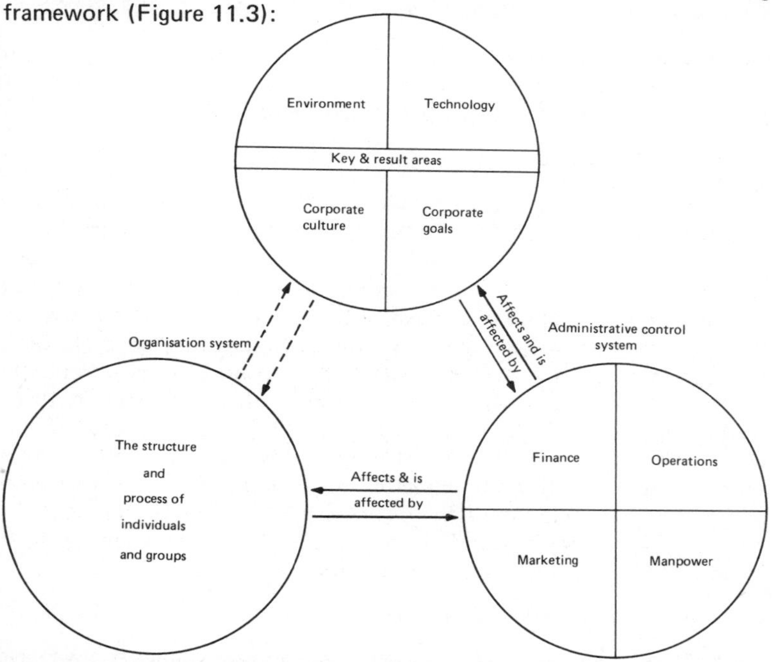

Fig. 11.3   Framework of interacting systems

We have been constantly examining each company to determine its unique characteristics and then design and implement an appropriate financial control system. These characteristics and circumstances change over time and some are within our own control to change, consequently our financial control systems are in a constant state of adaptation. We never seem to reach a steady state for any period of time. Indeed I would judge any financial control system in part by its adaptability to changing circumstances.

Question *What other criteria do you use in judging financial control systems apart from flexibility?*

John Marsh I would say *consistency* with the other control systems which we have mentioned, *consonance* with the other variables we have listed and, *educability*, that is the power to educate so that managers learn about their circumstances and take appropriate action. Very often I have noted companies in which a sophisticated financial control system exists, of which no-one takes any notice and certainly which does not influence actions. We have struggled to avoid that situation at Hardy Developments.

Question *Can you illustrate your approach with actual case histories with Hardy Developments?*

Derek Moore Yes, what we have done is to describe some significant events in the lives of some of our companies. If you wish, we could now analyse these, using the framework which we have described.

Interviewer *Let's do that.*

Derek Moore We have grouped our case studies into four sections and chapters. Each case study consists of a description of an incident, an issue or a problem together with our commentary, which is intended to highlight what are the main lessons to us. The commentary is not intended to be a complete analysis of the case and we have not tried to relate the case to the relevant literature, as I recall they do at Harvard. The commentary is a personal reflection by John and myself on why we think the case is worth bringing to your notice and what we think we have learned from it. We are often asked by business schools to discuss some aspects of the rise of Hardy Developments and we have found it useful to have the material in case study form together with our commentary. No doubt the business school lecturers will make the analysis more complete and refer to other literature when we have returned to base to make some more profits.

Question *How have you grouped the case studies?*

John Marsh We have so far compiled twelve case studies and we have grouped these into four sections and chapters. In the first group,

Chapter 12, we have concentrated on accounting for activities, which, in a group like ours, arise in many different forms. We think that we have captured the most interesting issues which have arisen during our period of rapid growth. The second group, Chapter 13, consists of two cases concerned with product profitability, whilst the third, Chapter 14, deals with issues in capital investment decisions. Finally, from 1974, we have developed corporate planning procedures to help us control our expanded operations and we have described four different aspects of this process in Chapter 15.

Question *But you have argued previously that each company within Hardy Developments is unique and must develop its own management accounting system. If that is so, how can anyone else hope to learn from your experience and apply it in his own unique circumstances?*

Derek Moore We do not argue that the lessons of Hardy Development are directly applicable, without modification and imagination, to other situations. What we do say is that we have taken a number of issues which are likely to arise in other enterprises and we have reflected on what we have learned. Any reader of these case studies must similarly reflect on what he has learned and how the lessons are to be applied in his unique circumstances. We cannot be responsible for all the thinking and all the doing; the most we can expect to do is to share our experiences with a wider audience. After all, whilst we are duly modest, we have been pretty successful, and our management accounting system has undoubtedly assisted our development.

Question *Where shall we start?*

John Marsh Well, let us take one of our favourites, which has many lessons for us, the case of Cresta Plating Co. Ltd.

12

Performance reporting of various activities

Case study no. 36 – profit centre reporting

Cresta Plating Co Ltd – background

Cresta Plating Company Ltd was purchased by Hardy Developments in 1974 and is now part of its materials processing division. The company is located in the London area, and this was a significant factor in the decision to purchase since the majority of the companies in the group were also situated in the south of England.

Apart from plating work for companies within the division and within the group generally, the company carries out a substantial amount of plating for companies outside the group. The proportions of work for group companies and non-group companies have recently been equal.

The company had its origins in the early 1940s and from tin-shed beginnings it expanded by the time of the purchase in 1974 to a reasonable size and had gained a sound technical reputation. All the remnants of private family business management have now disappeared. However, despite the efforts of the parent company, and a number of recent appointments which have been group-inspired, the 'group-image' is not well established.

Production and progress

The company is in the electro-plating jobbing industry, and this presents problems not met in a plating shop in a factory handling work produced in that factory alone. This is an important factor, for it results in the company having limited knowledge of the orders that are coming into the factory premises. Production planning and control is extremely difficult, especially when linked to the quick delivery so vital to secure orders. The company aims at a 48-hour turnround from the receipt of an order to its despatch.

Since 1970 the company has grown rapidly and now employs about 175 people at two factories in London, one in Newcastle and another in Sheffield. The last two factories being recent acquisitions of family businesses, which although technically sound, have not been satisfactory in the financial sense.

At Cresta both barrel plating and vat plating are used. Most of the vats are hand-operated in order to achieve a flexibility necessary to cope with the different mixes of products. On the barrel plating side, there are two large automatic plants to cope with the steady flow of work from group companies. There are also a few hand-operated barrels. The company handles a wide variety of work, ranging from small orders of a few pounds' weight, to huge orders where the total weight of the products involved could be as much as one ton. A wide variety of finishes is catered for, such as zinc, cadmium, tin, chromium, nickel, copper, precious metals like gold and silver, and also plastics.

The company has been profitable for a number of years and the continuation of this trend can be seen in recent results. This success has been partly due to the fact that the company has an assured market within the group. Intra-group pricing is a touchy matter within the company, and Cresta is under constant pressure to reduce transfer prices which, by the strength of its top management, it seems to withstand successfully.

Accounting methods

The accounting department has a staff of seven, who cover the duties of financial accounting, cost accounting and wages for all the factories. There are, however, two clerical workers on routine accounting and wages matters, both at Newcastle and Sheffield. Until a few months ago, the only costing work being done was the recalculation of cost rates for the purpose of estimating for price-fixing. This recalculation was undertaken annually and was on an absorption costing basis. Overhead costs are categorised as fixed or variable on a basis specified by head office, and this analysis is a requirement of the trading statement prepared and submitted to head office.

Just after the takeover a new man was appointed to the post of company secretary/chief accountant. He has proved to be quite an innovator, and one of the first tasks he under-took was to review the financial and cost accounting pro-cedures. At one of the early board meetings he attended it was stressed that better financial controls were needed. This attitude was supported by the argument that as the company was continuing to expand, control by observation became increasingly difficult. The new man formed the impression that a certain amount of lip-service was being paid to the idea of management accounting and information services. He found that monthly and quarterly interim trading statements were being prepared, but he was disappointed that these were only total trading statements for the company. He proceeded to give immediate thought to the departmentalisation of the figures. One of the factors which weighed heavily with him was the fact that during his four weeks' 'acclimatisation' at head office, he had been introduced to a management by objectives programme which was in the process of being launched throughout the group. Two points that particularly impressed him about this programme were:

1 the overall financial objective which was to be built into the programme, namely, a return on capital employed of 20 per cent before tax; and
2 the desire to set objectives and key tasks for individual managers and executives.

This second point matched comments which had been made at the Cresta board meeting that production managers needed measures which they did not have at the moment.

Budgets

The accountant also had work to do on accounting returns for head office. The statements include a budget and actual trading statement return (Figure 12.1), prepared to the

	September 1975		January to September 1975	
	Budget	Actual	Budget	Actual
Sales: To group companies	£22,000	29,161	£220,000	287,103
Outside group	38,000	27,277	380,000	285,046
	60,000	56,438	600,000	572,149
Variable costs of sales	35,000	32,231	350,000	335,203
Gross margin	25,000	24,207	250,000	236,946
Other costs				
Depreciation	2,600	2,416	26,000	24,270
Fixed works exes	5,200	6,637	52,000	58,643
Admin exes	2,800	3,029	28,000	29,327
Fixed sales exes	2,400	1,448	24,000	20,772
	13,000	13,530	130,000	133,012
	12,000	10,677	120,000	103,934

Fig. 12.1   Budget and actual trading statement, September 1975

group pattern. The budget is an annual affair and worries the accountant somewhat, since he believes that it should have its roots in departmental budgets. This is not so at the moment, because it is produced as an overall business budget.

Accounting developments

As far as Cresta was concerned, it seemed to the accountant that departmentalisation could logically be carried to profit centres. There was vat plating, barrel plating, and there were some less significant sections; further, there were natural sub-sections in each which were definite factory locations with directly identifiable sales. There was already in being a simple sales analysis to these profit centres. To develop the existing records into a departmental system of accounting was only a matter of arranging the necessary cost analysis procedures. These were partly in existence in a rough and ready fashion and were used to facilitate the task of recalculating cost rates annually. The extra work created by a full-scale cost allocation and apportionment exercise carried out each monthly accounting period was performed by two additional cost office staff specially appointed for the purpose.

There were, inevitably, some joint costs, and much thought had to be given to them, particularly on the matter of how these should be apportioned between the profit centres. In addition, there were service department costs, administration expenses and some general fixed costs, and for all of these, bases of apportionment had to be determined. It was a hard slog, but it was finally done and it was possible to produce interim profit centre trading statements.

Profit centre trading statements

The first man to see the new statements was the managing director, who took some time to warm to them, but he eventually did. The other executives were brought into a meeting to study them, and there was general agreement that they were very informative. This was the first information which top management had ever received on the profitability of different units, so that inevitably some surprise was registered about some of the figures. On this first set of departmental trading statements, the new accountant had gone no farther than to analyse sales, costs, and profits or losses. There was, however, a feeling at the meeting that the next statement should show an analysis of capital employed in profit centres in order that 'profitability' could be computed on a departmental basis. Interest was running high, and the accountant was pleased.

The next step was the analysis of capital employed, and the accountant and his staff found this analysis to profit centres was just as difficult as cost analysis. Some of the fixed capital could be identified directly with departments, but some was of a more general type. He was not at all sure about the working capital which he felt was very much more a function of the product itself and of the customer than it was of any production department. There was also the problem of capital employed in the service departments of the company. But again, the interest in departmental profitability was something to be cultivated, and he felt that the management accounting service had an opportunity here to justify itself. The net result of all these efforts is the type of trading statement which appears in Figures 12.2 and 12.3.

September 1975		Totals	Barrel	Vat	HD	Spec fin	Misc
Sales:	Group companies	£29,161	21,625	2,604	1,445	1,877	1,610
	Others	27,277	3,630	7,564	3,457	11,426	1,200
	Totals	56,438	25,255	10,168	4,902	13,303	2,810
Process materials		8,271	3,599	1,885	502	1,857	428
Direct labour		7,140	1,374	2,003	818	2,702	243
Indirect labour		1,501	497	474	28	455	47
Labour overheads		1,296	282	366	112	497	39
Consumables		2,308	127	470	195	857	659
Power		4,653	1,851	452	603	1,278	469
Maintenance		1,947	974	238	100	575	60
Jigs		576	—	133	203	240	—
Services		4,539	1,950	726	633	1,205	25
	Variable costs	32,231	10,654	6,747	3,194	9,666	1,970
Gross margin		24,207	14,601	3,421	1,708	3,637	840
Fixed works expenses		9,053	3,589	1,487	1,352	2,303	322
Admin and sales expenses		4,477	2,037	729	395	93	1,223
		13,530	5,626	2,216	1,747	2,396	1,545
Profit or (loss)		10,677	8,975	1,205	(39)	1,241	(705)
Jan–Sept 1975							
Sales		572,149	260,093	105,623	61,078	120,467	24,888
Profit or loss		103,934	77,909	8,101	4,568	9,356	4,000
% of sales		18.2	29.9	7.6	7.5	7.8	16.0
Annual rate of profit		138,578	103,879	10,801	6,091	12,475	5,333
Assets employed		350,000	130,000	58,000	43,000	109,000	10,000
ROI%		39.5	79.8	18.6	14.2	11.4	53.3

Fig. 12.2   Profit centre analysis

September 1975	Total barrel	A Automatic	B Automatic	Horizontal	Chrome	Small orders	Anodising	Spec fin
Sales:								
Group companies	£21,625	5,791	3,191	7,985	3,923	427	150	158
Others	3,630	247	1,926	1,177	63	217	–	–
Total	25,255	6,038	5,117	9,162	3,986	644	150	158
Process materials	3,599	516	533	2,105	137	213	18	77
Direct labour	1,374	282	226	474	165	112	40	75
Indirect labour	497	65	190	150	45	39	8	–
Labour overheads	282	50	67	94	30	25	6	10
Consumables	127	26	47	44	–	10	–	–
Power	1,851	520	568	570	118	40	15	20
Maintenance	974	65	261	375	209	64	–	–
Services	1,950	378	379	666	370	100	32	25
Variable costs	10,654	1,902	2,271	4,478	1,074	603	119	207
Gross margin	14,601	4,136	2,846	4,684	2,912	41	31	(49)
Fixed works expenses	3,589	754	1,095	1,065	465	170	20	20
Admin and sales expenses	2,037	486	412	738	324	52	12	13
	5,626	1,240	1,507	1,803	789	222	32	33
Profit or (loss)	8,975	2,896	1,339	2,881	2,123	(181)	(1)	(82)
Jan–Sept 1975								
Sales	260,093	73,424	57,916	82,491	35,228	7,326	1,802	1,906
Profit or loss	77,909	24,969	10,734	24,003	19,026	(700)	180	(303)
% of sales	29.9	34.0	14.6	23.1	54.0	(9.7)	10.0	(16.0)
Annual rate of profit	103,879	33,292	14,312	32,004	25,368	(933)	240	(404)
Assets employed	130,000	27,000	44,000	37,000	14,000	6,000	1,000	1,000
ROI%	79.8	123.3	32.5	86.5	181.2	(15.5)	24.0	(40.4)

Fig. 12.3   Profit centre analysis

'Can these assessments be right?'

The next phase in relationships between accounting and management generally at Cresta can best be described as a 'can these asssessments be right?' phase. Arguments raged about the allocation and apportionment of cost to profit centres. Time and time again the accountant made the point that any allocation is arbitrary, no matter how detailed the process by which the allocation rule is determined. On the other hand, he never failed to add that each profit centre must bear its fair share of all expenses. There is no doubt that many of the management team at Cresta had been shattered by the figures. Some profit centres were shown as not so profitable as they had been thought to be. Perhaps it was natural that there were recriminations. There were comments like 'we always felt that Bert was efficient, but look how much money he's losing us.'

All this worried the accountant. Surely it was logical to have profit centre reporting? But where were the ties between profitability and efficiency, if any?

Transfer pricing

Discussions between the accountant, managers and parties aggrieved by his efforts brought out many points which he felt deserved attention. The over-riding one seemed to be the subject of transfer pricing. The point was made that there were inconsistencies in pricing which stemmed from two main causes: first, insufficient work measurement had been done to enable the establishment of reasonable standards or synthetics for estimating: and second, the managing director had involved himself extensively in pricing decisions. On the first point, everyone agreed that proper work measurement was difficult in this type of manufacture. Then, since it had never been seen in this factory as providing much more than a basis for wage payment, no very clear need had been established. On the second point, the managing director had been very successful in price negotiations with group companies. Using the arguments of quick turnround and quality, coupled with his prestige in the trade and his forcefulness of character, he had been able to extract advantageous prices from group companies. Clearly, this was a factor in the profitability of the various profit centres.

Questions for consideration

Matters were brought to a head when the group chief accountant called a meeting of executives at head office to consider a wide variety of matters, which included the profit centre reporting at Cresta. The managing director and the accountant were invited to this meeting. On the subject of the trading statements, about which the group chief accountant was congratulatory, three specific points emerged for further consideration:

1 It was agreed that the pricing of completed work was an important factor in profitability. The group management accountant recommended that the relative profitability of group work and other work should be investigated and a report produced on the subject of the pricing of inter-company transfers.

2 The group chief accountant had work to do on instituting the management by objectives programme, and one of the first factors to be determined was the rate considered to be a reasonable return on investment for Cresta. This was likely to involve some difficulties, since Cresta was already making a better rate of return, or so it seemed, than the overall group requirement. Critical questions are: How is a target set in these circumstances? Does this target return apply to new capital spending?

3 Next was the question of objectives for individual managers and whether the latter should be expected to concentrate on profitability as shown by the profit centre reports, or efficiency. Consequent upon decisions being made on these matters, there was the problem of appropriate measures. At the moment, neither managers nor foremen saw any sort of detailed performance report of output, costs and efficiencies, though all managers saw the profit centre statements for the whole company. The management by objectives programme called for some means of measuring managers' performance in key results areas, and the accountant was, apparently, being called upon to play his part in this. He wondered to what extent basic budgetary control ideas might be useful in this connection, and how the performance report-

ing system should be designed, implemented and controlled.

Required

1   *Advise the accountant of Cresta on these three points,
    and on the implications of profit centre reporting as
    shown in Figures 12.2 and 12.3.*

Commentary by Derek Moore and John Marsh

We have often used this case when explaining our philosophy
of financial control because we consider that this incident
covers many of the essential features of designing and im-
plementing a management accounting system. As we see it
management accounting is very much concerned with
measuring and reporting what one might call 'the activities'
within the business, whether these are product groups and
products, channels of distribution and customers, or as is the
case in Cresta, departments, locations or process centres. One
of the problems in management accounting is exactly how to
view an activity; in the case of departments such as the process centres in Cresta, there are several alternatives. One can
either treat the departments as investment centres or profit
centres or cost centres or budget centres, or as a combination
of these. What are the essential differences between these
approaches?

A *profit centre* is a location to which both revenues and
costs can be attributed, so that it is possible to calculate the
profit made at that location, in other words, one can produce
a departmental profit and loss account.

An *investment centre* implies a profit centre to which one
can attribute the capital employed so that a return on capital
can be calculated.

A *cost centre* is a location to which costs can be attributed,
such costs being the subject of reporting and control. Frequently in this case the costs are related to a suitable way of
expressing the output, so that unit costs and/or cost rates can
be calculated.

A *budget centre* implies the use of budgetary control, a budget of performance and cost being set for each location, with which actual performance and costs are compared, and variances analysed and reported upon.

To us the guiding principle is that the approach used should be relevant to the purpose for which the financial information is required. Often the idea in using one of these approaches is to break down the total unit into sub-sections, so that departmental and managerial performance can be measured. Certainly, measurement of individual activities is imperative in a progressive organisation like Hardy Developments and the proper institution of managerial accountability is necessary also. The Cresta situation is, however, typical of the problems which can arise both from an accounting and a managerial point of view in pursuing a particular 'measurement and accountability' approach.

Although the term *profit centre* is used in the case, it could reasonably be argued that the approach being used here by the new chief accountant is really an *investment centre* approach, since there is an attempt being made to calculate the return on capital of each separate process centre. This has presented us with accounting problems, in particular:

1 how to allocate and apportion costs, and
2 how to allocate and apportion capital employed in its various elements.

These are critical issues in practice; we have found that managers can become very emotional when being judged on profitability, where the calculations include so many apportionment items. Our experience is that the aim must be to treat as much of revenue and cost as possible as directly attributable; but not all items can be so regarded. One way round the problem which we have tried is to abandon the idea of calculating profit on a traditional net profit basis, in other words, to stop short at a contribution figure or at a calculation of controllable profit; these approaches may or may not avoid the need for apportionments of cost.

Clearly there are also management problems. Rarely is an investment centre or profit centre manager in control of all the factors influencing profit and profitability, and this has been true in Cresta. Sales factors affecting profit can be summarised as volume, mix and price; in Cresta the process centre manager is given the volume (the amount of work to do) and the mix (long-run jobs or short-run work, group or outside work), and pricing is a matter of company policy, outside the manager's control. The latter is further complicated in this incident by the amount of work being done for other companies within the group, and the inevitable problems of transfer pricing. At the end of the day, the largest management problem can be the confusion between profitability and efficiency, brought out clearly in the case ('we always felt that Bert was efficient, but look how much money he's losing us'). Profitability is an accounting calculation, fraught with problems — what is profit? — what are the assets employed? Efficiency is really a physical thing, related to the effectiveness with which resources are used, e.g. what is the output per man or machine hour, how high is the scrap rate, how good or bad is the material yield?

An important question which we have constantly in mind is: how useful is the investment centre information in Cresta for operating control purposes? If one accepts that it is sensible to aim at knowing where the company profit is made; whether barrel plating or vat plating is the most profitable (important for strategic purposes), then it is really a separate issue to be in a position where individual departmental managers have relevant control information on a regular basis. It has been argued recently that the latter needs to contain the physical efficiency information plus information on controllable costs, perhaps compared with some sort of flexible budget.

From our view at the centre, it is very satisfying that Cresta is such a profitable company, with a 40 per cent return on capital against a target of 20 per cent for the MBO programme, but again, there are important issues for us to weigh in the balance. First of all, there is the question of transfer pricing which clearly has such an impact in the Cresta results. There is a clear indication in the case that transfer prices are high, because the Cresta managing director is a tough nut, and this brings the obvious possibility of sub-optimisation, in other words, that Cresta makes its profit very largely at the expense of other companies within the group. A question that is on the mind of the group accountant is: what might the effect on group profit be of lower transfer prices? Could it be that other group companies could be more competitive as a result and thereby attract more business and profit to the group?

On the three specific points emerging from the group chief accountant's meeting:

1 There is, of course, a need to be aware of the relative profitability of the different work, group and non-group, different customers, long- and short-run work. A very detailed cost analysis can be required, however, to satisfy this requirement. If a different approach to transfer pricing is judged to be necessary, there are so many possible approaches; clearly the one in use at the moment is 'what the managing director can obtain'. But a decision could be taken to restrict such prices to 'cost plus a set profit margin' or a 'break-even price.' The implications of any such decision on the motivation of personnel need to be considered, bearing in mind that we, at the centre, prefer to intervene as little as possible in the management of operating units.

2 We have become somewhat doubtful of the advisability of a target rate of return for all companies within our group, particularly if one bears in mind the problems of capital employed, or, put another way, the problems of asset valuation. Certainly, if a target rate is to be set individually for the company units, it needs to take into account not only the factor of asset valuation but also issues of company development, products' life cycle and industrial economics issues. The idea of a target return or cut-off rate for new capital spending has many proponents, but we would expect that such an approach would not be applied too rigidly, bearing in mind the different classes of capital projects, the welfare aspects of some and the risk aspects of others.

3 In our set-up, managers need to recognise the need for profit and for adequate profitability, but they also need to be aware of cash flow aspects of business operations, since they can so often affect these significantly. We have found that in order to develop an MBO approach within the organisation, consideration should be given to key results areas for managers which include physical targets of efficiency and cost-effectiveness. Certainly grass-roots budgeting and budgetary control, not currently used in Cresta, could

help in performance improvement; this would imply a
budget centre approach for performance reporting. To
develop this within Cresta would mean having reliable information on both physical and cost standards.

Conclusion

The main lesson to us from Cresta is that in the quest for
'measurement and accountability' one should not become
too hooked on a particular management accounting approach.
Because the unit in total is required to make a profit, it may
well be correct to break down that unit into investment or
profit centres. But the question of controllability should be
kept in mind; the manager of the smaller unit may well be
more in charge of efficiency in physical terms than profitability in financial terms. It is always a matter of aiming for
relevant information for each particular purpose. In terms of
the framework of analysis which we explained earlier, the
case of Cresta has taught us in Hardy Developments how the
technology involved in a particular company (here we have a
number of different processes) can affect the determination
of costs and their controllability by operating managers. This
then directly affects the design of the measurement and reporting system. Also we have learned that the translation of
corporate goals into key result areas which have to be
measured and reported upon is a key issue in the design of
an appropriate management accounting sytem for any
particular company.

Case study no. 37 – departmental budgetary control

James and Breasley Ltd – background

James and Breasley Limited was taken over by Hardy Developments in 1974. It is a well known name in the West Country. Its incorporation dates back to 1876, and its products have both a national and international reputation. When these products pass through its gates, they are usually very large and require special transportation, and many of the locals stand by to watch. The company is engaged in heavy constructional engineering production, with the emphasis between the turn of the century and immediately before the second world war on bridges, but with the current emphasis on a wide range of products, including constructional work for nationalised undertakings, such as the UK Atomic Energy Authority.

Much of the factory premises date back to the early 1900s and although the design and drawing office has a clinical-looking new block, the original office, a Victorian house, still accommodates three members of top management and the accounting department. The various production and service departments in the factory house 800 employees, many of whom have worked for the company since leaving school, and whose fathers and grandfathers worked there before them. In some production departments there are still family groups. All in all, this has been a business run by a benevolent management,

261

given only in recent years to a few and limited redundancies.
These have been occasioned by recessions in this very difficult and competitive market. The company has been
cushioned to some extent by its reputation and special expertise, and in particular, by its ability to meet delivery dates
much better than its competitors. Often this has been a
costly procedure, but the company has never failed to make a
profit in a trading year, in spite of one or two near misses in
recent years, when the return on investment has been very
low.

The financial director of the company, Milne, has in his
five years with the company done much to inculcate among
top management a better idea of financial objectives, and has
reorganised, with the enthusiastic assistance of two subordinates, a company secretary and a chief accountant, the whole
of the financial accounting, from basic ledgers to quarterly
financial statements. He has not found it necessary to devote
as much energy to the product costing side of the business,
which he considered to be quite well developed when he
joined the company. This product costing follows traditional
job costing procedures. Each contract receives a job number
followed by job part numbers to which direct materials and
components, direct labour and direct expenses are booked
through bills of material and material requisitions, wage
tickets and time sheets, and in some cases direct from
invoices, cash-book and petty cash-book. The factory is divided into departments, each with a departmental number, and
any part of prime cost booked to job numbers is identifiable
with the factory department in which the expenditure is
incurred.

Departmental overhead rates

Each department has its own overhead rate, which includes
departmental, factory, general administration, selling and distribution expenses. The departmental overhead rates are recalculated annually on the basis of budgeted labour costs and
overheads for each department. A little disturbing to the
financial director has been the fact that the departments are
factory locations, and in a sense budget centres also, but each
department contains several different operations, involving
the use of different plant, equipment and facilities. He senses

that a very good argument could be raised for using different overhead rates for each operation, but he fears the amount of cost analysis which would be necessary to achieve this. On the other hand, the present system has anomalies since the same operation is in some cases carried out in three different factory departments and carries, as a result, three different overhead rates.

Completion of contracts

A particular problem with which the financial director, Milne, has had to grapple, and was quite new to him when he joined the company, has engaged the attention of the chief accountant and the cost accountant. This is the problem of completions, which involves determining those contracts which can reasonably be regarded as complete at the end of a trading period, and for which credit can be taken for the sales income and the profit on the contract, if any. The decisions on this matter cannot be made on the basis of whether or not the job has left the factory premises; but whether it is felt from correspondence with the customer, or evidence from the representative on the site, that the product is to the customer's satisfaction, and whether there is any likelihood of any additional work or rectification which might involve James and Breasley in additional costs.

Departmental budgetary control

Some 18 months ago, Milne turned his attention to budgetary control. He had worked in Scotland for a business, in an entirely different line of trade, which had well developed budgetary control procedures, and he was convinced that these resulted in top management obtaining a better involvement in performance and cost control of all managers in the business, right down to supervisors on the shop floor. He was determined to get such procedures instituted in James and Breasley, and to this end promoted the best clerk in the cost office to budget officer. This young man, 23 years of age, Peter Franks, was reckoned to be a good prospect. He was already studying for a professional qualification, had a pleasing personality and was very acceptable to everyone in the organisation, having worked there since leaving school.

Milne had some doubt concerning Franks's ability to be firm when it was necessary, and this was a matter which he discussed with Franks very fully when he gave him his terms of reference. 'Installing budgetary control procedures is going to be a slow process. I want you to start at departmental, shop floor level so that as soon as possible we can involve the interest of departmental supervisors and their immediate superiors, the factory superintendents and so on up to the works manager. It's not going to be easy to involve the works manager. He's definitely anti-accounting, and in any conversations that I've had with him, he has been most unhappy about the idea that anyone below his level should receive control information. When we start producing control information, you must take upon yourself the role of presenter and interpreter, pointing out where things are going wrong, and this will mean you'll have to be firm and persistent. We will start slowly, on the basis of what we have already, that is a departmental analysis of costs produced mainly to facilitate the recalculation of overhead recovery rates. Build on that, I'm not expecting miracles.'

Peter Franks got moving. Existing financial and cost accounting procedures threw up a detailed analysis of costs, in a piecemeal fashion, which he could bring together to provide actual cost information for his departmental operating statements. His first shot at departmental budgets was carried out with some aid from production department supervisors, but consisted mainly of historical cost data. From the start he was worried about the setting of the level of activity. In fact, he was not even sure that activity could be measured in a realistic manner. In a few shops the production was reasonably standard and operators were paid on a piecework basis. But in most shops the work was one-off or small batch production, involving no piecework payments, and the only information available was the time booked to individual jobs and part numbers. His first thoughts were that in these circumstances the level of activity could only be assessed on the basis of actual direct hours worked or in relationship to direct wages. In any case, he did not see how he could start on flexible departmental budgets; he decided, in view of Milne's comments, that he would adopt a fixed budget approach, comparing actual costs of actual activity with the budgeted costs for the budgeted activity. It concerned him that departmental costing already existed to facilitate the calculation of overhead rates, and that the managing director himself showed a great interest in the under- or over-absorption of overheads. He felt that it should be possible to combine departmental budgetary control with a calculation each period of this under- or over-absorption of overheads.

Peter would have admitted to anyone that the first attempts were rough and ready, but he had made a start, and a typical departmental operating statement appears in Figure 12.4. At least, Peter felt, the one statement sufficed to give control information to departmental managers and supervisors, while at the same time providing the calculation of overhead recovery which the managing director was so keen to see each period. The actual overhead absorption of £19,326 is represented by the predetermined overhead rate of 375 per cent applied to the actual direct wages of £5,154.

Required

1 Critically appraise the existing departmental operating statement and consider possible improvements.

It was at this stage that Stokes, a friend of the financial director, arrived. Stokes had given some assistance recently to the company in recruiting staff, and Milne wanted his advice on budgetary control, particularly with regard to departmental operating statements.

After a detailed investigation on a part-time basis, Stokes sent the following memo to Milne:

Memo to Milne from Stokes
       Budgetary Control Procedures
My thoughts on the matter so far are:

1 Much of the present work which is done in a monthly accounting period is duplicatory. For example, general, service and fixed costs are allocated and apportioned at the budget stage, and then the process is repeated each month on the basis of actual figures. Apart from being duplicatory, the results of this exercise are quite meaningless. This is very clear to the man who is doing the job and gives him little satisfaction.

DEPARTMENT: PIPE-MAKING   No: 34   PERIOD 7   MONTH ENDING: 27th OCT.

OPERATING STATISTICS

	This month	To date			This month	To date
Budgeted direct hours	6,242	47,164	Budgeted direct wages		7,776	58,752
Actual direct hours worked	4,152	37,287	Actual direct wages		5,154	46,470
Capacity usage %	66.2	79.0	Direct wages variance		2,622	12,282
Predetermined overhead %	375	375	Budgeted indirect/direct %		24.3	24.3
Actual overhead %	442	402	Actual indirect/direct %		30.4	34.0

OVERHEADS

	Code	This month			Year to date			Remarks
		Budget	Actual	Variance	Budget	Actual	Variance	
DIRECT OVERHEADS								
Rent, rates & water		768	768	—	5,724	5,724	—	
Power, light & heat		4,008	4,599	(591)	25,074	26,487	(1,413)	
Sundry shop stores		48	18	30	366	225	141	
Repairs & maintenance		3,792	2,793	999	28,641	30,612	(1,971)	
Shop labour		1,887	1,569	318	14,277	15,807	(1,530)	
Process materials		—	—	—	—	—	—	
NHI & grad. pension		561	702	(161)	4,242	4,290	(48)	
EL & PL insurance		66	51	15	492	477	15	
Works bonus		108	108	—	816	852	(36)	

Added time	690	105	585	5,220	3,690	1,530
Works salaries	432	411	21	3,264	3,174	90
Depreciation	1,092	1,092	–	8,244	8,244	–
Holiday pay	573	459	114	4,326	3,861	465
	14,025	12,675	1,350	100,686	103,443	(2,757)
INDIRECT OVERHEADS						
Works expenses	96	162	(66)	732	867	(135)
Welfare	33	18	15	243	240	3
Transport						
Admin. salaries						
Admin. charges						
Printing and stationery					21	(21)
Selling expenses	129	180	(51)	975	1,128	(153)
ALLOCATED OVERHEADS						
Works services	4,065	4,848	(783)	32,499	38,037	(5,538)
Administration	5,007	4,182	825	37,041	40,179	(3,138)
Sales	1,206	1,164	42	9,114	9,126	12
General (credits)	(414)	(255)	(159)	(3,123)	(4,641)	1,518
	9,864	9,939	(75)	75,531	82,701	(7,170)
TOTAL OVERHEADS:	24,018	23,794	1,224	177,192	187,272	(10,080)
OVERHEAD ABSORPTION: BUDGET	24,018			177,192		
ACTUAL	19,326				174,240	
ACTUAL OVERHEADS	22,794				187,272	
UNDER-RECOVERY	(3,468)				(13,032)	

Fig. 12.4 Departmental operating and budget statement

2 The first task is to provide a clear division of the costs budgeted for individual departments into 'directly attributable controllable', 'directly attributable fixed', and 'general and fixed overheads apportioned'. In the long term there must be training of managers, foremen and the like, in order that they may all be involved in the budget setting. One would like to see them accepting the fullest responsibility for the 'directly attributable controllable' items.

I am not happy about what seems to be a complete lack of integration between the sales forecasting and shop floor manning which is built into the budget. Clearly, direct and indirect labour manning as contained in departmental budgets should be related to the budgeted level of activity, and I suggest that the level of activity can only be expressed in terms of the work content of individual jobs, orders and products. Further development in the measurement of departmental effectiveness will depend upon getting reliable measurements of work produced. The amount of work produced is not reflected by actual hours worked but by standard hours produced. I recommend that Franks should concentrate his attention on efficiency measurements in future, rather than on the present duplicatory clerical aspects of the budgetary control work.

3 I attach a proposed Departmental Operating Statement for a Production Department, (Figure 12.5). The particular points which I would like to stress about this are:

(a)   Operating measures
In this section we highlight, both in budget and actual terms, normal as opposed to overtime operating hours, waiting time, and a calculation of the activity percentage against budget. I would like to think that the 'hours produced' figures might at some time in the future be 'standard hours produced'. It is not sufficient merely to think in terms of numbers of people. The manning must be converted into normal working hours, and decisions must be taken about the extent of overtime which will be required and permitted. A further decision will be required regarding the 'standard' at which overtime premium shall be set. It will be necessary to decide upon a 'standard' for waiting

time, so that the total attendance hours can be scaled down to give a figure of budgeted productive hours.

(b)   Directly attributable/controllable

I want to interest the departmental supervisor initially in the first section, 'directly attributable controllable', in which the original budget can be flexed on the basis of hours produced. Any difference between actual costs and the flexed budget we would have to call a 'spending variance', until we have the standard hours information which would enable us to calculate an 'efficiency variance'. You will notice that I am recommending a more detailed breakdown of direct and indirect labour cost items in this section. They are significant enough to warrant the detail.

(c)   Directly attributable/fixed overheads

The second section of cost items is concerned with overheads which, though fixed, are directly attributable to the department. These items of cost should be carefully budgeted at the beginning of the year and included in a 'Fixed Cost Budget' or, if appropriate, a series of 'Fixed Cost Budgets', which are under the command of particular directors or senior executives. They are not controllable in the departmental budget. In fact, the only reason for having them there is in order that a capacity variance on these costs can be established. I am suggesting that this capacity variance should be calculated each control period in the operating statement by comparing the overhead absorbed by the actual use of capacity with the original budget. I do not see the point in putting the actual costs against the original budget in this departmental operating statement. Incidentally, if we could agree not to be involved in the apportionment of cost items each control period, this would very considerably reduce the amount of clerical work. This clerical work is not justified because it does not assist shop floor control.

(d)   General and fixed overheads

The third section of cost items is concerned with general, service and fixed overheads, which I suggest should be apportioned to each department at the budget stage on the basis of usage or potential usage; in other words, at an

DEPT: MACHINE SHOP **SUPERVISOR: J. R. MAY** **PERIOD: 15** **No. OF WKG. DAYS: 20**

OPERATING MEASURES

	Normal op. hours	O/T op.hours	Total op.hours	Waiting time	Net prod. hours	Hours produced
Budget	3,200	160	3,360	336	3,024	3,024
Actual	2,884	227	3,101	399	2,702	2,702

ACTIVITY % 90

OPERATING COSTS

Directly attributable controllable	Original budget (wkg days)	Flexed budget based on hrs produced	Actual	Spending Variance Over	Under	Cum
	£	£	£	£	£	
Direct labour	5,100	4,590	4,746	156	—	
Direct labour O/T prem.	90	81	129	48	—	
Waiting time	300	270	360	90	—	
Indirect labour						
Category 'A'	1,065	960	1,041	81	—	
Category 'B'	318	288	306	18	—	
O/T prem.	150	135	135	—	—	
Associated labour costs						
NHI/GP	195	177	189	12	—	
Holiday pay	288	258	270	12	—	
Insurance	60	54	57	3	—	

Production department

	Original budget		Actual use of capacity has absorbed	Capacity variance	
				Under	Over
Process materials	—	—	—		—
Other indirect materials	600	540	600	60	—
Coal, coke & oil	—	—	—		—
Elec. & gas apportionment	378	339	300	—	39
Repairs & maintenance	1,020	918	726	—	192
	9,564	8,610	8,859	480	231

Directly attributable fixed overheads

	Original budget	Actual use of capacity has absorbed	Capacity variance	
			Under	Over
Building occupation	510			
Depreciation	990			
Salaries	375			
	1,875	1,689	(186)	—

General & fixed overheads apportioned to department

	Original budget	Actual use of capacity has absorbed	Capacity variance	
			Under	Over
Service	1,440			
Administration	1,560			
	3,000	2,700	300	Over

Fig. 12.5 Production department – Departmental operating statement

agreed standard. I am suggesting the same treatment for this section of costs as for the 'directly attributable fixed overheads', namely, that capacity variances only shall be calculated in the Production Department operating statement.

(e)   Cost variances

It is possible to show a figure on the operating statement of total variance, comprising spending and capacity. This is the only over- or under-recovery of cost for that department which can be calculated. Certainly cost variance information will be more meaningful than the overhead recovery information which was formerly provided on the operating statement. The next step must be to use standard hours produced which will allow us to compute efficiency variances. This will be relatively straightforward in one or two departments, but much more difficult in others, since this does represent a significant problem in performance measurement in jobbing situations.

Required

1   *Appraise the comments and proposals of the consultant. The following questions are relevant:*
    (a) Is the revised departmental operating statement an improvement? Can you suggest refinements?
    (b) How can the company ensure that the operating statement is a key to effective and efficient management control?
    (c) Should the company have concentrated its attention at this end of the budgetary control process?

Commentary by Derek Moore and John Marsh

We feel that information systems are best if they are designed and implemented locally, reflecting local objectives, the particular technology, the local style of management and many other factors. Take the case of James and Breasley, which we purchased in 1974. It was engaged in heavy constructional engineering where the production is one-off or batch production on a job by job basis; it was inevitable that much of the work of planning and control would also have to be on a job by job basis. But some aspects of control are inevitably departmental; the factory is organised on a departmental basis, each department contains several centres for operational planning purposes and is managed by a person who is accountable for that department's performance and cost. It is also inevitable that control will reflect the paternalistic history of the development of the organisation and be influenced by the presence of family groups within the business; and it certainly was in James and Breasley.

Something very special that we learned from this particular company was that even with all the difficulties of its introduction in a jobbing company, one still needs an effective budgetary control system. We also learned a lot about the introduction of the procedures; first of all, that it is too important a discipline to leave to a junior officer in the business to try to design and implement on his own. Our conception is that budgetary control is one level of planning and control within an organisation, one could call it the management level, and it needs to be seen by management as a tool to guide them in running the business and the many parts within. It has to have complete top management backing, personnel need to be educated in its objectives, one has to ensure that the necessary prerequisites are present for the discipline to be effective.

What do we mean by prerequisites? Well, you need good management information systems in the first place, dealing in particular with the recording of production and its costs, material waste and production rejects; sound and acceptable ways of measuring output, knowledge of the behaviour of costs under different output conditions, and you certainly require an accounting service which is efficient, presents and interprets control information in a timely manner. This is well illustrated in the case.

In any business, the financial or stewardship accounting needs to be well organised; apart from the legal requirement for the financial statements which emerge from stewardship accounting, there is the need to conserve assets and cash in particular. Milne was right to put the general accounting in order first, was fortunate to have good and reliable job costing to depend upon, and again was correct in wanting to develop budgetary control. Mind you, James and Breasley was a different kettle of fish from his previous company, which was in flow production of standard products, where, to begin with, sales forecasting techniques were well established, and where physical and cost standards were available for products. We're not sure that Milne had fully appreciated the differences, or that budgetary control always needs a top-down *and* a bottom-up approach. In our experience there's a lot to be said for starting at the grass roots, in the departments where the inputs take place, but you've also got to start with top management; there's got to be some planning for one year ahead, it would be nice to think that the annual plan was a read-off from a longer-term, say five-year plan, and some sort of environmental anlaysis and sales forecast are essential preliminary exercises. This is certainly the basic approach which we encourage in all our companies.

There was a cost analysis by jobs and by departments for job costing purposes and also to enable the calculation of departmental overhead recovery rates on an absorption cost basis. One of the snags about building on that is the fact that it is an absorption cost approach, in other words all costs, directly attributable and apportioned, controllable and uncontrollable, fixed and variable, are included. And we have no doubt that you can't have a single costing view of things which gives you relevant information for all purposes. Even if you have decided that you want departmental cost rates for estimating and price-fixing; that doesn't mean that control information issued to departmental managers has to include the same cost data.

Whether it is cost-finding or budgetary control, there is the problem of output measurement, and you really have to measure it in a physical way. Using sales or wages paid really isn't adequate; there are manufacturing businesses, very few, where a weight basis is appropriate, but if one is to get a proper reflection of work content, then standard hours are needed. We put great store by standard hours; it means that there is the discipline of deciding how long operations ought to take to carry out, but these data are really required also for estimating for price-fixing; it implies that there is strength in work measurement procedures, of course. Peter Franks met this problem as he also met the difficulty of having a relevant budget with which to compare actual costs. In truth, the only relevant budget for variable costs is a flexible budget. We believe that it really is pretty useless comparing actual costs of actual production with the budgeted costs of budgeted production. And if you decide to flex budgets, then it is imperative that you have an appropriate way of measuring the level of activity.

One area in which we feel that Peter slipped up was in trying to combine operating control reporting with the much-loved-by-the-managing director examination of overhead recovery on a regular basis. The two really do not go together and what the departmental manager needs to be controlling are the variances in performance and cost.

Stokes was clearly trying to tidy up the approach and the form of reporting, as well as to put the emphasis in the right places, both from the point of view of the initial budgeting and in regard to departmental accountability. The first point about the duplication is very relevant; one really can waste resources on apportionments anyway, but to duplicate these month by month is quite ludicrous. He also pointed out an important requisite of the training of managers in budget involvement and the use of control information, something we have been committed to in our business careers. The revised operating statement was certainly a great improvement, getting rid of the awful conglomeration and confusion of items.

As far back as we can remember, there has been the argument about 'above-the-line' and 'below-the-line' items in operating statements. At best, Stokes was distinguishing between the two, and this must be sound. Many would argue that the uncontrollable costs should not be reported at all, but then there is the counter argument that there should be an awareness by managers of charges which they may not be able to influence, but which do have to be paid, and therefore contributed to by efficient production. It is a difficult argument to resolve, but we are quite clear that the main attention of managers must be directed to factors of both performance and cost which they can affect.

Conclusions

It is so easy to turn people off with irrelevant information; accuracy is important but so is the appropriateness and presentation of the data. It is also easy for accountants to forget the recipients of financial information when designing internal reporting systems. We happen to think that even the redesigned operating statement in James and Breasley was too much for managers to swallow. There is an argument for much less information, concentrating on the significant exceptions only or on what are agreed to be the real key results areas.

We do not feel that there is any point in constant recalculations of cost rates; that these are best calculated on the basis of a good sound budget, and then managerial attention directed to the variances, some of which will highlight problems of volume and capacity utilisation, others which will relate to efficiency and the ability to control cost.

Another point is that jobbing is different, and although job performance and cost need to be closely monitored, so do departmental efficiency and spending. There is a 'point of input' aspect to all activities, with a manager responsible for the input, and managerial accountability needs to be cultivated.

Finally, budgetary control is not just a technique or even a series of techniques. It is a management tool and must be developed as an organisational instrument.

Case study no. 38 – reactions to budgetary control

James and Breasley Ltd

Recently James and Breasley Ltd had been involved in developing budgeting control in their jobbing company (see Case study no. 37).

Disappointing results

With the help of Stokes, a consultant friend, the chief accountant Milne had revised the departmental operating statements so that the points stressed were:

1 operating measures;
2 directly attributable/controllable expenses;
3 directly attributable/fixed overheads;
4 general and fixed overheads;
5 cost variances.

Milne was not satisfied with the results and had asked Stokes again for his advice. Milne explained that the exercise seemed to have involved little more than a re-arrangement of information and, apart from cutting out some duplication of effort, small benefit seemed to have been obtained; indeed, shop floor performance and control had not improved.

Stokes was disappointed at the lack of improvement and promised to investigate. After some weeks, he was able to report back.

In Stokes's opinion, the application of the change in the departmental budgeting system still had not taken sufficient account of a number of particular factors affecting the behaviour and attitudes of the managers and employees. These factors, evident at the time of the first report, were:

1 Many employees had worked for the company since leaving school; fathers and grandfathers had worked there before them and in some production departments there were still some closely knit family groups.
2 The works manager was unhappy about the idea that anyone below his level should receive control information and was clearly acting as a brakeman.
3 The chief accountant had worked in Scotland for a business which had well developed budgetary control procedures but which operated in a different trade; in addition, Peter Franks, a young cost clerk, had worked for the company since leaving school and had been promoted to budget officer.

Technical characteristics

There were a number of technical factors, particular to the company, which had not been fully appreciated either in the design or application of the system:

1 The company was engaged in heavy constructional engineering production on orders which, for the main part, had a long time cycle.
2 The market was highly competitive and the company had been cushioned to some extent by its technical reputation and special expertise and, in particular, by its ability to meet delivery dates much better than competitors.
3 It was extremely difficult to forecast in a realistic way the level of activity and to measure actual activity.
4 In most production shops the work was one-off or small batch and did not involve piecework payments.

Existing weaknesses

Failure to appreciate to the full the implications of the social and technical factors had created certain weaknesses in the budgeting system:

1 The impression given to Stokes and other managers was that a textbook standard costing system, which happened to work well in an entirely different business in Scotland, was being forced into this jobbing company.

2 Departmental managers and employees represented highly cohesive groups which felt threatened by the emphasis of the new system and the way in which it had been implemented by the works manager; such cohesive groups with negative attitudes to the company represented a highly dangerous situation.

3 Negative attitudes had been engendered by the works manager's style of management; departmental managers were not joining in budget setting and the required standards of performance were imposed; some departmental heads considered that the budgets confirmed only what was already obvious and that they prevented supervisors from exercising real leadership.

4 The departmental operating statements were being used by the works manager to exact retribution; there was some evidence that some highly cohesive groups were intervening in the data processing system and that some unfavourable information was suppressed. For example, Stokes reported instances of scrapped work hidden in swarf bins or smuggled out to prevent the losses being recorded on the operating statement; some supervisors had justified this action by claiming that the budgets were misleading as a means of measuring performance because they did not explain why variations or excesses had occurred.

5 Emphasis in the departmental operating statements on the control of labour had lifted attention from the progress and control of individual jobs; since the labour cost percentage of total job cost was of the order of 20 per cent, this emphasis could be misplaced.

6 Departmental managers were confused about the objectives of budgetary control; the relative inexperience of Peter Franks in attempting to push through a textbook application of standard costing in an unsuitable situation, plus the management style of the works manager, had adversely affected attitudes.

Stokes had not been asked specifically to propose remedial action but he made suggestions to improve the situation.

First, he felt that there was a basic objective to design a budgetary control system which properly took into account the outstanding social and technical characteristics.

In dealing with the social factors, he thought that the departmental managers, the works manager and the chief accountant each had a different perception of the purpose of the budgeting system. Stokes recommended that the chief accountant should take immediate personal action to explain the objectives of the system, to review the ways in which the works manager involved departmental managers in budget setting and how he handled feedback of operating results.

Stokes further suggested that the negative attitude of the departmental managers should be studied. It might be necessary to remove the works manager unless he was prepared to change his style of management in line with the more participative approach which was being encouraged by the directors. The strong team spirit which still existed in departments should be channelled into activities favourable to the company.

Co-operative basis

The focus of attention of the group should be turned away from the works manager and the departmental budgeting system to the job, its progress and costs. In view of the difficulty of measurement and the presence of strong groups, departments should be encouraged to manage their activities on a co-operative basis.

Positive attitudes should be encouraged in a variety of ways such as competitions, suggestion schemes with cash prizes, outings or holidays, or even direct financial incentives. Stokes contended that in this type of industry, flexibility and adaptability was required to deal with a wide range of jobs. The company had a major asset in the strong, informal groups in operating departments. The budgeting system should not misuse this valuable asset.

Required

1   Consider how you would design and operate a control system, taking full account of the social and technical factors outlined in the case.

Commentary by Derek Moore and John Marsh

We often refer to this case within the group when we wish to demonstrate that it is not sufficient to produce a rational plan and then expect it to work well automatically. The likely attitudes and behaviour of the people who are going to work with the plan must be anticipated and any difficulties attended to. This sometimes means that the plan or system will have to be adapted to suit the requirements of the people concerned.

As we stressed when we were discussing our ideas on designing financial control systems, we encourage our managers to examine their company to determine its unique characteristics and then to design and implement an appropriate control system. We recognise that the process is one of continual adaptation as the circumstances of the company change. The basic questions are 'Does the management accounting system suit our company?' and 'Does it produce the outcomes which were intended?'

We recognise that each company within our group is different. In particular the technology which the company uses; the environment in which it makes its living; the company culture or way of doing things; all these variables will be unique and will influence in practice how any planning and control systems will operate. We also recognise that any systems have to work through individuals and groups, who become structured into formal and informal sets of organisation and who will have their own ideas on how to behave. The problem therefore is how to design and operate a financial control system which takes into account these unique characteristics and is sufficiently flexible to adapt as circumstances change. At any point in time there may be a very poor fit between these factors, and we have seen circumstances, fortunately for us not within our group, where the fit has been so poor as to put the company concerned out of business.

What are the unique characteristics of James and Breasley which are likely to affect the ways in which administrative control systems will work? First, the task and technology is that of heavy, one-off, constructional engineering with a long cycle time and the natural focus of attention is the individual job. To carry out such a task demands strong interdependence between the skills of individual operatives, functions and departments, and this in turn sets up a requirement for information on an uncertain, changing sequence of events. Second, the environment in which the company earns its living is highly competitive and the high degree of uncertainty makes it difficult to forecast the level of activity. This once again sets up a demand for information on situations external to the company, which are likely to change frequently and quickly. Fortunately at James and Breasley we have a corporate culture which has developed in response to many years of competing successfully in this environment. On the production side we have highly skilled individuals, who are organised informally into tight working groups and at first sight make an excellent fit with the technology and the environment. Yet we have learned that these apparent strengths can be turned against the company if they are not properly managed. The fit of the management group is much more doubtful. Franks is inexperienced and is likely to lack the sensitivity required to implement a successful system. Milne is much more experienced but is very much conditioned by his understanding of a management accounting system designed for structured tasks and standard products in Scotland. We have noted the tendency of managers to view current situations on the basis of their past experience; and on occasions this can lead to serious errors in the diagnosis of problems. The works manager presents a particular problem since his personal style of management does not seem to fit too well with demands of the task and the associated working groups. This personal style affects directly the way in which he uses management information, particularly performance reports. We do not argue that in some of our companies in some circumstances an autocratic style of management is not appropriate and we certainly do not regard 'participation' as some sort of panacea. As with the design and operation of the management accounting system we would argue that the appropriate style of management will be contingent upon a number of factors, of which the outstanding will probably be the task characteristics, the organisation structure and the personal characteristics of the individual manager.

In this case we have some clear evidence that the effect of

the works manager's particular style of management and the associated use of performance reports has produced some reactions by the people concerned, in their manipulation of the data. This is predictable behaviour; a reaction to relieve pressure applied by the works manager, probably perceived as unfair. We have observed other instances of this type of behaviour in other companies, and we are now constantly on the lookout for these adverse effects. For instance we have observed that on occasions managers have behaved in ways which make them look good in the terms of the measures emphasised by the management accounting system but which are not helpful in terms of meeting the overall goals of the company. In James and Breasley for example there is certainly a suspicion that the emphasis on cost control in the departmental operating statements may adversely affect quality control and delivery. This misfit between the goals set and understood at the centre and the measures and standards incorporated in the financial control system can be very expensive and we pay particular attention to it. Other reactions which we look out for are those intended to influence results so that they will look good or acceptable for a certain time period. We have had occasions when managers have deliberately 'smoothed' results to spread together good news and bad news; also there has sometimes been a drive for output at certain points in the month or year in order to make the results look impressive. We do not wish managers to put their ingenuity and initiative into such antics when they could be better employed in achieving the real goals of the company. Nonetheless, we do accept that from the managers' viewpoint such behaviour may be perfectly rational in the face of perceived pressure. We regard it as a challenge to design and operate our control systems so that the behaviour which is induced leads to the achievement of the goals intended for the company; consequently we are constantly on our guard for evidence to the contrary.

The role of the accountants in these interactions is important; it is fatally easy for the accountant to do things which are interpreted as the actions of an adversary; a fault-finder; an informer for the bosses. We encourage our accountants to be communicators and facilitators and stress to them the importance of designing and communicating financial statements in ways which encourage behaviour intended to further the goals of the company. We acknowledge that the manager has personal goals, as has, incidentally, the accountant; the problem is how to fit these together so that the goals of the company are realised in the most effective and efficient manner.

Conclusions

We think that this case brings out the importance of establishing the unique characteristics of the external and internal environment of the company and then designing and managing an information system which represents a good fit. In practice there may, for a number of reasons, be a poor fit and the problem is to calculate the direction and strength of the required adaptation. This is a continual process; as environmental circumstances change so the financial control system should be adapted. Some of these adaptations will be minor but there will be occasions where more fundamental changes are required. For an example of a major adaptation, since 1974 the change in rates of inflation has been so great that we have found it necessary, in all our companies, to be able to express the results of our activities after making adjustment for price level changes. Who should decide upon these adaptations? We believe that there is a strong case for involving the users of the accounting information in the design of the reporting system. This may require a change in attitude and style by management but should lead us to using the undoubted strengths of the existing highly cohesive groups. We like to stress the importance of not only formal controls but also informal controls and our present strengths in group form should be used to this advantage.

Finally, an analysis of the task characteristics in this company leads to a focus on the project and it may be necessary to restructure on a project basis both in terms of organisation and information. This could lead to an appropriate reporting package for projects which would cover all major key result factors: costs, completion dates and quality; in turn departmental operating results might also be presented on a project basis.

Case study no. 39 – the control of administrative costs

Star Components Ltd – background

Star Components, a main division within Hardy Developments, is concerned with the manufacture, packaging and distribution of a large range of electrical products and electronic components. The division was created in 1974 by bringing together the hitherto separate activities of Hardy Heating, Merrydale, K. S. Hunter and Disco. Three general managers covering manufacture, packaging and distribution report to the divisional managing director and an ambitious, aggressive young accountant. John Gillett has been appointed to the post of divisional director of accounting and administration, with particular responsibilities for the planning and control of computer applications and the development of budgetary control. There are also divisional directors of marketing, production and personnel.

John Gillett has put forward draft proposals for an integrated management information system, which are currently being considered by his colleagues. He claims that the computer has been used as a book-keeping machine, and its full potential has not yet been realised. John Gillett has also investigated the accounting procedures at the three main producing units, and is impressed by the sophisticated system of

control information which is available to production management. He is, however, very unimpressed by the use which
is being made of this information, and his main efforts in
this field have been designed to stimulate effective action
based on the information system. This has included the replacement of the existing factory accountants by men who
have been told specifically that factory economics is an essential part of their job, and that they will be judged, in part, by
the future improvement in factory productivity and efficiency. Their job does not end with the provision of reliable
and relevant information; they must ensure that the relevant
action is taken. On occasions, this attitude has produced
some difficulties with senior production managers, but the
managing director has supported the views of John Gillett.

John has now turned his attention to budgetary control,
and in particular to the control of administrative costs. He
has produced a detailed report which he has circulated to his
fellow directors. Summarised extracts follow.

Productivity in the factory

An examination has been made to find out what lessons
applicable to offices could be gained from experience in the
factory. A comprehensive plan has been operating over a
period of years for the improvement of product quality, an
increase in productivity and cost reduction through the
rationalisation of product design, and the improvement of
manufacturing processes. Deliberate and continuous efforts
have been made in three directions: in generating the right
organisation and systems so that productivity can be
increased; in generating the right atmosphere; and in developing an information sytem to report on the various factors
which contribute to productivity; including labour utilisation, product quality, content and works costs. In this way,
it has been possible to measure the relative improvements of
each factory and to make comparisons of productivity gains
between product groups. Changes in organisation have also
been introduced, with an emphasis on the creation of product teams.

The numbers of staff (and inevitably their costs) have increased significantly over the past five years, and it is clear
that determined efforts must be made to control and to im-

prove staff productivity. It is equally clear that the lessons learned in the improvement of productivity in the factory must be applied to the offices. These lessons are:

1 The need to set up an appropriate organisation to plan and control administrative costs.
2 The need to measure productivity in the office.
3 The need for a sustained programme to improve staff productivity in the right atmosphere and with enthusiasm.

The proposed management services department

It is proposed that the planning and control of administrative costs be centralised in a newly-created management services department responsible to the director of accounting and administration.

The recommended organisation charts are given in Figure 12.6.

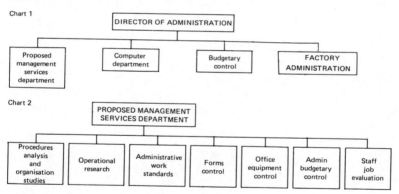

Fig. 12.6   Recommended organisation charts

The management services department must be organised to handle the following activities:

(a) Procedures analysis and organisation studies
(b) Operational research
(c) Administrative work standards
(d) Forms control
(e) Office equipment control
(f) Administrative budgetary control
(g) Staff job evaluation.

Procedures analysis and organisation studies. All studies of procedures and organisations should be centralised, and this section should be responsible for the issue of operating manuals and standard procedures. Procedures analysis for computer operations should also be the responsibility of this section, leaving computer programming and computer operations as the responsibility of the computer department.

Operational research. An operational research section should be established, which will work very closely with the above section and also with the computer department. This section should be concerned with the application of management science techniques to business problems.

Administrative work standards. A specialist section should be established with specific responsibilities for the establishment of work standards. Without measurement and standards there are no yardsticks by which improvements in productivity can be assessed. This section will provide these yardsticks.

Forms control. Administrative effort is expended on forms, which are also costly. The design and production of all forms within the company should be subjected to the central scrutiny of this section. This would reduce duplication of forms, improve design, reduce stationery costs, and reduce clerical costs.

Office equipment control. At the present time, office equipment can be purchased or rented by individual departments. This field deserves specialist attention. The specification of office machinery, and its subsequent purchase or rental, should be subjected to a central control which should be given the responsibility of establishing contracts, including maintenance agreements with outside companies. This responsibility should extend to EDP equipment and office furniture.

Administrative budgetary control. With the central control of organisation, procedures, standards, forms, and office equipment, the function of this section should involve their co-ordination into a system of budgetary control. After rigorous examination of these aspects, staff levels and associated expenditures should be determined before the commencement of the financial year. It should be the function of this section to report actual performance against budget, to have any significant variances investigated by the relevant section of the management services department, and to report on requests for additional staff and expenditure.

Staff job evaluation. Organisation and procedural changes will affect the nature of individual jobs and, consequently, their worth to the company. It is essential that changes in duties and responsibilities are speedily evaluated. Also, if necessary, investigations by the appropriate sections should be carried out when job re-gradings are sought by other departments. The administration of the company staff job evaluation scheme should be the responsibility of this section, leaving the determination of salary scales to the personnel department.

The need to measure staff productivity. At present there is little information to provide a realistic basis for staff budgeting. The problems are how to determine the basis for the relative allocation of expenditure to each staff department and, within each department, to determine how the expenditure allocated can most profitably be deployed. These problems are at present tackled by considering:

1 what funds are likely to be available;
2 what allocation has been requested by the departmental managers;
3 what allocation has been made in the past.

Problems arise when margins reduce with a drop in production or sales volume and, invariably, reductions of staff are made on an arbitrary basis. However, it is clear that, whilst the workload in some staff departments is directly related to the volume of production and sales, in many departments the relationship is indirect and, in some, the workload either remains static or actually increases in the face of a reduction in production volume. It is also clear that the workload in some staff departments is absolutely unrelated to what is happening in the factory, but is governed by quite separate

factors, e.g. the programme of new models being introduced
to customers. In the other direction, it is equally important
to control increases in staff. This can be achieved only if
information on workloads is available, so that effective decisions can be made on whether requests for additional staff
should be approved or not.

Firm information on the workloads in each department
would enable a more effective approach to be made in the
preparation of staff budgets. This would also enable a regular
assessment to be made of the staff position and would create
effective control. It would also provide a firm basis for the
calculation of the training requirements for each department.

The need for a sustained programme. The efforts made to
establish the information necessary must come from within
each department and must not be arbitrarily imposed from
outside. In any office, there is normally an input of information, a processing of information, and an output which are
capable of definition and measurement. The form of measurement used must be custom-built to suit the requirements of
each office. A typical example is found in routine clerical
operations, which can be measured using parallel techniques
to those used by time-study engineers in the factory. This
applies to such operations as typing, the use of accounting
machines and punched-card equipment, record maintenance,
filing, etc.

Routine clerical operations cover only one part of the
work of the staff departments. Such techniques could not be
applied to the work of sales engineers, cost estimators,
buyers, draughtsmen, and production planners. Here, the
techniques used must be adapted to suit each job. A careful
and detailed analysis must be made of the cycle of work in
each job and of the factors which affect the workload. It is
thus possible to determine the amount of productive and non-
productive time in each job and to ensure that non-productive time is reduced to a minimum (e.g. where a sales engineer
has to spend time carrying out routine clerical work which
could be done by lower-grade staff). By analysis, it is possible
to arrive at the factors which affect the workload of each job,
e.g. number of items bought, number of customers dealt
with, number of items planned, frequency of new models,

etc. In this way, it will be possible to estimate how much work one man in any job can reasonably be expected to carry out and how many staff are required in relation to the work-load of the department. In addition to the quantity of work which can be measured it is also necessary to measure, where possible, the quality of work performed. In this way, it will be possible to set an index of performance for each staff department, fulfilling a similar purpose to the index used in the factory.

It is important to stress that the impetus for the work must come from within each department, since the system of workloading will vary with each department and within the section of each department. To enable this to be done, it is recommended that staff productivity teams be set up in each department, headed by the departmental managers and appropriate members of the department. These teams should be serviced by a specialist from the management services department; a service similar to that given by product engineers to product teams.

In this way, it will be possible to devise a yardstick for each department so that productivity can be measured and targets can be set, against which progress can be ascertained. It will encourage departmental managers to pursue and sustain a continuous programme of improvement, simplification and cost reduction. An overall method of assessing relative performance is desirable. Until it is possible to refine such a method, it would be useful to measure:

1 the proportion of the cost of £1 turnover which arises in each department;
2 the ratio of total works employees to the staff in each department.

When a comprehensive sytem of workloading and measurement has been introduced, the relationship of measurement to individual performance must be considered.

At present, individual appraisal is carried out on the basis of merit-rating and the procedure for executive appraisal. These are, to a large extent, based on subjective factors. A system of work measurement makes it possible to introduce an objective factor into such appraisals, i.e. the performance of the individual against the standard established for his particular job.

In many cases, it would be possible to set quite specific standards. For example, a buyer is responsible for controlling a particular section of the stocks of raw materials or bought-out components. He must keep the factory satisfied, but must not build up excess stocks. It is possible, therefore, to set such standards. Other elements are present which can also be measured, e.g. the effectiveness of the buying in terms of price. It would not be necessary to establish an elaborate machinery to set the standards—in many cases the individual would be required to set his own standards or targets. The measurement of accomplishment would then become an objective factor in the appraisal of individual performance, in addition to being part of the normal managerial process.

Training can also play an important part in fostering a positive attitude to staff productivity. It could play an important part in encouraging departmental managers, executives and senior supervisors to realise that productivity is their business and highlight what can be done.

The reaction of managers

The report of the director of accounting and administration created considerable discussion within the company, and also some critical reactions. The divisional production director was afraid that the company was about to create an administrative 'Frankenstein's monster' which would suck out initiative by its paperwork and systems. He argued that the efforts of operational research workers would be best applied to the production planning and control systems, in which case the unit should be responsible to him.

He had already expressed the view that the factory administrators were exceeding their authority. The responsibility for the economics of a factory rested clearly and unequivocally with the factory manager. The role of the factory administrator was to supply information. The divisional sales director was concerned at the high degree of centralisation which was proposed. In his view, the proposed computer-based management information system affected every functional department and should not be regarded as an off-shoot of the accounting department. Some organisational arrangements must be made to ensure that the functional views and interests were respected.

With regard to staff productivity, he suggested that, as a test piece, the director of administration should advise him on the number of sales engineers to be employed and on the ways in which their productivity should be measured. He felt that too much emphasis was being placed on expense control, which might lead to situations in which opportunities to earn revenue were neglected and stifled.

The personnel director saw that it might be sound to site staff job evaluation in a 'neutral' department; after all, functional responsibility for the evaluation of works jobs rested with the work study department. However, he would like to be reassured that the management service department would be able to deal with the problems arising in three geographically distinct sites.

Required

1 *Evaluate the control system which is proposed for administrative costs.*

Commentary by Derek Moore and John Marsh

We like to use this case as an example of some of the particular problems which we have met as we have expanded our operations. When Hardy Heating was small, the administrative or non-manufacturing issues and their costs did not represent a terribly difficult management problem; also a great deal of the operations could be controlled by direct observation and attention. As we have grown, we have found it necessary to delegate responsibility and hence the problems of centralisation/decentralisation; the balance between line and staff departments has become tricky; and further, the administration costs have now become a very significant element in our cost structure. We have found that, at the centre, we have needed to give a great deal of attention to

these organisational relationships, so that we are able to delegate effectively, making individual managers feel responsible
for their sphere of operations, and yet still ensuring our own
overall control of the business. As our individual units have
grown, the same issue of delegation and control has been
worked out at another level. Within these units, it has been
necessary to develop specialised departments to assist our line
managers and it is the matter of a correct balance which is
difficult to maintain. These specialised departments, sometimes unkindly referred to as non-productive or overheads,
can be expensive and it is difficult to judge whether the company is receiving value for money from them. It is relatively
easy for us to know what they are costing but very much
more difficult to evaluate their output. Nonetheless although
it is admittedly an intractable problem, it has to be controlled, for in our observation, after they have gone public
many companies turn in disappointing results because they
fail to control their overheads. When we have discussed this
problem with some outsiders, they have said 'easy, just set a
budget for each overhead expense and keep to it'. But this is
not very helpful in our experience — at what level should we
set the budget? What activities should be included and excluded from the budget? If we keep our spending just within
the budget, should we congratulate ourselves on doing a good
job? Well maybe we should, but it is equally possible that we
might have wasted money even though our activities were
efficient. Keeping within the budget certainly helps us to
predict our cash flows but does not necessarily ensure that
resources have been used effectively and efficiently. Our
observation is that many institutions in both the public and
private sector use a 'historical–incremental approach' to the
setting of overhead budgets which leads to 'last year plus a
bit for inflation' being quoted as the main and sometimes
only criterion. This may be a convenient approach but it certainly is not logical and undoubtedly has led to massive problems. For example, we understand that the level of the
budgets for building maintenance in some hospitals can be
traced back to those levels which existed in 1948, the beginning of the Health Service. In other words, those hospitals
which had relatively low maintenance budgets in 1948, had
low budgets for the next 30 years, irrespective of what was
required by the physical condition of the buildings.

Perhaps we should start by stating that at Star Components the term 'administrative costs' covers all 'non-manufacturing costs' and therefore includes the costs of the accounting department, the marketing department, the research and development department and the personnel department. On the manufacturing side, we have put considerable emphasis on work measurement which has allowed us to measure manufacturing efficiency pretty accurately, in the sense of the degree of success achieved in converting inputs of labour and material into outputs. We have found that for these manufacturing costs, increased efficiency leads automatically to increased effectiveness, in the sense of enabling organisational objectives to be achieved. However we must admit that for some non-manufacturing activities it seems to us that increased efficiency by itself does not necessarily guarantee effectiveness. For example, we have experienced the situation where our efficiency in transport, measured by cost per mile and vehicle down-time, has been high, but simultaneously we have been dissatisfied with the overall quality of service given to our customers by our distribution function. We have learned that we must distinguish 'efficiency' from 'effectiveness' and have control sytems which cover both aspects in probably very different ways. In Star Components, we applaud John Gillett for taking such a determined approach to the measurement, and control of, basically, the *efficiency* of non-manufacturing costs, but we have some lingering doubts concerning the assessment of the *effectiveness* of these activities. Our view is that it is necessary to get behind the total cost of the function, to consider in detail the specific activities which make up the functional cost and then to decide upon the form of control which is needed for each sub-activity. We have found that it sometimes helps to distinguish different categories of activities. For example we can distinguish relatively easily between routine tasks; projects/*ad hoc* tasks; regular tasks and finally general activities of a non-routine nature. For many routine tasks, the work study and work measurement techniques, which we are accustomed to using in factories manufacturing standard products, can be applied with considerable success. The basic approach of John Gillett is particularly strong for these routine tasks and has led to tight measurement of administrative efficiency. However, we have found that, in addition to routine tasks there are other activi-

ties which are less structured and for which the temptation
exists to force-fit them into a control system which works
well for structured activities, but which produces some un-
intended consequences if applied insensitively elsewhere. The
proposed management services department with its control of
procedures, organisation, work standards, forms and office
equipment will ensure that all activities, but particularly
structured, routine activities, will be rigorously monitored.
Our doubts surround the treatment of unstructured, non-
routine activities and the possibility of inflexibility being
created as a result of the inevitable tendency to centralise
control. From our experience we can predict that the proposed management services department will be strong in the
pursuit of efficiency but less able to grapple with the more
difficult problem of assessing effectiveness. We like the idea
of developing productivity teams, providing their terms of
references are drawn sufficiently broadly to cover the assessment of both efficiency and effectiveness. Elsewhere in the
group we have tackled the control of non-manufacturing
costs by using the techniques of zero-based budgeting (ZBB)
and management by objectives (MBO) and we have learned to
adapt these techniques to the local circumstances of the particular company.

Conclusion

As we explained, when we described our model of control
systems, the structures and processes of the individual control systems for operations, marketing, personnel and
finance, interlock. One advantage of the recommendation of
John Gillett is that this interlocking system will be constantly
under review and any changes will be quickly observed and
evaluated. However the establishment of the proposed
management services department will tend to centralise this
review and also place more power in the hands of John
Gillett. The existing balance between line and staff departments will be upset and the resulting new position may produce more inflexibility and may stifle initiative.

The proposed system presents an opportunity to critically
examine in detail the activities of the non-manufacturing
departments; although the main emphasis seems to be placed
on the measurement and control of mainly routine activities.

The non-routine activities, in our view, present the most diffi-cult problems. We do not regard management by objectives schemes as general panaceas because we know from experi-ence that the programme must be tailored to local circum-stances. Nonetheless, we do believe that such an approach has a part to play in the measurement and control of unstruc-tured, non-routine activities and also in the assessment of the effectiveness of activities generally. Such schemes do have the merit of allowing a regular review of the expectations of top management, functional heads and their subordinates regard-ing the purpose and the success of the different categories of activities provided by each function.

13

The measurement of product profitability

Case study no. 40 – product profitability (1)

Merrydale Ltd – background

Merrydale Limited was acquired in 1969 (the first acquisition), and has been placed for present organisational purposes in the Star Components division. The company is a supplier of components to the electronics industry and was formerly a part of the large conglomerate Falco. Originally a private family business in an old factory 1½ miles from Birmingham city centre, it moved to a trading estate in the Black country. At the time of its purchase by Falco, it was making a loss, never really became sufficiently profitable, and was purchased by Hardy Heating at a time when losses were again appearing. In the 1970 financial year the loss was £5,000 on a turnover of £300,000 and in relation to assets employed of approximately £240,000.

Not being at all satisfied with the results, and wanting a speedy improvement in the fortunes of Merrydale, Derek Moore decided to take action.

Meeting with the divisional managing director

The three executives, the general manager, works manager and sales manager, were summoned to group headquarters, and there is little doubt that they feared the worst. However, the meeting was a pleasant one, though the group managing director, Derek Moore, made it quite clear that the position must be improved. In his opinion 12 months was a reasonable period in which to get Merrydale back into a break-even position, and one of the prime jobs was to carry out a comprehensive exercise into the profitability of the various products. Moore suggested that unprofitable products should be dropped and that marketing attention should be concentrated on the profitable items. The group managing director had now decided to attend a meeting of executives at Merrydale in two months' time, at which he expected to see a statement of product profitability and some firm recommendations on the future of the product range, including the treatment of new products.

Production and accounting methods

The executives took stock of the existing situation at the earliest opportunity. The works manager was confident of a reasonable level of efficiency in the factory which he had tended very carefully in the last five years. All agreed that production planning and control was effective and the work study engineer, appointed four years ago, had done a first-class job in both method study and work measurement. Standard times were available for almost every production operation on every product, and the piecework method of remuneration applied to over 90 per cent of direct employees. The executives agreed that no dramatic improvement in operating efficiency was likely to be achieved. On the other hand, there had been doubt for some time about the relative profitability of the products. Ninety-five per cent of the sales stemmed from 150 standard products, and recent costings suggested that many of these products were sold at inadequate prices, mainly because of fierceness of competition, and because of the willingness of the larger manufacturers to subsidise part of their output.

The accountant, Frank Berry, was called in to summarise the existing accounting methods. As a relative newcomer to the firm, having joined a year ago, Berry was struggling to make an impression. The executives had deliberately recruited a middle-aged, unqualified man and regarded him as a 'reliable plodder'. Nevertheless, the accountant had made a number of suggestions, some of which had been implemented. He had recently calculated departmental overhead rates for the first time and had produced a report on standard costing which was still under consideration. As part of the report on standard costing, Berry had produced a sample standard cost for one of the main-line products and had plans in hand to expand these calculations through the product range, as soon as the executives gave their approval. Within three days he supplied the following statement of the actual costs for the first 25 products for which information was readily at hand from current production records (Figure 13.1).

The statement was examined and there was a general air of disbelief. The general manager noted that, if the instructions of the group managing director were implicitly followed, 16 lines from the first 25 products should be dropped. The works manager, Frank Key, was so alarmed at the figures that he insisted on a detailed explanation of the costing procedures which had been used. Berry outlined the procedures as follows:

1 For material costs, I work from the product specification, adding what I think are reasonable allowances for waste, then I extend these quantities at the current prices.'

2 For labour costs, I check on the most recent batch made, satisfy myself that all the operations on the product specification have been carried out, and take the labour cost per unit from the batch order.

3 For overheads, I use the departmental overhead rates which I showed you recently and which are revised annually. Administration, selling and distribution costs are recovered as a percentage of works cost.

4 Frank Key made a special point of asking Berry about production rejects and Berry explained that he kept some figures summarising inspection records and that he included the current reject rate in the unit product cost.

Berry made it clear to the three executives that Merrydale did not have a system of product costing which threw out the figures regularly, but that any request which they made for

Product no.	Average selling price	Total product cost	Profit	Loss
02	15.2	9.2	6.0	
15	50.8	61.3		10.4
17	50.8	61.3		10.4
27	70.8	75.4		4.6
32	117.6	145.4		27.8
35	224.2	238.8		14.6
36	282.1	288.8		6.7
40	272.9	234.2	38.8	
41	368.3	393.3		25.0
42	355.0	347.1	7.9	
51	51.7	52.1		0.4
67	16.7	13.8	2.9	
73	208.8	209.6		0.8
74	228.8	233.8		5.0
76	6.7	7.3		0.6
82	215.8	220.4		4.6
92	195.0	224.2		29.2
93	242.5	258.8		16.3
95	81.7	95.0		13.3
100	7.9	5.8	2.1	
107	7.9	6.7	1.2	
137	132.5	117.5	15.0	
402	275.0	285.0		10.0
403	275.0	268.3	6.7	
404	275.0	268.3	6.7	

Note: all figures in pence

Fig. 13.1   Actual costs for first 25 products

product costs called for an *ad hoc* exercise which he carried out along the lines indicated. As far as he was concerned the product cost statement was reasonably accurate, but he felt that his ideas on standard costing should be implemented without delay.

The three executives were undecided.

1 Should they rely on the statement as presented and work out the marketing policy based on these figures? or
2 Should they wait until Berry had implemented his ideas on standard costing?

Required
1 *What action would you recommend?*

The sales manager had serious doubts about his ability to assess product profitability from the figures supplied, and suggested that they should seek some outside help in order to obtain a proper interpretation of the situation. It was at this point that the three executives agreed to take the opinions of James Martin, a management consultant and friend of Frank Key.

Martin was familiar with the firm and its procedures. He was supplied with a file of working papers by Berry which included: the total product cost statement; and a sample standard cost for one main-line product.

The approach of the consultant

Martin studied these details and quickly concluded that the total product cost statement might be misleading as it stood. Indeed, he thought that even if a total *standard* product cost statement was produced it would still not represent reliable and relevant information for assessing product profitability. He would be surprised if all 25 products were not making some contribution towards overhead expenses, in which case to drop any of the products might well worsen the company situation.

The first sample standard cost for one main-line product included overhead standard costs arising in the six manufacturing departments through which the product passed. This overhead standard cost represented the absorption of total overhead into the cost of the product, and was based upon the budgeted total overhead costs for a budgeted level of activity. Martin felt that the latter was a snag, that he needed to use a cost per unit which would not vary with the level of activity and to achieve this it was necessary to calculate a variable or marginal standard overhead cost.

He went back to the department cost analysis which had been used to calculate departmental overhead rates, and studied the behaviour of each cost item in turn.

Some items he quickly classified as fixed or period costs such as supervision, rent and rates, depreciation of fixed assets. Other items required much closer examination, and he

found it useful for these items to show graphically the relationship between cost and activity (see Figure 13.2). Using
the least squares method he was able to distinguish between
the fixed and variable element of each item of cost. He was
now in a position to concentrate on the standard marginal
costs of products, which would be constant irrespective of
varying levels of activity. In respect of the same 25 products,
he insisted on decisions being taken regarding standard
material cost and standard labour cost. The large amount of
work measurement which had already been undertaken at
Merrydale helped the calculations of standard labour costs,
and made it possible to calculate departmental variable overhead rates on a time basis. Standards were established for
production rejects and after three weeks a new product cost
statement emerged.

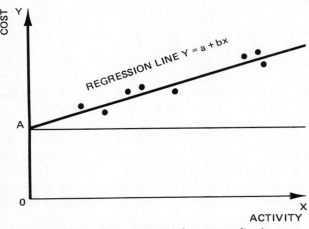

Notes: a (the regression constant) represents fixed costs
b (the regression coefficient) represents marginal
or variable costs

Fig. 13.2   Relationship between cost and activity

Explanation of the revised statement

Martin introduced the statement by making the point that, in
his opinion, in this case, the most relevant way to look at
product profitability was on a standard contribution basis.
His first argument was that no product made a profit but that

each product made some sort of contribution towards fixed overheads and profit. It was important to establish the amount of the contribution, preferably on a standard cost rather than an actual cost basis, since factory inefficiencies should not, he suggested, be allowed to confuse the issue. It was tempting when product contributions had been calculated to relate those contributions to product selling prices to obtain a ratio or measure of profitability, but this was not accurate. He argued that contribution should be related to the resource which was the limiting factor in the business at that time. This might be material, such as was currently the case with nickel. In future, he suggested it might be a particular class of labour which was difficult to obtain, but it might be space or capital. His summing up of the Merrydale situation was that they were busy fools, since capacity and facilities were almost fully used in every department and yet they were making losses. In his opinion, the standard contribution of each product should be related to the standard production time, and this he had done on the statement. Then he had ranked the products according to the standard contribution per hour which they made. The results had been quite staggering (Figure 13.3), with a top rate of contribution per hour of 123p and a bottom rate of 8.6p, the latter being almost equivalent to no contribution at all.

He suggested that the statement now gave a clear picture of those products which should be pushed and which should be contracted. In future, he suggested that Berry should connect the monthly sales analysis figures with the standard marginal product costs and the revised statement would then be a useful tool in determining the production/sales strategy of the company.

Martin was also keen to explain the three contribution classifications A, B and C on the statement. Contribution classification A, he said, represented those products which made a contribution better than 60p per production hour. This contribution rate represented a return of more than 20 per cent on the capital employed by the company. Contribution classification B, he explained, bore contribution rates between 33p per hour and 60p per hour, the 33p rate being a break-even rate of return. Contribution classification C included products making contributions of less than 33p per hour, that is less than break-even rate.

Product number	Average s.p.	Standard marginal cost	Standard contribution	Total standard time	Standard contribution per hr.	Contribution classification
	pence	pence	pence	(hrs)	pence	
137	132.5	87.5	45.0	.366	123.0	A
74	228.8	158.5	70.3	.67	104.9	A
73	208.8	151.7	57.1	.67	85.2	A
40	272.9	174.2	98.7	1.17	84.4	A
2	15.2	6.9	8.3	.106	78.3	A
67	16.7	9.9	6.8	.1	68.0	A
403	275.0	198.3	76.7	1.3	59.0	B
404	275.0	198.3	76.7	1.3	59.0	B
100	7.9	4.2	3.7	.065	56.9	B
42	355.0	262.1	92.9	1.92	48.4	B
82	215.8	160.4	55.4	1.25	44.3	B
51	51.7	36.3	15.4	.366	42.1	B
41	368.3	293.3	75.0	1.84	40.8	B
402	275.0	216.7	58.3	1.456	40.0	B
107	7.9	5.0	2.9	.077	37.7	B
93	242.5	193.5	49.0	1.45	33.8	B
92	195.0	164.2	30.8	1.07	28.8	C
36	282.1	218.8	63.3	2.3	27.5	C
35	224.2	178.8	45.4	2.0	22.7	C
27	70.8	56.7	14.1	.706	20.0	C
76	6.7	5.4	1.3	.078	16.7	C
32	117.6	110.4	7.2	.486	14.8	C
17	50.8	46.1	4.7	.54	8.7	C
15	50.8	46.1	4.7	.54	8.7	C
95	81.7	73.7	8.0	.093	8.6	C

Fig. 13.3   Comparison of product standard marginal costs with selling prices

The general manager said that he found the exercise novel and easy to understand. He confessed that the fluctuations of unit cost with changing volume had always confused him. He asked Martin to explain how the 33p and 60p contribution rates per hour had been calculated. Martin said that these were not precise rates, but the 33p rate was the result of dividing the annual fixed cost bill of approximately £60,000 by the annual figure of production hours available, 180,000. The top rate had been arrived at by dividing the £60,000 fixed costs plus a £48,000 profit budget by the 180,000 production hours.

Other advantages of this approach

The sales manager asked whether this approach could be used when considering adding new products to the range. Martin replied that, in his opinion, new products should only be introduced if they could be classified A or B in the reasonably foreseeable future. The sales manager thought this procedure might be unduly restricting and argued that even class C products made some contribution which might otherwise be missed. Martin justified his opinion by pointing out that the calculation of the marginal cost figures was not a black-and-white affair. Some arbitrary allocations and apportionments were unavoidable and it was only reasonable business conservatism to cover this point by expecting some acceptable minimum above marginal costs. The acceptable minimum would also take into account that the addition of a product might well involve some slight increase in fixed costs, such as sales promotion or product design, and that the management team would have yet another problem to consider. The works manager, Frank Key, thought that this approach should help him to control costs. He had noted that the standard marginal costs were those that fell within the control of departmental managers, and he hoped that Berry would produce statements which not only dealt with product profitability but also assisted shop floor control. It seemed to him that the same basic data could be used for a number of purposes. Martin agreed with these points and suggested also that the isolation of fixed costs should help senior management to appreciate their significance and to assist their control.

The reaction of the divisional managing director

The general manager thanked Martin for his speedy and helpful advice. Frank Berry was asked to continue the exercise for the remaining standard products, and in the meantime they would consider the action which should be taken consequent upon the revised information. A copy of the revised statement was sent to Derek Moore.

At the meeting of executives, the general manager explained to Moore what had taken place, and was quick to point out the benefits which had already stemmed from the product profitability exercise. He mentioned that the selling prices of certain products had been increased, with more or less certainty that this would not have any effect on the volume of sales of these products, that value analysis work was being carried out on several of the products in order to improve the contributions, and it was already clear that this would meet with some success. All of this was very interesting to Moore, but he asked if he might see Martin to discuss the costing work.

When Martin arrived, Moore told him that he was intrigued by the exercise, though he felt that it had been unnecessarily complicated. He said that he believed the basic idea to be sound since it was very similar to the gross profit approach, used in the distribution industry, where for years, he said, it had been customary to assess product profitability on the basis of the gross profit percentage of sales. He used as the examples in support of his argument product numbers 137, 41 and 95 on the standard marginal cost statement. The contribution percentages to sales came out at 34 per cent, 20 per cent and 10 per cent respectively.

Martin reacted strongly to this, saying it was sheer coincidence that the figures came out in this particular way. He suggested that Moore should also look at product numbers 137 and 40, where the contribution percentages were 34 per cent and 36 per cent respectively, yet the contribution rates per hour were very different, being 123p and 84.4 p. Then, there was product number 100 where the gross profit rate was even higher at 47 per cent, though the contribution rate per hour was only 56.9p.

Moore was not too sure how to answer this, but reiterated his interest in the work which had been done. 'I have just two more doubts', he said. 'First of all, I am a little worried about the way in which you've added together the various production department times in order to arrive at a total standard time. Then, what about the facts that the capital employed by each product, and the value added by the company to the raw materials cost of each product, vary considerably? The selling and distribution efforts might also differ considerably between products. Does your method of costing take this into account?'

Required
1 *Consider whether you support the attitude of James Martin towards the new marginal product cost statement, and consider how you would deal with the points raised in the last paragraph.*

Commentary by Derek Moore and John Marsh

We didn't buy Merrydale Limited on the basis of the profits it was making, because it wasn't making any, but it did seem to fit the planned development.

When a company is turning in losses rather than profits, the reasons can be many. The main factors affecting profitability may be sales factors, i.e. the volume may not be high enough, the mix may be wrong, the prices may be incorrect; in fact, there are some combinations of these which can have a devastating effect on profits. For example, prices may be set too high for products which would utilise underemployed capacity so that the total product mix becomes slanted towards underpriced items where capacity is already being used to the maximum. Of course, there are so many other possible factors affecting profitability, the ability to control costs and operating efficiency being amongst the forerunners. But there is no doubt that product profitability and mix predominate in the quest for an adequate return.

We have discovered that in all our businesses, a sizeable management accounting problem is the one of determining the profitability of individual products in a product range, and there are many possible views which can be taken. Perhaps a first question here is: should the cost which is compared with the selling price be an actual cost or a standard cost? A second question is: what do we mean by an actual product cost? Is it the absorption cost, the marginal cost, the direct cost or what? A third question is: when one has discovered the margin between cost and selling price, to what should this be related in order to determine the relative profitability of different products? Should it be the cost, the selling price, could it be the capital employed, or should it be some expression of the use of resources?

A further problem which can arise is the volume of production/sales of the individual products, and the fact that some products are short-run items, whereas other products may offer long production runs. We would feel that these factors should all, somehow or other, be reflected in the assessments. A tricky problem, but one confronting our businesses.

We had to correct the situation in Merrydale and it seemed

sensible to give the three executives running the plant a dead-
line, as well as some advice. We felt that a basic problem was
one of mix and product profitability, so we left them to get
on with the exercise of sorting out the product range.

As you can see, the accountant pursued a total or absorption costing approach towards costing the products, and this
requires that a lot of problem areas be tackled. There is a
first decision to be taken upon whether the cost of the product should be based upon the last batch put through or an
average over the month; there can be sizeable problems in
estimating the actual consumption of material in relation to a
number of products produced; in regard to labour cost, the
costing may be eased by the presence of piecework prices,
but excess operations and the inevitable excess costs need to
be collected. Our experience is that in manufacturing an
awful bogey of product costing is the scrap rate, knowing
what it is, having the basic production records, and then the
problem of dealing with scrap rates which vary enormously
according to the operator, the machine, the material worked
on and other factors.

Also we would argue that a problem which surmounts all
the difficulties of obtaining accurate direct cost data is how
to absorb overheads in the product cost? Is a blanket rate
adequate? You may recall that Hardy Heating changed from
a blanket rate to overhead rates for the departmental cost
centres; this is a lot of work, involving time and expense.
There is a question as to whether such rates should be based
on an actual production/trading period (never to be repeated)
or whether the calculations should be on a predetermined
basis (perhaps, related to the next budget period). And
wherever we have worked, there has been difficulty in arriving at satisfactory methods for the recovery of overheads
outside the production departments.

It is a little worrying to us how much faith so many people
in manufacturing have in absorption costing, seemingly for-
getting the assumptions which have just been referred to. It is
very difficult to use absorption cost and net profit figures in
determining product profitability. We would go along with
those who say that a product does not really make a profit at
all.

Another factor which we all need to consider is: should the
profitability of the product be based on the actual cost of the

product, containing all the inefficiencies of production, or on a standard cost; if you like, what the product ought to cost? One could make the mistake of eliminating a product from the range because one is failing to manufacture it to reasonable performance standards, not because the product has no profit potential. Berry's idea to introduce standard costing has much to commend it, particularly in a situation where you not only want to assess product profitability, but you also wish to know what the variances and excess costs are so that these may be corrected.

We certainly didn't object to the fellows at Merrydale obtaining some outside help in the form of James Martin. He brought yet another, and important, slant to the exercise. He insisted on a breakdown of operating costs into variable and fixed; in our experience this is essential if one is going to make correct decisions. Having said that, costs are not either fixed or variable; it isn't quite as simple as that, and getting to grips with cost behaviour can be difficult. But you can see from the case how Martin approached the problem. It was all aimed at arriving at a product cost on a standard cost basis, and on a marginal rather than absorption cost basis. This was the 'marginal coster's' argument that a product doesn't make a profit anyway, but does, hopefully, contribute towards profits. This certainly fits in with experience which we had both had in distribution, where ideas of gross profit tend to prevail.

We would go along with the idea of finding out whether each product makes a 'standard contribution', but there you must have a base to which that measure of profit can be related if you wish to rank the products in a range. From our experience, the selling price is not a satisfactory base, because that is a policy figure, and may not reflect in any way the use of resources, one or more of which may be seriously limited. So the idea of 'contribution per unit of limiting factor' is one that we like to see applied throughout our businesses. Further, the notion of some sort of target of contribution to limiting factor is sensible. A practical problem, however, which we have frequently met, is the presence of more than one limiting factor; and it can become very complicated under this circumstance; linear programming can help in this sort of situation.

We have seen other approaches, one of which got a men-

tion in the Merrydale case. If one argues that more and more
costs are becoming fixed, certainly less variable, then the concept of added value begins to be significant. There are those
who would say that the bought-out costs are the essential
variables in their business, the internal costs being pretty well
entirely fixed. If this is so, then added value, that is the selling price less the bought-out cost, is a good indicator of profitability, and can be used in the same way as contribution.

Conclusion

We both can remember the costing textbook which said that
an estimate is an opinion, a cost is a fact, and a selling price is
a policy. No doubt the intention here was to distinguish
between these three very different things. Having said that, we
would hope that it is clear from this incident that a cost is
not a fact. There is a standard cost and an actual cost, an absorption cost and a marginal cost, and they relate to different
concepts like: what ought the cost to be, what was the cost
the last time we made it, what is likely to be the cost of one
extra unit of production, what is an average all-in cost including appropriate apportionments of establishment costs?

But one has decisions to take about products: which to
drop, which to try to extend the production and sale of, and
one needs the most relevant financial information one can get
as an input to those decisions. Two important things to remember are: you do not obtain good cost information without reliable basic shop floor procedures, good recording,
effective production planning and control and sound work
measurement; and the information inputs to the product
decision are not entirely financial. We have learned the hard
way that you sometimes continue with particular products
even when they earn negative contributions.

Case study no. 41 – product profitability (2)

R. B. Ling & Co Ltd

R. B. Ling and Company Limited was taken over in 1974 as a result of the decision to establish a materials processing division. The company manufactures aluminium castings, though when it was formed in the pre-war years, it was a small general engineering company, engaged primarily in machining for the motorcycle trade. The latter trade started to use aluminium castings, and the company was turned over to their manufacture. No machining has been done, therefore, for many years, but it is being considered again, because of the many customers calling for machined castings.

There is not a wide range of customers; there is no demand from the motorcycle trade, and the level of activity has now been low for the last two years. It is thought that the presence of machining capacity might attract more casting work as well as make its own contribution to profits. At the moment the average number employed in the business on its own site is 105.

Three product groups

The company secretary/chief accountant, who was appointed two years ago, is beginning to restructure accounting procedures, and one alteration introduced since January can best be understood by reference to the trading statements for January and for February (Figures 13.4 and 13.5).

The products of the factory fall into three groups and, therefore, it has been decided to break down the monthly trading results into these three groups; the toolroom has been added as a fourth column on the trading statement. The three product groups (pressure diecasting, gravity diecasting and sand casting) are indicative not only of separate products but also of separate factory locations and plant and equipment.

Each casting shop has its own coremaking and fettling facilities, though melting and heat treatment facilities are common to the products; these costs are apportioned without too much difficulty to the three product groups.

In the toolroom, some dies are made for customers for new products and, in these cases, customers are charged a selling price for the dies. Some toolroom work is on die maintenance for which materials and labour are charged as overheads to the three product groups. Figure 13.6 shows the relationship between the operating shops and the workflow.

To determine the relative profitability of each product group, the first task was to arrive at the saleable value of output shown at the top of the trading statement. There is no problem in determining sales and returns figures but work in progress quantities have to be extracted from production planning schedules and valued. Work in progress is classified as cast only and near-finished and priced at average total costs per ton.

The directors and the accountant know that saleable value of output is a misnomer but they are uncertain about a satisfactory alternative.

Against saleable value of output is set the variable cost of production, which leaves the gross contribution made by each product group. Fixed overhead is budgeted at the beginning of the year and charged to each trading period according to the actual number of working days. Further, at the time of the preparation of the budget fixed overheads were sub-divided into those directly attributable to the product groups and those which are general.

On the trading statement, the period portion of the directly attributable fixed costs is deducted from the gross con-

	Pressure	Gravity	Sand	Tool-room	Total
	£	£	£	£	£
Sales	29,105	20,060	3,617	3,108	55,890
Less returns	873	712	–	–	1,585
	28,232	19,348	3,617	3,108	54,305
Add closing W I P	10,311	13,812	1,263	8,043	33,429
	38,543	33,160	4,880	11,151	87,734
Less opening W I P	6,413	9,782	1,027	8,161	25,383
Saleable value of output	32,130	23,378	3,853	2,990	62,351
Variable costs of production:					
Metal	13,868	9,891	1,214	–	24,973
Melting	1,658	1,409	327	–	3,394
Coremaking					
Direct labour	–	143	83	–	226
Variable overhead	–	137	159	–	296
Total	–	280	242	–	522
Casting (casting hours)	(2,544)	(2,702)	(793)		
Direct labour	1,782	1,814	474	–	4,070
Variable overhead	2,691	2,119	327	–	5,137
Total	4,473	3,933	801	–	9,207
Fettling					
Direct labour	1,287	675	50	–	2,012
Variable overhead	1,566	1,070	72	–	2,708
Total	2,853	1,745	122	–	4,720
Toolroom	389	527	–	4,099	5,015
Heat treatment	63	384	100	–	547
Distribution	582	385	45	–	1,012
Outwork	115	1,291	–	–	1,406
Total variable costs	24,001	19,845	2,851	4,099	50,796
Gross contribution	8,129	3,533	1,002	(1,109)	11,555
Direct fixed costs (budget)	1,609	1,023	398	200	3,230
Net contribution	6,520	2,510	604	(1,309)	8,325
General fixed costs (budget)					10,109
			Trading loss	£	(1,784)

Fig. 13.4 Trading results, January

	Pressure	Gravity	Sand	Tool-room	Total
	£	£	£	£	£
Sales	37,996	24,342	4,804	2,298	69,440
Less returns	1,470	86	362	–	1,918
	36,526	24,256	4,442	2,298	67,522
Add closing W I P	7,422	10,107	808	7,813	26,150
	43,948	34,363	5,250	10,111	93,672
Less opening W I P	10,311	13,812	1,263	8,043	33,429
Saleable value of output	33,637	20,551	3,987	2,068	60,243
Variable costs of production:					
Metal	13,141	8,062	826	–	22,029
Melting	1,612	1,358	280	–	3,250
Coremaking					
Direct labour	–	112	70	–	182
Variable overhead	–	112	140	–	252
Total	–	224	210	–	434
Casting (casting hours)	(2,256)	(2,414)	(640)		
Direct labour	1,578	1,600	382	–	3,560
Variable overhead	2,309	1,818	361	–	4,488
Total	3,887	3,418	743	–	8,048
Fettling					
Direct labour	1,198	607	50	–	1,855
Variable overhead	1,422	973	70	–	2,465
Total	2,620	1,580	120	–	4,320
Toolroom	420	554	–	3,082	4,056
Heat treatment	30	332	119	–	481
Distribution	473	385	30	–	888
Outwork	63	1,228	–	–	1,291
Total variable costs	22,246	17,141	2,328	3,082	44,797
Gross contribution	11,391	3,410	1,659	(1,014)	15,446
Direct fixed costs (budget)	1,609	1,023	398	200	3,230
Net contribution	9,782	2,387	1,261	(1,214)	12,216
General fixed costs (budget)					10,109
				Trading profit	£ 2,107

Fig. 13.5   Trading results, February

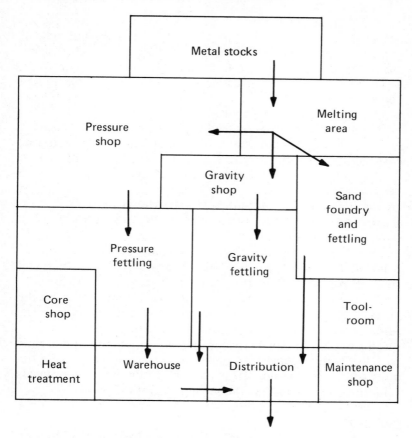

Fig. 13.6   Factory layout and workflow

tribution made by each product to leave a net contribution. The period portion of the general fixed costs is then deducted from the grand total of net contributions to give the trading profit for the period.

The directors find this layout acceptable because of the simplicity of the contribution approach and also since they believe that it should enable them to assess the likely effect on company profit of changes in the level of activity and the use of capacity. Previous statements of the profitability of product groups reflected the apportionment of all fixed costs and left them in doubt about the actual contribution made by each product to overall profitability.

There are problems, however. None of the product groups has shown a significant variation in cost per unit of output expressed on a tonnage basis, on a sales value basis or in relation to actual production hours. The gross contribution, which the accountant has claimed to be the most realistic and consistent measure of profit, shows no sign of demonstrating a constant relationship to output.

In the last three weeks, the current products of the pressure diecasting section have been examined on a marginal cost basis to determine individual contributions (Figure 13.7). It was hoped that an extension of the output of each of these products, in February, by the contributions per unit would give a figure which would equate to the gross contribution shown in the February trading statement. In fact, there was a significant difference.

This has highlighted another problem—the method of stock and work-in-progress valuation, not being at marginal cost, is also distorting the monthly figures of contribution. These points are brought out clearly in a comparison of the gross contribution figures for pressure diecasting on the January and February statements of trading results.

This has led to a more recent exercise in which the marginal cost per unit of each product has been compared with the unit total cost arising from the monthly work-in-progress valuation; again, this has shown significant differences.

Required

1 *Consider how to explain the movement from a trading loss in January to a profit in February.*

2 *Consider whether the trading statements give a fair reflection of the operating position for the two months.*

Product no.	PD 5067	PD 5132	PD 4417	PD 3982	PD 4617	PD 1022	PD 1428
Sales price	£0.0625	£0.0753	£0.2516	£0.0318	£0.2125	£0.1945	£0.0388
Marginal costs							
Metal	.0128	.0258	.1500	.0140	.1100	.1180	.0140
Melting	.0012	.0026	.0150	.0014	.0110	.0118	.0014
Casting DL	.0028	.0037	.0122	.0019	.0125	.0121	.0030
VO	.0056	.0049	.0200	.0053	.0167	.0205	.0077
Fettling DL	.0037	.0035	.0092	.0007	.0044	.0051	.0020
VO	.0052	.0049	.0129	.0010	.0060	.0071	.0028
Totals	.0313	.0454	.2193	.0243	.1606	.1746	.0309
Contribution each	.0312	.0299	.0323	.0075	.0519	.0199	.0079
% of S P	50%	39%	13%	22%	24%	11%	20%
Per casting hour	£5.05	£5.50	£1.44	£1.28	£2.75	£0.88	£0.83

Fig. 13.7 Product costs and profitability, pressure diecastings only

Commentary by Derek Moore and John Marsh

There are very few businesses, in our opinion, where the monthly profit and loss account could not be broken down into appropriate activities. In many instances these activities would be product groups; if there are closely identifiable groupings of products, then it is logical that one should want to know their relative profitability. Having said that, the decision to do so presents management accounting problems. Profit measurement for the business as a whole is fraught with problems, for example, stock and work-in-progress valuation, the calculation of and provision for depreciation, the correct ascertainment of sales–reserves; and accruals and prepayments, provisions and reserves generally. When one decides to break down the profit and loss account into product groups, more problems arise, many in the area of cost allocations and apportionments, and costing concepts come into play, in particular the absorption and marginal costing theories. Once again, it is a matter of which costing approach is most relevant for the particular case.

Then there is the inevitable further requirement to have information available about individual products within each product group, and the likelihood that the financial information which is relevant to this exercise is not that which is relevant to the product group study.

We would applaud the attempts made in the business to establish product group profitability, stressing the inevitable limitations of the figures. Obviously there is the bogey of stock and work-in-progress valuations; there are those who would feel that since the whole approach is really a marginal cost layout, the stock valuation should really be on a product by product, marginal cost basis. It is not really satisfactory to use average total costs per ton, but whether one could change this to an individual product marginal cost basis would depend first of all upon whether one could obtain actual stock quantities identified by stage of completion at each month-end, or whether one could operate work-in-progress records at marginal cost. Since these accounts would need to be credited monthly with a cost of sales figures, there would be a requirement for a product by product master file; this could be achievable where reasonably standard products are involved, but assumes sound basic cost information and the facilities to update regularly.

Cost allocation and apportionment will, in our experience, always present problems. The aims should be to allocate costs wherever possible, and treat as much cost as feasible as 'directly attributable'. In Ling, we know that a very large proportion of the so-called variable costs were directly attributable to the individual product groups, that in fact the majority of apportionable costs were included in the fixed costs category. It is interesting to see that fixed costs are divided into 'direct' and 'general' headings, the 'direct' being those capable of direct identification with a particular product group, the 'general' being what might be called establishment expense or policy costs. The idea of the split and their charging only the direct fixed costs into the profit measurement calculation for each product group was novel to us, but makes good sense.

The fact that one does not apportion the general fixed costs means one does not arrive at a profit figure for each product group, but at a net contribution. We would accept this approach, because in our view an individual product group does not make a profit. It is hoped that the business in total makes a profit, and each product group contributes. What is not acceptable to us is an arbitrary apportionment of the general fixed costs, say, for example, on the basis of what is called the saleable value of output. Taking the figures for February, if one used this basis of apportionment, the general fixed costs charge to the gravity diecastings product group would be

$$£10,109 \times \frac{20,551}{60,243} = £3,437$$

There would then be the suggestion in the statement of trading results that gravity diecastings make a loss; there might even be the debate as to whether this product group activity should be lopped off. This would be unfortunate, because clearly the activity contributes in no small measure.

There can, of course, be some argument about the use of budget figures for fixed costs rather than actual. Clearly, at the end of the day, the profit and loss account must contain the actual charges, but it is not unreasonable to argue that if fixed costs are fixed, then at least in the short term the method used is suitable, particularly if the fixed cost budget is in the hands of a particular person to control.

We believe that it is unrealistic to expect a constant relationship between variable costs and sales, or between contribution and sales. And when sales are adjusted by work in progress calculated on an average total cost basis, there really is no chance of a constant profit/volume ratio, as the textbooks call it. On the other hand, it is quite correct to be looking for reasons for the variations. Whatever the business, a likely significant reason will be product mix, and this is why in our view it is correct to do as they did in Ling and take a further look at individual product profitability.

This was done on a strictly marginal cost basis, to determine product contributions, then express these as a percentage of selling price and per casting hour. We would not feel the relationship of contribution to sales price to be meaningful, but that the ratio to limiting factor is a very useful measure.

There is a reference in the case to an attempt made to reconcile gross contribution for February, with a calculation of output multiplied by contribution per unit, and that there was a considerable difference. We have found that the method of stock valuation can contribute significantly to this, but that cost variances from product marginal costs could be factors also.

A factor which is not mentioned in the case, which we know received some attention in Ling at the time, is the question of product group profitability in relation to the input of resources, and capital in particular. The analysed trading statement, subject to its limitations, certainly gave a good breakdown to net contribution, but there is then the question, taking the February figures, as to whether the net contributions of each product group are adequate. For example, pressure diecastings are showing 2.6 times the net contribution of gravity diecastings; but something which we know that the reader will not, is that the capital employed in the pressure diecasting shop is 10 times that employed in the gravity diecasting process. How far is it possible to break down the capital employed in a business to product groups? Once again we find that this will differ from one business to another.

Incidentally, as a closing shot, could we remind our reader that there is no mention anywhere in this case of measuring the efficiency of departments — that is a separate issue. This case is looking at outputs in the form of product groups.

Conclusions

One conclusion must be that management accounting is not only something of a science but also an art. One wants to obtain some information about product group profitability and there are many different approaches, each one with its own problems of procedures and techniques. What must be clear is that there is no such thing as 'right' information, but the aim must be for the approximate information to be relevant. This is clearly brought out in the point that whereas direct fixed costs are relevant to the profitability of the pressure diecasting product group, they are not relevant to the profitability of individual pressure diecastings.

We believe that a profit and loss account is of little use if the reasons for profit variations cannot be adequately explained and point to the action required. The marginal cost layout together with product marginal costs and contribution analyses can be a considerable aid to this. With the help of a computer, computer bureau or mini-computer, it is now possible to use the product marginal cost data extensively in the search for improved company performance.

14

Management accounting and investment decisions

Case study no. 42 – takeover negotiations

K. S. Hunter & Sons Ltd

Until the takeover by Hardy Developments, Paul Hunter was managing director of K. S. Hunter and Sons Ltd, a manufacturing business with 100 workpeople on a trading estate at Redditch, Worcestershire. K. S. Hunter was Paul's grandfather and founded the business, in 1912, at Small Heath, Birmingham. The move to Redditch, in 1957, was prompted by space problems plus an opportunity to sell old-fashioned premises; labour problems, including high wage rates, proved added impetus for a change of location.

The company was in a traditional trade, based on sheet metalwork, with emphasis on quality finishing. Some production was hand-made but the majority was long-run repetitive work. The original products had been tin boxes of all sorts, including some office equipment and waste paper bins.

These were still the main products at the time of the move to Redditch but, within a year, there was a serious drop in demand for the traditional work. It needed 18 months to find sufficient suitable new work, which came from two main sources. One source was an office equipment distributor who was interested in placing contracts for a range of three new-design files which needed to be precision-made. This distributor seemed happy to have found a supplier able to work to the required limits of quality and reliability.

Planning for growth

Preliminary contacts were made also, late in 1959, with potential customers in the electronics industry and a major decision was taken to enter this field which was assessed to have significant growth possibilities. It was recognised that this market would be highly competitive and a works manager was appointed who could make a major contribution in this development. The first piece of plant and equipment for this activity was bought in 1961 for £6,000.

The demand was for custom-made metalwork which had to be manufactured alongside the traditional tin box business. The factory layout had to be changed on many occasions to meet customer demand.

Then, at an electronics industry exhibition in 1966, the need for a range of standard products became apparent. Designs, prototypes and plans were prepared — a programme which soon called for greatly increased investment in equipment, staff expertise and marketing. The development of marketing skills proved difficult for a company which had not previously required them in any great depth.

Hunter saw the need for the company to be recognised as a manufacturer of quality products with speedy delivery. He hoped for a significant share of the market within five years. Two years later, new additions to the standard product range were well received at another exhibition.

Financial results for five years

Figures 14.1 and 14.2 show the financial results over this period. Results were good in 1967. Turnover rose by more than £25,000 on the previous year and profit increased 20 per cent. Although the 1968 results showed a fall in turnover, the considerable change in the mix of products provided a further profit increase. In this year, the return on net assets stood at 17.1 per cent compared with 15.4 per cent two years previously.

Unfortunately, two difficult years followed in which profitability declined to a return of 11.2 per cent on net assets, in 1970. The main reasons for the decline were judged to be:

1 fierce competition for all products, with keener prices and margins;

2 large cost increases, particularly for labour, and the need to strengthen considerably the administrative side, including the appointment, for the first time, of a company secretary/management accountant; the revised structure was capable of supporting the continued growth of the company but, meanwhile, the increased costs adversely affected profits;

3 a fall in factory efficiency apparently due to problems of increased throughput and variety.

Decision to sell out

To add to the managing director's worries, he became ill in December 1970, which led to an operation and long convalescence and rest. Paul Hunter and his wife agreed that whatever activities he might wish to follow later the immediate step should be to sell the business.

Michael Dodd, a family friend who was an accountant working for a large industrial organisation in Birmingham, was called in. He had been concerned recently in a series of mergers and acquisitions carried out by his employers.

One of the first points made by Dodd was that businesses were rarely sold on a 'balance sheet basis'. With regard to the financial history of the company, he pointed out that the recent return on investment of 11.2 per cent was barely adequate. He asked also if Hunter knew the market value of individual assets in the balance sheet. Hunter replied that a comment made to him recently suggested that the land and buildings might be worth £90,000.

Dodd recalled a discussion between himself and Sir Frederick Adam, a director of Bonnelle Industrial Investments which operated in the field of industrial marriage-broking and was always on the lookout for the smaller type of business which might sensibly be merged with another, larger, one.

Dodd and Hunter recognised that this approach might not bring the best results for Hunter but it was worth exploring. Dodd telephoned Adam giving the nature and size of the business, capital employed, annual turnover and profits. Adam replied that at least one company on the file might be interested.

Year ended December 31		1966	1967	1968	1969	1970
		£	£	£	£	£
Fixed assets						
Freehold property and buildings	(net)	60,046	61,175	65,366	65,629	66,239
Plant and machinery	(net)	13,566	18,779	20,075	21,213	20,705
Factory fixtures and fittings	(net)	1,079	1,482	1,334	1,260	1,346
Office equipment	(net)	1,843	2,302	2,231	2,857	2,827
Motor vehicles	(net)	2,167	1,789	1,342	1,688	2,786
		78,701	85,527	90,348	92,647	93,903
Current assets						
Stocks and work in progress		21,529	23,331	28,911	29,746	33,821
Loose tools		4,000	4,250	4,500	5,000	5,500
Debtors		26,634	38,059	39,787	47,075	45,980
Cash		156	113	203	106	71
		52,319	65,753	73,401	81,927	85,372

Less current liabilities					
Creditors	19,004	14,951	17,028	23,617	26,618
Taxation due	8,500	9,000	10,000	8,500	7,800
Bank overdraft	6,251	20,925	16,121	15,258	10,735
Net current assets	33,755	44,876	43,149	47,375	45,153
	18,564	20,877	30,252	34,552	40,219
Net assets employed	97,265	106,404	120,600	127,199	134,122
Financed by:					
Share capital	40,000	40,000	40,000	40,000	40,000
Revenue reserves	47,265	56,404	66,600	73,199	80,122
	87,265	96,404	106,600	113,199	120,122
Unsecured loans					
P. Hunter	10,000	10,000	14,000	14,000	14,000
Total sources	97,265	106,404	120,600	127,199	134,122
Profit before tax	15,032	18,197	20,703	16,552	15,020
Return on net assets	15.4%	17.1%	17.1%	13.0%	11.2%

Fig. 14.1   Financial results for past five years: balance sheets

Year ended December 31	1966 £	1967 £	1968 £	1969 £	1970 £
Sales	166,914	192,197	182,432	237,049	253,964
Costs					
Materials and components	53,343	64,798	60,381	81,175	83,483
Works wages	48,578	55,357	42,275	70,531	79,304
Works salaries	10,925	12,078	12,115	14,397	16,816
Fuel and power	3,109	3,787	3,400	3,865	4,027
Rates	4,301	4,537	4,812	5,000	5,062
Office salaries	12,022	12,457	13,901	17,582	19,307
Advertising, printing, stationery	9,278	8,543	11,099	14,078	16,242
Pensions fund	907	907	1,037	1,038	1,106
Audit fees	485	521	530	620	600
Directors' remuneration	6,317	6,500	7,530	7,530	8,848
Bank interest and charges	1,010	2,378	2,210	2,138	1,509
Bad debts	–	–	–	63	102
Depreciation	1,607	2,137	2,439	2,480	2,538
	£ 151,882	174,000	161,729	220,497	238,944
Profit before tax	15,032	18,197	20,703	16,552	15,020

Fig. **14.2** Financial results for past five years: trading statements

Meeting with the broker

Soon after, Paul Hunter and his adviser attended a meeting in London, where they met Arnold Churchman, chairman of a well known group of companies.

Churchman said that his first, cursory look at the Hunter organisation showed a satisfactory state of affairs regarding the reputation of the company and its products. His own group, however, was run on a strictly 'return on investment' basis and his approach was not to buy assets, or any hypothetical potential, but earnings.

Hunter told him that the average profit before tax made by the company over the past five years was £17,000. Churchman replied that the required return on investment within his group was 20 per cent, so that his first, and possibly final, thoughts for a purchase price for the business would be around £85,000.

Dodd was not entirely surprised by this approach but it was so unsatisfactory to Hunter that he pointed immediately to the figure of assets in the balance sheet adding a comment about the likely increase in value of land and buildings.

Churchman repeated that his group was interested in earnings, not asset values, and he suggested that Dodd and Hunter might care to withdraw for a time before returning to discuss in the detail which would be necessary prior to a settlement.

Back in his office, Hunter was indignant and surprised by the comments made at the meeting. The price offered fell short of his requirement by at least 50 per cent but, more important, he was annoyed at the manner of its presentation. Dodd had been right when he had said that the balance sheet did not show what the business was worth, any more, it seemed, than did any objective valuation on an assets basis. Hunter was particularly disturbed that repute and goodwill apparently counted for nothing.

Widening the search

Dodd pointed out that to many businessmen, Churchman included, if repute and goodwill did not reflect above average profits, they had no worth. It was agreed that further contact with Churchman or Bonnelle seemed undesirable at that time.

Dodd thought that they should seek a situation in which the purchaser considered that rationalisation would be possible in adding the Hunter business to the existing enterprise. It was decided to concentrate on companies in similar lines of business which might add to their competitive position by taking over the strengths of the Hunter company.

The news of an impending sale was carefully leaked to selected points within the electronics industry by financial contacts of Dodd. This resulted in an approach from Derek Moore, the managing director of Hardy Developments, to discuss the possibility of a merger. A meeting was arranged.

Valuations by the owner

Hunter and Dodd were agreed that considerable preparation would be necessary to ensure that this particular interview went more favourably than the earlier one. Dodd suggested that they should have some positive figures in mind, backed by detailed valuations of the market value of the business as a complete entity and the value if the assets were realised piecemeal.

The most recent balance sheet showed a net worth of the business to Hunter of £134,122. He was aware that freehold property and buildings were now worth considerably more than the £66,000 shown in the balance sheet and he took immediate steps to have this particular asset revalued. He was somewhat surprised when the valuer suggested that an appropriate current figure was £110,000, an increase of £44,000, which gave a revised net worth of the business of £178,000.

This figure was already far removed from the offer of £85,000 by Churchman. On the other hand, Hunter and Dodd felt that this was not the only asset which might be undervalued. Clearly, there was the possibility that other fixed assets might be worth more than their book values; stocks and work in progress had inevitably been valued conservatively for stewardship accounting purposes, loose tools were shown in the balance sheet at a very arbitrary figure and there was the debatable problem of goodwill.

It was agreed that Hunter should pursue in some detail the general problem of asset revaluations and produce a statement of his findings. Dodd would then add to this some ideas on the valuation of goodwill.

The statement which they prepared appears as Figure 14.3. Two values are shown. The first is based on assessments of the market values of assets held by the company as a going concern; the second is based on assessment of the break-up values of individual assets if realised on a piece-meal basis and represents the lowest price which Hunter would accept.

Negotiations for takeover

At the meeting, Moore explained that his company had recently reviewed its capital budgeting system and all projects were now evaluated prior to board approval. The proposed purchase of K. S. Hunter and Sons represented a complex investment which must be evaluated.

The financial history of the company over the past five years was of some interest but Moore was mainly concerned with estimating the incremental net cash flow attributable to the merger. The capitalised value of this incremental net cash flow and the worth of any surplus assets represented the value of the business to Moore.

To estimate the incremental net cash flow, Moore proposed that Hunter should allow a team to investigate in depth Hunter's internal efficiency and also external competitive strength. The assessment of internal efficiency would take into account the turnover and age of assets, while the assessment of competitive strength would concentrate on estimates of growth and stability.

These assessments, with a capability profile of Hardy Developments, would enable some measure of the joint effects of the merger to be evaluated. Moore anticipated favourable reports on sales synergy arising from the use of common distribution channels, common warehousing and sales administration. It was also likely that favourable joint effects would result from increased use of personnel and facilities, common tooling and machinery.

Hunter and Dodd explained the approach taken in drafting Figure 14.3. Moore examined the statement with interest but pointed out that an important factor in his calculation of the value of the business would be his estimate of surplus assets. In this connection, the item of land and buildings valued at £110,000 was critical. It was possible that his team's report

		Market value as a going concern	Piecemeal break-up value
Property, freehold		£110,000	110,000
Other fixed assets at written down value as per 1970 balance sheet		27,664	30,000
Addition to above for re-valuation		7,500	
Current assets 1970			
Stocks	£33,821		35,082
plus additional overheads	3,000		
Loose tools	5,500		5,000
plus re-valuation	2,750		
Debtors	45,980		45,000
plus doubtful debts written back	1,786		
Cash	71	92,908	71
		£238,072	225,153
Less current liabilities			
Creditors	£26,618		
Tax due	7,800		
Bank overdraft	10,735	45,153	45,153
		£192,919	180,000
Goodwill at two years' purchase of the average profits for the last five years, say,		34,000	—
		£226,919	180,000

Fig. 14.3   Valuation of the assets of K. S. Hunter and Sons Ltd, as at December 31, 1970, to establish a price for merger

on internal efficiency would affect his attitude towards this asset — particularly if use of space was low and if activities could be transferred to other premises.

As part of the calculation of the value of the business it would be necessary also to estimate the timing and costs of future replacements of assets since this would affect the net cash flow. In addition, Moore noted that it would be necessary to take advice on all taxation aspects of the takeover.

Hunter agreed that a team should examine and report on internal efficiency and external competitive strength. At the very least, he would receive information which would be useful in negotiating with other purchasers if Hardy's bid proved unacceptable.

Required

1   The reader is invited to consider the programme of investigation required to estimate the incremental net cash flow arising from the merger and the assets which will be surplus to requirements.

Commentary by Derek Moore and John Marsh

There's no doubt that one obtains a lot of experience as a result of pursuing a policy of progressive growth, in the same way that one can learn a lot from the difficulties of decline and entrenchment. In the first instance, there are management problems of actually dealing with increased activity, maybe even new activities, but an even more critical problem is that of deciding where growth shall take place, and in what form. In the second instance, which must have confronted many groups and individual companies recently, the management problems are very different; there is regret associated with a reduced activity or having to chop off certain activities altogether, but the critical issue is once again a decision-type problem, where the decline is to be recognised and entrenchment implemented. In other words, in either case there is an investment decision, or if you like, in the second instance there is a divestment decision.

We've all heard the old story going the rounds that Lord Thomson of Fleet would hop onto a train at Glasgow Central with the financial statements of a company over a ten-year period, study these, and be in a position when the train pulled into Preston station to hop out, make a telephone call and communicate to underlings a decision as to whether the purchase of the company should be made or not. We don't believe the story. Lord Thomson was too wily a bird and too successful a businessman to take such a narrow view of an organisation as this. Of course, the financial statements provide some useful historical information for such a decision, but a decision must concern itself with future happenings, and with relevant data.

The first point which the case makes, very clearly in our opinion, is that there can be very many reasons for making an acquisition, and that the particular reason in a particular case can drastically affect the offer made and the deal in general. Churchman made the point about 'buying earnings', though one can't be certain that he was telling the whole truth; after all he was about to commence negotiations, as he thought. Then there is the point that he was not at this early stage taking into account changes, rationalisation or whatever other steps he might take to improve the earnings from the present base; or if he was giving thought to these possibilities, they were not going to be mentioned at the beginning of negotiations. We wouldn't dare suggest that he might have indulged in some asset-stripping, but it has been done; after all, the freehold property and buildings could have been worth more than his offer.

The second point concerned a balance-sheet valuation of a business, or an amended balance-sheet valuation. Although Dodd made the point that businesses are rarely bought and sold on this basis, we know that there are still a few naïve businessmen about who are terribly hooked on the financial statements as decision-making documents as well as periodic reporting statements. Then, looking at it from Hunter's viewpoint, aided by family friend Dodd, it must have seemed quite logical to 'reconstruct the balance sheet' in the two ways which they did. One could say that it gave them some ideas on a top price and a bottom price for a deal. And the nice thing about that approach is that it is essentially an 'accounting approach' in that one has started off with a good solid and respected balance sheet and updated it by information relevant to each particular possibility. No doubt in the approach there are a number of estimates and opinions, but the approach seems logical enough. We entirely endorse Dodd's point about goodwill. There has been, quite rightly in our opinion, a new view taken of goodwill in recent years, and that is that the company name, repute, client and order book is only as good as the profits likely to accrue in the future, not upon the reported historical profits.

Having made that point, we're right into the arena of what Derek wanted done as soon as he got involved in the discussions. We both see an acquisition as an investment which must be evaluated in terms of future cash flows, whether these be the incremental profit cash flows or cash flows from assets released as being surplus to requirements. So these need to be estimated, and to do that, a very detailed investigation is called for; now let's make the point that however detailed the investigation, there's no way that the estimates are going to be right, but we are not going to be guilty of buying a 'pig in a poke', as for instance the Leyland Motor Corporation did when they purchased Standard Triumph in 1961. You've just got to be more systematic than that.

What does the programme of investigation need to look like? Well, it's very much a management accounting approach which is needed. In this respect we mean management accounting of a very broad type, including all aspects of *internal resources*; their utilisation and operating efficiencies, the strengths and weaknesses in resource areas; the worthwhileness of *plans* already laid and the extent to which they can be seen as coming to fruition or having failed, with a particular and special look at *personnel*, including management personnel, how they are welded together organisationally and the nature of industrial relationships within the organisation. Bearing in mind what was reckoned to be one of the main reasons for the profit decline in 1970, namely a fall in factory efficiency, the reasons for this need to be fully understood, as well as the extent to which any corrective action would seem to have any chance of meeting with success. The emphasis in the internal enquiry should always be, we feel, on highlighting the present and likely immediate future strengths and weaknesses.

And what about the necessary external enquiry? Well, there may not be too much to be done in the case of the Hunter company in regard to what might be called the broad external environment of the business, but there are instances where we've had to look very closely at government actions, social and cultural changes in viewing the present and likely future position and capability of a business. More important in this case was the rather closer to home product/market enquiry, particularly bearing in mind the recent product developments within the organisation, such as the move to standard products. We had a clear impression that Hunter wanted to be seen at the quality end of the market and put great emphasis on speedy delivery; couple this with fierce competition for all products and keener prices, and there's an argument for a pretty comprehensive investigation, looking at the likely market, possible share, competition and its features, and particularly on the likelihood of growth or otherwise.

The third aspect of the enquiry needs to be on the subject of synergy of resources generally coupled with asset policies in regard to joint use and replacement. Clearly, one hopes to get benefits out of a merger, except in a conglomerate situation, stemming from commonality in regard to administration, centralisation in regard to certain aspects of financial management, and there are many other possibilities. Evaluation of these is difficult but should be attempted. Incidentally, it is worth making the point at this stage that there should always be the hope of setting up what are believed to be possibilities and potentials as targets and aims should the acquisition go through.

There is a fourth aspect directly concerned with accounting aspects, and this is of two parts; first, much of the investigative work is inevitably related to basic management accounting. For example, the analysis of present performance and the determination of likely future performance depends upon sound and reliable management accounting information on product and customer performance. Second, and somewhat different, but very important, the taxation aspects of a likely takeover need to be thoroughly understood.

Conclusion

God forbid that we should ever buy a 'pig in a poke'; it would not be good for investors, employees, for us, for our other stakeholders, and there really is a lot of information that one wants before one can evaluate the likely investment in a fairly traditional capital investment manner, that is to be able to compare the investment with the cash flows likely to stem from it subsequently. One can be very tempted by the ease with which one can obtain data which is really not so very relevant to the exercise, namely historical accounts.

Case study no. 43 – capital investment in new venture

Kent Aluminium Castings Limited

Prior to the takeover by the Hardy group of companies in 1974, Kent Aluminium Castings, with its main factory at Dartford, was an old established private company. Though in its early days the company was engaged in the founding of grey iron castings, for 25 years its product has been aluminium castings.

Production of castings at Kent is by three methods: high-pressure diecasting, gravity diecasting and sand casting. High-pressure diecasting involves the forcing of molten aluminium under pressure into metal dies which give 6 or 8 impressions of the product: this lends itself to high-volume repetitive production. High-pressure diecasting machines are expensive and running costs, tooling, tool repairs, and maintenance are high. Gravity diecasting involves less capital equipment and is suitable for lower-volume production with a mixture of cored and uncored work. Sand casting is a very skilled occupation and the operation is suitable for one-off, small batch production of prototypes and production development work.

All castings have to pass through the fettling shop where they are trimmed on presses, ground, bobbed and dressed. There is a finishing shop in which a variety of operations and processes are carried out, machining, shotblast and anodising being amongst these. Finally, there is a warehouse and des-patch function.

There is considerable interdependence of the three pro-duct groups, and the willingness of Kent to engage in the development work, which is a feature of the output of the sand foundry, has often produced gravity and pressure die-casting work. Pressure diecasting contributes much the greater sum to fixed overheads and profit, while sandcasting does only a little better than break even. Judged on a basis of the profit return on capital employed, pressure diecasting is still the most profitable process, though it does depend for its profitability on double-shift working; it is recognised throughout the industry that a single-shift operation on this process cannot produce a reasonable level of profit.

1974 was a good trading year for Kent which produced a net profit before tax and dividends of £217,000, which was a great improvement over the previous five years (see Figures 14.4 and 14.5). The previous two years, in particular, were dismal with annual profit figures of a little over £70,000. The success of this last year is due to a variety of reasons. A new managing director of some 18 months has imparted a new dynamism and thrust to the business, additional customers and work have been attracted, there have been considerable improvements made to working conditions and operating efficiency, some new ancillary plant has added to the overall capacity of the factory, and these factors apart, trade has been much better after almost two years of mild recession in the foundry trade. Control procedures in Kent have been much improved. At the operational level of planning and control in the company, production scheduling and progres-sing have assumed a new importance, and there is an involvement of managers and supervisory managers in the control of costs; there has recently been much tighter finan-cial planning and control through the use of budgetary con-trol procedures and, in addition, more thought given to longer-term aspects of company planning and growth. Recen-tly there have been thought and discussion about new fields or extensions of the existing field of activity in which Kent might sensibly become engaged. Most of the discussions have centred around the ideas of a proprietary product and enter-ing the field of leisure. The latter has brought Kent into con-

	1974		1973		1972		1971		1970	
	£		£		£		£		£	
Fixed assets										
Land and buildings		237,196		227,789		228,755		232,813		231,688
Plant		320,353		287,750		231,922		214,707		202,996
Investments (at cost)						56,697		46,998		34,676
		557,549		515,539		517,374		494,518		469,360
	£		£		£		£		£	
Current assets										
Stocks and WIP	71,454		86,613		54,990		52,817		48,922	
Debtors & payments in advc.	359,117		273,296		270,438		267,132		241,558	
Bank balance & cash	10,086		515		387		894		727	
Total assets	440,657	998,206	360,424	875,963	325,815	843,189	320,843	815,361	291,207	760,567
Less current liabilities										
Trade and other creditors	135,477		119,157		124,916		130,708		112,967	
Taxation	105,433		26,000		27,500		36,200		37,800	
Dividends proposed – gross	25,289		25,289		20,232		20,232		20,232	
Bank overdraft	—		10,114		20,918		5,693		19,596	
Net assets	266,199	732,007	180,560	675,403	193,566	649,623	192,833	622,528	190,595	569,972
Financed by										
Share capital		252,892		252,892		252,892		252,892		252,892
Share premium a/c		43,010		43,010		43,010		43,010		43,010
Reserves		436,105		349,501		323,721		296,626		244,070
Shareholders funds		732,007		645,403		619,623		592,528		539,972
Debentures		—		30,000		30,000		30,000		30,000
		732,007		675,403		649,623		622,528		569,972

Fig. 14.4 Kent Aluminium Castings Ltd – Balance sheets as at March 31

	1974		1973		1972		1971		1970	
	£	£	£	£	£	£	£	£	£	£
Turnover		1,889,406		1,314,694		1,418,793		1,364,898		1,265,303
Trading profit, before charging		280,379		141,536		130,280		166,113		173,408
Depreciation of fixed assets	26,360		32,800		27,745		28,327		25,916	
Auditors' remuneration	765		765		910		875		765	
Directors' emoluments	40,870		36,420		30,320		30,164		30,627	
Compensation for loss of office	2,500		—		—		—		—	
Pensions to widows of former directors	950	71,445	1,000	70,985	1,000	59,975	1,000	60,366	1,000	58,308
		208,934		70,551		70,305		105,747		115,100
Add Income from:										
Investments (gross)	6,939		4,717		3,206		2,317		1,902	
Rents (net)	1,453	8,392	1,801	6,518	1,316	4,522	924	3,241	817	2,719
Profit before taxation		217,326		77,069		74,827		108,988		117,819
Deduct taxation		105,433		26,000		27,500		36,200		37,800
Profit after taxation		111,893		51,069		47,327		72,788		80,019
Deduct transfer to reserves		86,604		25,780		27,095		52,556		59,787
Dividends proposed		25,289		25,289		20,232		20,232		20,232

Fig. 14.5 Kent Aluminium Castings Ltd — Profit and loss accounts for the year March 31

tact with British Boats through an external director of the company who has a keen interest in power-boat racing.

British Boats is a very large company which manufactures and distributes a wide variety of boats, cruisers, day boats, runabouts, dinghies and inflatables through many hundreds of outlets and stockists. They have in the past not concerned themselves with many of the fringe products of the boating trade. Any accessories made and sold by them have been optional extras for their own boats, and they have relied entirely upon the dealers for purchase and supply of inboard and outboard motors, Z-drives and all servicing arrangements, including modifications to boats and supply of canopies, trim gear, special towing and water-ski equipment. More recently, they have been considering these important fringe aspects of their trade.

They have been particularly conscious of the limitations of the outboard motor market; that anyone in the UK requiring such a power unit attached to a boat has to choose between Mercury, Chrysler and OMC (Evinrude and Johnson), all American suppliers, and can only obtain very small outboard power units from one British manufacturer, Gull, the supplier of the Seagull outboards up to 4½ horsepower. They have believed that, with the considerable expansion of leisure and leisure industries in general, and boating in particular, with the growth of power-boat racing and the increasing number of marinas springing up throughout the country, there might be some considerable scope for business and profit from being able to offer a small range of medium-sized outboards to fit to a part of their range of boats and, in particular, to the smaller runabouts and the inflatables. They have discussed in some detail around the trade the idea of 'boat packages' to include boat, engine and trailer at a competitive price and have had talks with both Kent and Gannet on this subject.

Some two years ago, British Boats set up an outboard motor development team. This was an expensive operation, but British Boats has been extremely profitable during the years of steady increase in boating, having been the first company in the trade to cash in thoroughly on new fibreglass moulding techniques. The directors believe that this investment in development work could pay off. The team has thoroughly researched the possibilities of the manufacture and sale of 20, 30 and 45 horsepower outboards and has come to the conclusion that there is enormous business and profit potential therein, provided that it can be part of 'boat package' trading. They are clear that any expansion in the next three to five years is likely to be in safe and stable family run-abouts and inflatables taking the medium-size outboards. They take the view that the higher horsepower models are outside the purse of the normal family man and are, in any case, more suited to more hectic pursuits than the average family will wish to contemplate. With the permission and enthusiasm of top management there have been discussions with Kent on the possibility of a joint venture in outboard production, designs have been finalised, and the production and assembly has taken place of prototype. Kent have been actively involved in the development work and have produced all the prototype castings required — this has involved them in the use of many expensive resources at an estimated total cost of around £30,000 over a 15 month period almost immediately after the takeover by Hardy. It has come to the stage where the managing director and sales director of Kent have joined in a combined Kent–British Boats project team which has finalised its proposals for offering the new packages, including outboards in the Spring of 1975. Kent's managing director and sales director have summarised the proposal as far as it affects Kent with the help of the works director, and this summary appears as Appendix A. Kent's chief accountant has evaluated the proposal and appraised it in detail, his report appearing in Appendix B.

At a recent Kent board meeting, the proposal and the accountant's report have been laid on the table, together with supporting Tables 1–4.

Appendix A   Summary proposal on the Kent–British Boats joint venture

It is not necessary to recount the complete history of this project, because the board has been fully informed during its progress. It should suffice to say that the combined companies' project team has finalised its ideas on the offering of the new packages to the market in the early spring of 1975, and a decision is now urgently required as to whether the project shall go ahead. Essentially, this decision is ours, since British Boats seem to be entirely committed. It is our recommendation that we should go ahead, subject to the accountant's report on all financial aspects. This recommendation is not based upon the sort of financial evaluation which the accountant will obviously undertake; indeed, the only calculation which we have made on the profitability aspects of the project appears in (e) below. It is based on our belief in the expansion of this particular leisure market, the need for us to diversify and the requirement that there is for us to use more profitably the money which we have currently in external investments.

Below are certain summary aspects of the project which you will wish to examine and which will need to be taken into account in a full financial evaluation; they can, of course, be amplified as required:

(a) Kent is to be the sole supplier of the outboard motor castings to British Boats. Production quantities have been forecast for a 10-year project period in line with the anticipated life of the required plant and equipment. Some castings will be required by British Boats during the autumn of 1974, these to be made within our existing factory. Forecast prices for sales of castings to British Boats have been agreed within the project team. The net result of this is forecast casting sales of £224,000 in 1975 rising to a maximum of £490,000 by 1982, a good growth rate, and no account having been taken of changing price levels.

(b) We will now need to acquire the factory premises at Hilverham which we have been eyeing for some time.

350

It appears that this 20,000 square feet factory can be purchased for £210,000, comprising the separate purchases of land £80,000 and buildings £130,000. These premises are somewhat larger than are required for this project, but will allow for further expansion or diversification.

(c) Purchases will need to be made of additional plant and equipment as follows:

	1974	1975
Additional melting pots and equipment	£20,000	—
Pressure diecasting plant	£78,000	£39,000
Gravity diecasting plant	£38,000	£6,000
Trimming presses	£22,000	—
Other fettling equipment	£13,000	£8,000
Ancillary service plant	£24,000	£8,000
	£195,000	£61,000

(d) Precise and detailed specifications are now available of all the castings required and have been put through our standard costing procedures. It is pleasing to report that the planned mix shows a contribution percentage of sales, or profit/volume ratio of around 40 per cent against a present average of around 35 per cent on diecastings. This is a very strong point in favour of the project.

(e) A very rough check on profitability has been based on the fifth year of the project, where we see possible sales of around £350,000 yielding a contribution of £140,000, meaning a net profit of around £70,000. If we relate this to an input of capital of £210,000 for land and buildings, £256,000 for plant and equipment and say a further £80,000 for working capital, a total of £546,000, the project will show a return on capital of 12½ per cent.

Appendix B   Accountant's report on the proposed
Kent–British Boats joint venture — evaluation of the project

There are accompanying this report three appendices which evaluate the project in terms of annual cash flows and overall profitability. Taking the 'most likely' figures of castings sales, all estimated costs, capital requirements, taxation aspects of the project and two possible figures for the terminal value of land and buildings, Table 1 indicates the 'most likely' internal rates of return as 9.24 per cent, assuming the terminal value to be the same as the purchase price, and 12.91 per cent, assuming the terminal value to be double the purchase price. Table 2 indicates the 'optimistic' assessment of castings sales and gives internal rates of return of 16.28 per cent and 18.97 per cent respectively, while Table 3 takes the 'pessimistic' view of sales and comes up with percentages of 4.60 per cent and 9.08 per cent. These are net after tax returns.

A further table, Table 4, shows how the capital requirements of the projects have been arrived at. The 14 per cent working capital requirement has been calculated with a fairly accurate knowledge of the stock and work in progress requirements of the project, having agreed with British Boats the terms of credit, and knowing from our experience in the trade the extent to which we can depend upon creditors to provide our working capital. In regard to other assumptions in the cash flows:

1 Capital allowances on plant and equipment have been taken in the first year, while on buildings the 40 per cent initial allowance has been taken with an annual writing down allowance of 4 per cent, the balance having been allowed in the final year. Corporation tax has been assumed at a 50 per cent rate, with a payment in year 10 for both years 9 and 10, otherwise one-year time lag throughout.

2 In estimating the costs of castings produced and sold, all directly attributable variable and fixed costs have been taken into account including some special 'learning' costs in the first year. The directly attributable variable costs include metal, melting casting, fettling and distribution, and amount to approximately 60 per cent of the

352

Table 1
Project cash flows — most likely

	1974	1975	1976	1977	1978	1979	1980	1981	1982	1983	Total
Sales	52.500	240.000	285.000	352.500	390.000	427.500	472.500	502.500	525.000	447.750	3,695.250
Contribution	21.000	96.000	114.000	141.000	156.000	171.000	189.000	201.000	210.000	179.100	1,478.100
Deduct directly identifiable fixed costs	68.000	58.000	63.000	68.000	73.000	77.000	81.000	86.000	90.000	95.000	759.000
Net contribution (1)	−47.000	38.000	51.000	73.000	83.000	94.000	108.000	115.000	120.000	84.100	719.100
Deduct tax allowances	−252.200	66.200	5.200	5.200	5.200	5.200	5.200	5.200	5.200	31.200	386.000
Taxable income	−299.200	−28.200	45.800	67.800	77.800	88.800	102.800	109.800	114.800	52.900	333.100
Tax payable (2)	0	+149.600	+14.100	−22.900	−33.900	−38.900	−44.400	−51.400	−54.900	−57.400 −26.450	
Capital expenditure (3)	−412.350	−87.250	−6.300	−9.450	−5.250	−5.250	−6.300	−4.200	−3.150	−83.850 +283.500 (1) +493.500 (2)	−166.550 −256.000 −46.000
After-tax cash flow 1−2−3	−459.350	+100.350	+58.800	+40.650	+43.850	+49.850	+57.300	+59.400	+61.950	+283.750 (1) +493.750 (2)	296.550 506.550 (2)
Internal rate of return										9.24% (1) 12.91% (2)	

Table 2
Project cash flows — optimistic

	1974	1975	1976	1977	1978	1979	1980	1981	1982	1983	Total
Sales	70.000	320.000	380.000	470.000	520.000	570.000	630.000	670.000	700.000	597.000	4927.000
Contribution	28.000	128.000	152.000	188.000	208.000	228.000	252.000	268.000	280.000	238.800	1970.800
Deduct directly identifiable fixed costs	68.000	58.000	63.000	68.000	73.000	77.000	81.000	86.000	90.000	95.000	759.000
Net contribution (1)	−40.000	70.000	89.000	120.000	135.000	151.000	171.000	182.000	190.000	143.800	1211.800
Deduct tax allowances	+252.200	66.200	5.200	5.200	5.200	5.200	5.200	5.200	5.200	31.200	386.000
Taxable income	−292.200	3.800	83.800	114.800	129.800	145.800	165.800	176.800	184.800	112.600	825.800
Tax payable (2)	0	+146.100	−1900	−41.900	−57.400	−64.900	−72.900	−82.900	−88.400	92.400 56.300	412.900
Capital expenditure (3)	−414.800	−96.000	−8400	−12.600	−7.000	−7.000	−8.400	−5.600	−4.200	148.700 308.000 (1) 518.000 (2)	−256.000 (1) −46.000 (2)
After-tax cash flow 1-2-3	−454.800	+120.000	+78.700	+65.500	+70.600	+79.100	+89.700	+93.500	+97.400	+303.100 (1) +513.100 (2)	542.900 752.900
Internal rate of return										16.28% (1) 18.97% (2)	

Table 3
Project cash flows — pessimistic

	1974	1975	1976	1977	1978	1979	1980	1981	1982	1983	Total
Sales	41.650	190.000	226.100	279.650	309.400	339.150	374.850	398.650	416.500	355.215	2.931.565
Contribution	16.660	76.160	90.440	111.860	123.760	135.660	149.940	159.460	166.600	142.086	1.172.626
Deduct directly identifiable fixed costs	68.000	58.000	63.000	68.000	73.000	77.000	81.000	86.000	90.000	95.000	759.000
Net contribution (1)	−51.340	18.160	27.440	43.860	50.760	58.660	68.940	73.460	76.600	47.086	413.626
Deduct tax allowances	252.200	66.200	5.200	5.200	5.200	5.200	5.200	5.200	5.200	31.200	386.000
Taxable income	−303.540	−48.040	22.240	38.660	45.560	53.460	69.740	68.260	71.400	15.886	27.626
Tax payable (2)	0	+151.770	+24.020	−11.120	−19.330	−22.780	−26.730	−31.870	−34.130	−35.700 −7.943	−13.813
Capital expenditure (3)	−410.831	−81.825	−4.998	−71.497	−4.165	−4.165	−4.998	−3.332	−2.499	−43.643 +268.310 (1) +478.310 (2)	−256.000 −46.000
After-tax cash flow 1-2-3	−462.171	88.105	+46.462	+25.243	+27.265	+31.715	+37.212	+38.258	+39.971	+271.753 +481.753	143.813 353.813
Internal rate of return										4.60% (1) 9.08% (2)	

Table 4

Project estimates of capital requirements and tax allowances

	1974	1975	1976	1977	1978	1979	1980	1981	1982	1983	Total
1 Most likely											
Working capital	−7.350	−33.600	−39.900	−49.350	−54.600	−59.850	−66.150	−70.350	−73.500		
14% of sales		7.350	33.600	39.900	49.350	54.600	59.850	66.150	70.350	73.500	
Fixed capital	−7.350	−26.250	−6.300	−9.450	−5.250	−5.250	−6.300	−4.200	−3.150	+73.500	
	−405.000	−61.000								+210.000 (1)	
										+420.000 (2)	
	−412.350	−87.250	−6.300	−9.450	−5.250	−5.250	−6.300	−4.200	−3.150	+283.500 (1)	
										+493.500 (2)	
2 Optimistic											
Working capital	−9.800	−44.800	−53.200	−65.800	−72.800	−79.800	−88.200	−93.800	−98.000		
14% of sales		9.800	44.800	53.200	65.800	72.800	79.800	88.200	93.800	98.000	
Fixed capital	−9.800	−35.000	−8.400	−12.600	−7.000	−7.000	−8.400	−5.600	−4.200	+98.000	
	−405.000	−61.000								+210.000 (1)	
										+420.000 (2)	
	−414.800	−96.000	−8.400	−12.600	−7.000	−7.000	−8.400	−5.600	−4.200	+308.000 (1)	
										+518.000 (2)	
3 Pessimistic											
Working capital	−5.831	−26.656	−31.654	−39.151	−43.316	−47.481	−52.479	−55.811	−58.310		
14% of sales		5.831	26.656	31.654	39.151	43.316	47.481	52.479	55.811	58.310	
Fixed capital	−5.853	−20.825	−4.998	−7.497	−4.165	−4.165	−4.998	−3.332	−2.499	+58.310	
	−405.000	−61.000								+210.000 (1)	
										+420.000 (2)	
	−410.831	−81.825	−4.998	−7.497	−4.165	−4.165	−4.998	−3.332	−2.499	+268.310 (1)	
										+478.310 (2)	
4 Tax allowances											
Plant & equipment 100%	195.000	61.000									256.000
Buildings (40%)	52.000										
+ 4%	5.200	5.200	5.200	5.200	5.200	5.200	5.200	5.200	5.200	31.200	130.000
	252.200	66.200	5.200	5.200	5.200	5.200	5.200	5.200	5.200	31.200	386.000

planned sales mix, leaving a 40 per cent contribution, from which has been deducted those fixed costs which are incremental and directly identifiable with the project.

3 Though the whole area of the Hilverham factory will not be taken up by the new project, it has been thought fit to charge all the capital expenditure and building occupation costs to it. There has been the difficulty of setting a terminal value, which has been dealt with by two separate assumptions:

   (a) that this will be the same as the purchase price;
   (b) that it will be double the purchase price.

Financing the venture

Obviously, the decision on the project will be a joint one between ourselves and the group, but the way I look at it, there should be no great difficulty in obtaining the necessary funds, and the cost of the capital should not be prohibitive.

It could be that the group will want to accept the entire responsibility for funding and providing the funds, but I know that ICFC could be persuaded to provide a term loan of some £400,000 and I imagine that the additional requirement could come from a bank overdraft. At the very top limit, this would not mean a cost of more than 14 per cent per annum gross, therefore 7 per cent per annum net of tax.

Changing price levels

No attempt has been made to allow for changing price levels in the evaluation. There is no doubt that, as a result of our discussions with British Boats, we will be able to pass on cost increases as they occur, so that we should be able to preserve the profit margins which are included in the evaluation.

Conclusion

I have talked to the project team and they have assigned the following probabilities to their three estimates:

	Pessimistic	Most likely	Optimistic	Expected value
Probability	2/10	7/10	1/10	
Assumption (1)	4.60%	9.24%	16.28%	9.00%
Assumption (2)	9.08%	12.91%	18.97%	12.73%

Since the expected rates of return under both assumptions are greater than the cost of capital, I conclude that this is an attractive investment opportunity which should be exploited.

Required

You have been called in at short notice to advise Kent Aluminium Castings on their capital expenditure decision.

You are required critically to appraise the contents of Appendices A and B, Tables 1–4 and the financial statements (Figures 14.4 and 14.5) paying particular attention to:

1 *the method of assessing the profitability of the project, including the treatment of uncertainty;*
2 *the question of the cost of capital;*
3 *the treatment of changing price levels.*

Tomorrow morning you will report to the board of directors who are determined to make a decision.

Commentary by Derek Moore and John Marsh

For most businessmen, the major new product project comes along only occasionally. It's always an exciting affair for a whole variety of reasons: the fact that it's new; there is the challenge of a whole host of problems, from financial to organisational, production to industrial relations; the pulse runs a little faster because of the risks, and with a bit of luck and a lot of good management, it comes out right, or nearly right.

We take the view that good management implies, apart from the market research and marketing aspects, apart from the determination to get the production aspects right, real care in evaluating the project, taking snapshots from all possible angles, being as comprehensive as possible in estimating the likely outcome of the project. And that calls for a teamwork approach; information is needed and there are many sources, internal and external to the organisation, which need to be tapped. No trouble is too much, especially when a project decision affects the livelihood of personnel as well as the financial fortunes of the business.

Having said that, we know that every project, and notably a new product project, is packed with uncertainties. There is no certainty even about the fixed asset requirements, in our experience; we have seen plenty of instances where completely wrong estimates were made of this important item; and working capital requirements not only depend on the ability to sell the product and the resulting stock levels, but also upon the credit aspects of both sales and purchases.

And then there is the difficult problem of sales forecasting, never done completely accurately. No; project evaluation is fraught with problems.

In our view, the approach taken by the managing director and sales director at Kent is to be applauded, because although they did not apply the accountant's rigorous approach to project evaluation, they pulled out the essentials in their report. For example, there was a partial attempt to estimate the capital requirements of the project, clear evidence of volumes and prices of sales having been tackled, and reference to the estimates of product costs. Though one could quarrel with the summing up on profitability, they did appreciate that it was only a 'rough check'.

The accountant's approach is very detailed and deserves appraisal. First of all, there is the attempt to tackle the uncertainty aspects with the optimistic, pessimistic and most likely sets of figures; this is surely a considerable improvement and much more realistic than single estimates. The forecasting of demand at a single point is really quite unrealistic, and our experience shows that a management team will respond much more enthusiastically if the 'bracket' approach is applied. And this enthusiasm is important, because the estimates required come from functional heads, and the approach needs to be one which they consider possible, and which will give meaningful results when they have made their contributions.

Then there is the ascertainment of the likely capital requirements. Fixed assets do not normally prove to be difficult to estimate, though silly errors have sometimes been made; one must not forget the installation costs and, in certain instances, the costs of extensive relayouts to accommodate new product plant. Working capital assessments are much more difficult. We feel a certain amount of doubt with the 14 per cent of sales approach adopted here. It is true that working capital really should bear a relationship with the final output of the business, indeed this is a well-known accounting ratio, but there is an argument for a cash budget type of approach, at least for the first two or three years of the life of a new project. If such a project cash budget is prepared, then apart from giving more detailed period figures of project cash flows, the information is then available to feed into the general cash budget for the business.

The cost aspects of project evaluation are extremely important, and sometimes not particularly well tackled. We like the very logical way in which this problem has been addressed in Kent. There are standard costing procedures on a bureau computer master file, and the new products/components have been fed through this system; this means that the strictly product variable costs have been accounted for, but then the whole question of other incremental costs has been tackled. This is an important area, because a slavish adherence to marginal costing ideas really will not suffice; one must recognise incremental costs in both variable and fixed costs areas; one feels that in Kent this has been carefully done. The test applied to contribution on a profit/volume ratio basis is useful, indicating as it does a percentage better than normal, something one would hope for in a situation where the risks would seem to be greater.

The premises aspect of the evaluation is really difficult, in two senses. First, there is the problem that not all the premises will be required for the new project, and then there is the question of terminal value. There can be no golden rule over either of these. In regard to the first problem, one is presumably always hoping to fit other projects into the premises to improve asset utilisation, but one does have to make a verdict upon this as objectively as possible. The project being examined could be killed off at the financial appraisal state under the weight of capital costs and running costs of the whole building, but on the other hand, it must bear the whole charge if no other use is likely to be made of the premises. In regard to the terminal value of the buildings, no accurate prediction is possible, so that the Kent approach of applying two possible values seems eminently sensible; certainly, it would seem very correct to have in mind, at the worst, a terminal value the same as the purchase price after only a 10-year period. We have always felt that a big question mark hangs over the extent to which one should allow the influence of purchase prices and terminal values of premises to influence project evaluations; our view is that in a new project appraisal, the property aspect is really a secondary issue. Thank goodness some organisations still believe in making things and set out to make profit on those products rather than depend for 'profit' upon the appreciating values of buildings.

As far as financing is concerned this is always a separate issue, in that it is a question of what sources of funds are available at a particular time and at what cost. Of course, the group wanted to be involved in this decision; it really is not sensible to have your individual companies dashing off and doing their own thing, but we were pleased that the local accountant had explored the matter. This view of the cost of capital was quite reasonable looked at on an incremental basis, but naturally we also looked at it on a group overall basis, with reference to the weighted average cost of capital, which, in fact, at this time, was somewhat lower than the incremental cost. One thing that we would not have in the group is a rigid cut-off rate for capital projects; this is so stultifying and must have been the reason for some pretty unadventurous (and poor) investment decisions over the years in the UK.

There has been a lot of discussion about allowing for changing price levels in project evaluations; we are not aware that any clear conclusions have emerged. The line taken in the Kent evaluation was that if cost increases could be passed on in price increases, then the figures in the evaluation would still ring true. The alternative to this line is to attempt to estimate likely inflation rates applying to cost inputs and capital requirements, estimate what this would mean to prices in the market, and then apply the adjustments to the evaluation. We would conclude that testing the sensitivity of the rate of return to movements in as many variables as possible should be undertaken, where the computer facilities are available. This seems better than point estimates of inflation rates, which are more than a little difficult to predict. Then the probability approach already being used can be applied.

Conclusion

The last thing one needs is to be lacking in innovation in a business, but because it is a business, there need to be disciplines to ensure continuity and survival. Continuity demands both — innovation and disciplines. The disciplines applied in the Kent case were fairly sophisticated, not in general use, but even these could be improved, as has been seen. What one has to watch in practice is that the financial appraisal does not become of itself the decision taking. Apart from the rigidity which can enter such an appraisal, it is sometimes forgotten how uncertain are the figures entered into it. And one should never forget the very important factors incapable of quantification.

15

Management accounting and corporate planning

Case study no. 44 – aspects of corporate planning: 1 Preparation of plans

Hardy Developments Ltd

It was late in 1975, after the flurry of takeovers, that Moore and Marsh started to give special consideration to the question of planning for the group as a whole with the next decade in mind. Both of them felt that now was the time for consideration and that any further acquisitions were unlikely for a year or two.

There were signs of a difficult economic period ahead in the world and in the UK in particular, the inflation rate within the UK had soared, and it was felt that it was time to take stock.

By now the group was operating within its three divisions and with eight companies on different sites, of itself creating some problems of overall planning. There was a ready acceptance by Marsh and Moore that operational planning and control was an individual company matter, with some need for co-operation divisionally; certainly there was no intention to set up group specialists in this area, as some groups have done. Marsh in particular was opposed to the idea of group production directors and group sales directors. Budgetary planning and control, of course, had group implications, but budgets started out at the divisions and were subject to the inevitable vetting and scrutiny at group head office. The feeling now was that it was the longer-term and corporate aspects of planning which needed to be pursued, with steps being taken to implement this additional feature of managing the business as soon as possible.

Moore's feeling was that not enough thinking was really taking place about the future, either at the centre or the divisions, and that corporate planning procedures ought to be implemented. Not being certain how to get this off the ground, he decided, with the agreement of the three divisional managing directors, to engage a firm of management consultants, Stroud Wallace, to advise upon and implement corporate planning procedures.

The consultants discovered that budgetary planning and control procedures were applied to all companies within the group but for rather few years in some cases; they determined that there were considerable differences in the success of these procedures as between one company and another. Most of these differences seemed to stem from the type of production and the lengths of production time cycles, but it was felt that there were other reasons to do with organisational structures and management attitudes.

After a detailed survey the consultants produced a document on the outline procedure to be followed in each division for corporate planning; see Appendix A.

Required

1   *The reader is invited to appraise and criticise the suggested procedures.*

Appendix A   Outline of procedure for corporate planning

Preparation of plans

1   In order to achieve a co-ordinated corporate plan, it is suggested that the following outline procedure should be followed in each division.

2   A meeting should be held of the divisional executives at which the managing director should outline his objectives for the coming year. The managing director should appraise the problems facing the division, and its strengths and weaknesses, assessing the factors that are limiting performance under the headings of:

(a)   sales
(b)   production capacity:
   (i)   buildings
   (ii)   machinery
   (iii) labour
(c)   material availability
(d)   technical
(e)   financial
(f)   skills of management

3   At this meeting, the managing director should review the economic situation as it affects the division and any specific significant problems. He should conclude with a statement of the action and timetable to be followed in overcoming the problems and meeting objectives. Functional heads should emerge from the meeting with a clear idea of the division's objectives, the problems facing the division and their relation to his own function, and the outline of his plan of action.

4   In the light of decisions made and targets set at this meeting, each function, assisted by a member of the finance director's staff responsible for budgeting, should prepare its functional plan and budget, supported by detailed budget sheets prepared at lower levels after functional budget meetings have been held.

5   The functional budgets should be co-ordinated and summarised by the finance department, then reviewed by the managing director.

6   A further meeting of the divisional executives should be

held to discuss any revisions to objectives or budgets required after the review of the detailed plans submitted by each function.

7   After amendment by the persons responsible for preparing the original budgets and further review, the managing director should prepare a summary of the divisional plan, for which the various functional plans and schedules will provide supporting detail. The agreed plans should then be forwarded to group.

8   Group will then review the divisional budget and either approve it or return it to the division for further discussion and revision.

9   At each stage that revision is required, where a change in the plans or activities of the unit under consideration is involved, the change should be reflected in the written plan. Revisions should be agreed with the persons preparing the original budget.

Divisional plans

In order to facilitate review, managing directors are asked to write their divisional plans under the references and report heads listed below. These report heads are in no way intended to limit the items to be covered. Some items will fall under more than one head, in which case a cross reference will be sufficient.

Reference	*Report head*	*Explanation*
A	Objectives	A statement of the division's objectives
B	Current performance	A brief review of the division's performance in relation to its long-term objectives
C	Review of strengths and weaknesses	An analysis of the major strengths and weaknesses of the division in relation to its objectives and its environment
D	Strategy	A summary of the main business develop-

		ments proposed, dealing particularly with any changes
E	Projects	The major projects which the division is proposing to undertake in order to achieve its objectives including major, general, and specific programme activities setting out for each:
	1 Programme	A statement of the situation with which the programme is to deal
	2 End result required	The objectives of the programme
	3 Action	A step-by-step breakdown of the major stages in completion of the project
	4 Dates	The dates by which each major step will be started and completed
	5 Responsibility	The persons responsible for each step
F	Review	
	1 General	Any other business points not previously covered
	2 Intra-group co-ordination	A statement setting out how the divisions plans are to be co-ordinated with those of other group companies, where appropriate
	3 Organisation	A review of the organisation of the division, the jobs to be done by

		functions and any proposed changes, and the relationship of these changes to the divisions business plans (confidential)
4	Training and development	A review of the training and development of senior staff, stating probable successors to key points (confidential)
5	Capital and special projects expenditure	A general review of projects
G	Summary	Summary

Functional plans – general

1   As the organisation of activities within each division does not follow a uniform pattern throughout the group, it is not possible to write a guide for each function's plan that will apply throughout the group. However, in order to facilitate review, and so as to ensure that all points are covered, functional heads are asked to submit their written plans under the report heads and references listed below, covering all points mentioned. This layout is in no way intended to limit the items to be covered. Some items will fall under more than one head, in which case a cross reference will be sufficient.

Reference	*Report head*	*Explanation*
A	Objectives	A statement of the function's objectives
B	Review of strengths and weaknesses	A review of the strong and weak features of the function in relation to achievement of its objectives
C	Appraisal of specific problems	The following heads are to be used for each problem reviewed:
	1 Problem	A statement of the

2	End result required	problem The solution desired
3	Action	A step-by-step break-down of the action to be taken to achieve the solution
4	Dates	The dates by which the steps will be started and completed

D   Review

1	Specific func-tional points	See section of guide for each function
2	Group functions	A statement of the use to be made of, and services required from, group functions where these are in existence
3	Intra-group co-ordination	A statement showing how the function's plans are to be co-ordinated with those of other group companies where appropriate
4	General and specific pro-gramme activities	A statement of the objectives and a review of the programme and achievements of all general and specific programme activities
5	Organisation	A review of the organ-isation of the function, the jobs to be per-formed in the function and any proposed changes to the func-tion's plan (confiden-tial)
6	Training and development	A review of the train-ing and development

		of staff, proposed recruitment and probable successors to key posts (confidential)
7	Capital expenditure	A review of projects for capital expenditure
8	Cost reduction	A review of projects for cost reduction and improvements in productivity
9	Systems	A review of systems, control and procedures
E	General	Any other points to be mentioned
F	Summary	Summary

Marketing diagnosis

1   In this section the division should outline how it sees its market situation in relation to its financial objectives, existing resources, competition, social or economic factors and trend in demand. Short- and longer-term considerations are both involved. Since this analysis effectively determines strategy, it is a crucial topic.

2   The factors to be considered and the conclusions to be drawn will vary with different divisions and over time. The following are some that may be involved:

(a)   the size of the market at home and overseas
(b)   the importance of the world market, export distribution by territory
(c)   market growth at home and overseas
(d)   the division's share of the markets and situation in relation to competitors, effect of any new competitors entering the market
(e)   local overseas manufacture
(f)   licensing operations
(g)   dependence on certain industries
(h)   trends in numbers of customers and their size
(j)   price trends
(k)   the level of R & D expenditure

(l) technological change at all levels, product, customer, customer's customer
(m) new product policy
(n) profitability in relation to objectives
(o) the scope for economies of scale in production and promotion
(p) the total production capacity available in the markets covered
(q) political situation
(r) economic situation
(s) tariffs
(t) takeover situations of customers and competitors
(u) changes in sales distribution channels

3   Divisions must provide a qualitative analysis of the major competitors including:

(a) the reasons for their success
(b) their weaknesses
(c) their market shares and trends

Examples

Division A: diagnosis

4   Currently has 10 per cent of its turnover going directly overseas. Total business gives 5 per cent pre-tax return on capital employed; unit is currently working at about 60 per cent of effective capacity. UK market is characterised by low growth rate and seven other competitors have between them 60 per cent of UK market. The unit has 5 per cent of UK market. UK market is at the moment static.

Division B: diagnosis

5   Is in an area of rapid technological development leading to a high rate of product obsolescence and high R & D costs. UK demand is limited and division must sell in world markets. A minimum essential level of R & D expenditure is £0.3 m per annum and this currently represents the equivalent of 10 per cent of total sales turnover. In spite of rapid growth and a good record of innovation, the division is still only returning 9 per cent pre-tax on capital. Furthermore analysis of sales

records shows that despite rapid expansion of sales the market has expanded even faster.

6   There would of course be other issues involved in these examples. Only a few have been highlighted.

7   The division should also state in this section what factors, if any, are acting as constraints in realising its stated financial objectives; for instance no UK competitor is achieving even the minimum target and the division's market position is also unfavourable because of its size (perhaps it is neither big enough nor small enough).

Marketing strategies

1   In this section, in relation to its long-term objectives, the division should outline the broad lines of approach it has decided to adopt and the reasons for their adoption.

Examples

2   Division A: strategy

The division A above could propose that it must both rationalise and expand internationally, concentrating particularly overseas on growth economies.

3   Division B: strategy

The division B might propose that it should pursue two main strategies: increase its manufacturing capacity and pursue a more positive policy towards licensing in particular and marketing in general.

Marketing – quantification of strategies

1   Having established the broad strategic policies, the division must aim to quantify these so that it can measure progress, and assess cost and profit.

Examples

2   Division A: targets

The division A might propose to rationalise within the year with one or more of the leading competitors.

3   Division B: targets

The division B might aim to propose to cover 10 per cent of
R & D costs by licensing and to expand capacity by 30 per
cent. Marketing expenditure must be increased by 20 per
cent, aiming at an average annual increase in the order intake
of 25 per cent over the next five years.

Marketing – tactical plan

1   In this section the division should broadly indicate how it
intends to achieve the subsidiary objectives.
   The following are points that might be covered in the plans.

Profitability

2   Set out the profitability of each product group. If segre-
gated trading results for each product group are not available,
state the measures in hand to obtain the best indication of
contribution made by each product group.

Market mix planned

3(a)   Selection of industries to take account of:
   (i)   growth areas
   (ii)   cyclical investment
   (iii)   vulnerability to legal or fiscal change
  (b)   Selection of territories to take account of:
   (i)   growth and/or concentration
   (ii)   those territories less hampered by foreign ex-
      change problems
   (iii)   cyclical trends
  (c)   Selection of customers within industries to take
      account of:
   (i)   distribution of business within an industry over
      customers
   (ii)   growth customers in non-growth industries
   (iii)   size of customer
   (iv)   vulnerability
   (v)   costs of promotion
   (vi)   costs of providing an overall service relative to
      size of customer

Pricing policy

4(a) Overall attitude to pricing policy in respect of:
     (i)   price leadership
     (ii) buying into a market
  (b) Use of 'market price' as well as 'cost plus' approach
  (c) Pricing over the life of a product
  (d) Policy in regard to size of orders and volume requirements
  (e) Price in relation to the other economic variables to influence customer behaviour
  (f) Charging of special tools, development and pre-production costs
  (g) Influence of royalty or commission payments
  (h) Charging of distribution costs, packing and delivery
  (i) The impact of 'capital over time'
  (j) Volume/cost/profit relationships and the use of marginal cost information.

Product developments

5(a) Requirements for research and development
  (b) Products or work areas that are to be abandoned or run down
  (c) Rate of product obsolescence
  (d) Impact of new products or techniques
  (e) Requirements for value engineering
  (f) Implementation of policy regarding standardisation or special products
  (g) Design
  (h) Need for services such as:
     (i)   technical advice
     (ii)   engineering applications
     (iii) systems applications
     (iv)   installation
     (v)   spares and repairs and after sales service
  (j) Ability to lead in turnkey contracts.

Sales promotion proposed

6(a) Product publicity
  (b) Exhibitions

(c) Council for Industrial Design Awards
(d) Technical articles by staff
(e) Queen's Awards to Industry
(f) Public relations.

Distribution plans

7(a) State stock policy
 (b) Proportion of production made for stock
 (c) Rate of stock turnover aimed at
 (d) Delivery service
 (e) Overseas agents and distribution arrangements.

Requirements from production

8(a) Reductions in cost of product
 (b) Steps to improve delivery performance or reliability
 (c) Margin of spare capacity needed for business obtained on the basis of urgent delivery or to provide a 'breakdown' service.

Marketing personnel

9(a) Distribution and control of field sales force
 (b) Co-ordination of tender/order/contract functions
 (c) Technical service.

Marketing — areas of interdependence

1 Comments should be included here on any situation where it is thought that other group interests can reinforce the division's efforts, and also possible areas of current or future competition. The latter is most likely to arise from technological change.

Marketing — integration and rationalisation

1 In this section we are concerned with the division's views on whether a major move such as merger or takeover, or a joint manufacturing agreement overseas, or rationalisation or capacity, or a move into entirely new markets would in fact be the best solution for realising the division's financial objectives.

Finance

1   The financial plan should cover under the main head 'review':

   (a)   Cost, profit and capital control objectives for the division
   (b)   The improvement of management control information
   (c)   The improvement of clerical systems
   (d)   Co-ordination with other group divisions.

Personnel

1   The personnel plans should cover under the main heading 'review':

   (a)   Implementation of group policies, and coordination with group personnel function
   (b)   Training programme
   (c)   Recruitment programme
   (d)   Salary and wage policy for the year
   (e)   Negotiations outstanding or proposed with the unions
   (f)   Changes in employees' terms or conditions of service or benefits
   (g)   Health, welfare and security matters.

Administration

1   The administration plan should examine the divisional organisation in the light of its declared objectives, covering under the main head 'review':

   (a)   Proposed organisational changes (confidential)
   (b)   Proposed physical relocation.

Technical

1   Objectives and realistic timetables should be given for each development or research project. Major projects should be listed to show their expected duration, cost, the return expected and the numbers and quality of the staff employed. Long-term projects covering periods longer than the year under consideration should be budgeted separately from short-term projects to be completed in the current year.

2   Points to be covered in the functional plan under the main head 'review' should include:

(a)   The research and development needed to achieve the marketing objectives of new or modified products, techniques or processes

(b)   The development of existing products needed to maintain, achieve or anticipate technological changes

(c)   The requirements in terms of manpower and facilities to achieve these objectives to the required timetable

(d)   Assistance to be given to production or sites to reduce costs through improved processes.

Manufacturing

1   The manufacturing plans for each product group should be given. These must be related to the marketing plan of the division and associated companies where appropriate, and should cover under the main head 'review':

(a)   Any changes in volume or production, showing available capacity not matched by orders

(b)   Any requirements for sub-contracting work out or facilities available for taking in sub-contracted work

(c)   A review of the production facilities by budget centres

(d)   A review of manpower capabilities and recruitment

(e)   A review of machinery capabilities and plans

(f)   The control of stock and work in progress investment, including target levels for work in progress, stocks and stores inventories, related to forward sales

(g)   Works and plant maintenance

(h)   Major layout and method changes.

Quality assurance

1   The quality assurance plan should include under the main head 'review', a review of quality costs, showing the costs of:

(a)   Prevention

(b)   Appraisal

(c)   Failure, including rectification.

2   The plan should indicate action proposed to reduce defects.

Purchasing

1   The purchasing plan, which should be related to the
manufacturing plan and co-ordinated with the group buying
panel, should include a review of the markets for major raw
material and bought in items, and cover under the main head
'review':

    (a)   Major suppliers' plans in respect of production, selling
policies, discounts

    (b)   The comparative economics of bought out and made
in parts and components, bearing in mind group
sources

    (c)   The supply position, likely delivery and lead times

    (d)   Stock levels and stock control

    (e)   Price movements

    (f)   Quality assurance in respect of purchased items

    (g)   Any technical developments, new materials, components

    (h)   Target savings on material, parts and stores purchasing

    (j)   Surplus and redundant materials and parts, and
arrangements for their disposal

    (k)   New sources of supply to be investigated.

Commentary by Derek Moore and John Marsh

In any company, there needs to be at least some long-term planning activity. In addition to the inevitable attention given to day-to-day planning and control, essential for survival, and to the often annual target aspects of budgetary control, there must be someone or some small group of persons giving thought to the question of long-term objectives and how those objectives might be met. We are practical businessmen, not academics, and we believe it to be logical to be constantly looking way ahead to try to determine the future path of the organisation. But one has to put some procedures to this work if there is to be a proper discipline, and there is a lot to be said for engaging outside consultants if this is to be organised quickly and competently.

It must be remembered that we were not just a single company, but eight all told, operating in three divisions, and that makes things very much more difficult in many ways. First of all, you need the long-term planning even more; the organisation is bigger and the activities more diverse; you are in more different production activities using diverse resources and serving differing product markets. It is inevitable that one has a swings and roundabouts situation. There is the problem of divisional and company management personnel and other employees, all with individual goals and aspirations, inevitably all fighting for their own causes. And then there is the rationing out of resources, funds in particular, because it would be very unusual if one did not have capital rationing. There really is no way in which the latter problem could be solved without corporate planning, that is, establishing strategies to reach objectives, evaluating the strategies, being aware of priorities and then allocating resources.

The greatest difficulty often proves to be the interface between group headquarters and the divisions. We would sum this one up by saying 'what is good for group may not be good for an individual division, and vice-versa.'

The first thing to be absolutely clear about is that the consultants only produced a procedure to be followed within each division; they did not tackle the other related problems of 'group corporate planning', in other words, what happens in the group, the relationship and interface within the group, and the ultimate agreement and issue of long-term plans which are at the basis for programming the necessary activities.

We believe that they did not adequately tackle a root problem that one so often meets — patchiness in existing planning and control procedures at the two lower levels. Not that their terms of reference were to tackle the patchiness and attempt to put it right — that in itself can be a pretty long job — but there obviously are some risks in attempting to build the top level on insecure foundations, and we would have welcomed some indication as to the things which needed to be put right. We believe that the effectiveness of planning and control is initially very dependent upon organisation structure and managerial accountability and attitudes. Of course, as our consultants recommended, an early look must be a 'position audit', or if you like, an appraisal of where the division stands at the moment, but this is essentially a 'technique' aspect of long-term planning. First and foremost, in our opinion, one needs to ensure that the prerequisite of an effective organisation and the constituent parts within it is met.

There is much to commend in the suggested divisional procedures, which are logically laid out. The first recommendation of what we would call a team spirit meeting is often not a part of what is done in businesses, but is essential for proper motivation. The writing of the divisional plans based on carefully thought-out functional plans, with report heads following the natural elements of the corporate planning process is good stuff. We are proabably carping a little, but something which did worry us a little was the many references to 'budgets' on the first page. One does have to be careful, we know from experience, that one does not give the impression that a long-term plan is just the annual budget extended for, say, four more years ahead. We may need the financial projections, we may not. When Sir Michael Edwardes was the chief executive of the Chloride Group before his secondment to BL, there was a time when he declared a moratorium on the accounting projections, 'so that personnel could get on with the real work of corporate planning'. The point is that one needs to do the planning, the plans can be pretty important, but the budgets really are no more than the financial expressions of the plans.

Now, we must not give the wrong impression — it is sensible to be aware of the likely financial outcomes; there are no doubt, financial objectives to be met; one needs to know what cash resources are likely to be needed. But over-attention to the budget aspects would defeat the main objective of longer-term planning, which is to get answers to the question: where do we want to be in five years' time and what have we to do in order to get there?

It will be understood by the reader that the reference to 'reviewing the divisional budget' is a big topic in itself, and something which needs to be tackled with care. This brings us to another point of criticism. There is a very strong argument for some information being issued from the group before the divisional planning activities take place. After all, it could be argued that at the end of the day, it is a group corporate plan which will emerge, so that divisions really need to have a knowledge of the total business objectives, any changes which the group feel are desirable in the strategic structure. Apart from this, group headquarters may be a very good collecting place for much of the general evidence needed for long-term planning. For example, it is not unknown for a group of companies to employ someone as an economic advisor, or at least as the person who pulls all the economic indicators together.

It was our feeling that, compared with the internal operational aspects of review for planning purposes, the marketing emphasis was very strong. Again, we must not be misunderstood — knowledge of the market is tremendously important; it is almost certainly correct to pursue the market research and diagnosis with all the zeal which the consultants intended. But an adequate internal appraisal is also essential, of physical assets and monetary capability, of manufacturing resources, manpower including management, of information systems and control procedures.

Conclusions

It is obvious that one should engage in long-term planning, and it's true that a lot of the work in it is 'thinking' work. But it does need to be a discipline, not rigidly timetabled, but obviously with some annual deadlines. You do not want it to be seen as 'something we do once a year', but on the other hand there have to be some formal procedures. It is very important in a group situation to get these procedures as right, and yet as economical, as possible. The consultants appeared to be stressing a grass-roots, bottom-up approach; in other words, functional plans preceding divisional plans, preceding group plans. And this must be right providing one recognises the inevitability of a top-down aspect to the planning as well.

Case study no. 45 – aspects of corporate planning: 2 Cost structure analysis

Hardy Developments Ltd

Profit planning

1   In order to maintain the return on assets on a continuing basis in all trading conditions that may be encountered, and in order to improve the group's competitive position, it is vital that costs are closely controlled. The profit planning procedures outlined below are designed to help managers to appraise their costs with a view to concentrating attention on those areas where savings can be made. They are intended to ensure that the best possible profit can be made at each level of activity.

2   To establish a yardstick for the appraisal of budgets and plans, a budget at normal activity should be developed. It is intended that this yardstick should remain in being for five years. Accordingly, in fixing the level of normal capacity regard should be paid to:

(a)   past performance;
(b)   existing facilities;
(c)   factors limiting performance:
    (i)   sales;

(ii)   production capacity: buildings; machinery; labour; number of shifts to be worked;
(iii) material availability;
(iv)   technical;
(v)   finance;
(vi)   management skills.

3   Normal capacity is usually set at around 80 per cent of the theoretical maximum on single-shift working, where this is normal. Each year's budget is expressed as a percentage of normal. Normals of capacity should be set on the basis of existing facilities and those to be brought into use in the current budget year. They should only be altered for major changes in facilities.

4   All costs should be considered for levels of activity, 60 per cent, 80 per cent, 100 per cent and 120 per cent, of normal. Each level of activity should be envisaged as enduring for the whole year. The consideration of costs to be incurred at different levels of activity allows management to plan the adjustments that will have to be made if business activity differs substantially from the level expected. In making plans for different levels of activity, management should consider and state the signals that will trigger the decision either to 'gear up' to the extent necessary to take advantage of favourable trade conditions, or to make the cuts in expenditure required to move to a profitable position at lower levels of activity. The length of time that an indicator will be allowed to show trends which indicate action, and which show no sign of reversal, before action is taken, should be stated.

Cost structure analysis

General

1   To identify those costs that can be most easily controlled, the cost structure of each function within a division must be examined and the costs classified as:

(a)   constant or bedrock;
(b)   general programme;
(c)   specific programme;
(d)   operating costs: fixed;

(e)   operating costs: variable.

It is not intended that records of actual costs analysed to these categories should be maintained. The classification is for appraisal and planning only.

Constant costs

2   Constant (bedrock) costs are those incurred for the company to be able to open its doors to do business. They will include:

(a)   depreciation and rental of premises and installed plant and equipment;

(b)   insurance of fixed assets, rates;

(c)   maintenance required to maintain assets in a serviceable condition (but not maintenance required as a result of operating machinery);

(d)   utilities required to maintain assets as above;

(e)   other costs of ownership of assets not listed above;

(f)   expenditure resulting from statutory obligations;

(g)   maintenance of patents or agreements in respect of trade;

(h)   salaries and associated costs of key staff, including works personnel who by virtue of their qualities, qualifications, experience and training must be considered necessary to retain a cadre of direct labour, who would be available to train others.

3   The determination of what is or is not a constant cost is a matter of judgement. As a guide, it is helpful to envisage the hypothetical situation that would occur if the division were to transact no business at all for one year, but it was decided that the facilities and organisaton should be maintained in order to recommence business at the beginning of the next year. The costs incurred in this hypothetical situation are the constant or bedrock costs. Once these costs are clearly established for the facilities in being, apart from control exercised over price or salary increases, very little can be done to control their amount. Changes should correspond to changes in the facilities provided, which will reflect major changes in the pattern or volume of business, leading to the acquisition or disposal of assets.

General programme costs

4   These are costs incurred by decision of management with a view to improving the business position of the division. They are not specifically identifiable with any particular product or service. General programme costs include such items as:

(a) research and development expenditure of a general nature;
(b) public relations, publicity and advertising expenditure not associated with a particular product or service;
(c) general training programmes;
(d) non-contractural employee benefits;
(e) entertainment expenditure;
(f) subscriptions and donations.

Specific programme costs

5   These are costs incurred by decision of management with a view to improving the business position of the division. They can be identified to a specific product or service or project with a circumscribed objective. Such are:

(a) development expenditure on a particular product or process;
(b) promotional expenditure incurred for a particular product or process;
(c) specific training for manufacture of a new product or operation of a new process;
(d) installation of a new control or data processing system.

Operating costs

6   These are the costs incurred as a result of doing business and handling the daily work of selling, making contracts, preparing drawings, production, accounting and some aspects of administration. They are costs that are much more closely associated with the level of activity of business than the previous categories.

7   Operating costs are divided into fixed and variable. Fixed costs are those that are expected to remain fixed for a parti-

cular range of activity. Variable costs are those that will vary more or less directly with the level of activity.

8   Direct labour on piecework and material costs should normally be variable. Ascertainment of the different rates applicable to different levels of activity should be mainly a matter of taking into account any changes in efficiency, methods, or quantity discounts applicable. A cadre of direct labour which will form a base from which to expand for each level of activity may be considered as a constant cost. Retention of some direct labour at lower levels of activity may be justified where the length of time required to recruit, train or develop the necessary skills exceeds three months.

Determination of structure

9   The classification above is intended as an aid to action on cost control. Costs should therefore only be split in severable units, i.e. the wages and salaries (except overtime) of individuals must be allocated wholly to one category or another. It is appreciated that when dealing with individuals, it is not always easy to assign them to categories, as their time is frequently split. Regard must be paid to the possibility of redistributing the work load, according to the functions performed, and according to levels of activity.

10   The following approach is suggested as a guide:

  (a)   select the key personnel on the principles outlined in paragraph 3 above, i.e. those personnel whose qualities, qualifications, experience and training make it imperative that their services be retained;

  (b)   select those personnel whose activities are mainly associated with general or specific programmes and allocate them accordingly;

  (c)   the remaining personnel should be those who are required for transacting the company's business, but who could be replaced or released at less than three months' notice. Amongst these should be distinguished those who are required at the 60 per cent level of activity, and those whose services are required to cater for increased levels of activity.

Required

1   *The reader is invited to consider the strengths and weaknesses of the proposed cost analysis.*

Commentary by Derek Moore and John Marsh

We have previously described our approach to corporate planning and this case outlines the cost structure analysis to which each division must adhere in preparing its corporate plan. It is an adjunct to the planning process; a means of marshalling the evidence from eight different companies and from our view at the centre, it is important to have a mechanism like this which ensures that plans are being expressed in a uniform fashion. It certainly makes much easier the task of preparing the group corporate plan and also our discussions with the individual companies and with their divisional managing directors are assisted by our ability to speak a common language. Without doubt, in any decentralised enterprise, it is important to develop procedures which act as linkages between the various segments; the corporate planning procedures are an outstanding example of an aid in this linking process and the cost structure analysis defines in even greater detail, the uniform view which is to be taken. All of this helps in the process of obtaining 'goal congruence', that is general agreement at all levels of the enterprise to the objectives, goals and plans which are to be followed. These procedures should therefore be designed so that on the one hand the centre is better able to plan and control the activities of the group, and on the other hand the individual company is helped to develop ways and means of controlling its own unique position in its environment. Our observation of other companies is that the corporate planning procedures and cost structure analysis often seem to have been designed to assist the control of group activities but do very little for the individual company. The danger is that the individual company sees the exercise as involving 'doing something for head office' rather than a process which is most important for its own progress. When we received the report from the consultants, Stroud Wallace, we wanted to be reassured that the recommendations would assist the individual company as much as ourselves at head office.

We have found that one of the strong points of this cost structure analysis is that managers become accustomed to thinking about their operations at a number of different levels of activity; indeed each year's budget is expressed as a percentage of normal capacity. The definition of 'normal' capacity certainly raises considerable problems, but we would argue that the very fact that this point has to be debated, agreed and defended, is a most important element in the process of corporate planning. To arrive at an agreed definition involves a discussion of existing facilities and also an assessment of external opportunities; and this represents the very essence of corporate planning. The outcome of this thinking and discussion is that managers find it easier to see the financial consequences of physical actions, which may or may not occur or which may occur at different levels of activity. We call this the 'management of whifs', because managers keep on asking each other 'what if this happened?', or 'what if that happened?'.

The classification of costs into constant or bedrock; general programme; specific programme; operating costs — fixed; operating costs — variable has allowed us easily to switch our attention to various scenarios of the future. We have been able to reflect on the effects of expanding or contracting specific programmes, the effects of operating at different levels of activity, and the results of increasing or reducing discretionary or general programme costs. Without this ability to examine different scenarios the overall quality of our corporate planning would have been much reduced. We have certainly felt the benefit of this system over the two years, 1979 and 1980, when a number of companies have been forced to adapt to lower levels of activity during a period of recession. Indeed we have used this lull in activities as an opportunity to better equip ourselves to tackle the long-term future by developing our corporate planning skills.

Yet, we must not be complacent. Certainly the implementation of this cost structure analysis caused some confusion initially, because the case is not clear whether we were restricting the classification of costs to 'appraising and planning' only or whether the classification was intended as an aid to action on cost control. The consultants did say that it was not intended that records of actual costs, analysed to the five categories, should be kept. However, we have found in practice, that whilst in time the planning process can be distinguished from the control process, nonetheless it is important to have a common language or cost analysis for both.

Perhaps a more fundamental doubt is that we might have been refining our budgetary control processes rather than dealing with corporate planning. After all, the essence of planning is to consider alternative courses of action and what is required are reliable and relevant data for such decisions. It has been argued within the group that this cost structure analysis helps to develop projected profit and loss accounts and balance sheets under varying assumptions, but data will be required in quite different forms to evaluate alternative causes of action, which often boil down to investment or divestment decisions. In these instances, we wish to see the future incremental costs and benefits arising from the decision under review and we now have a separate capital budgeting system where large sums of capital are required.

Conclusion

Perhaps we should see this cost structure analysis as part of the general evolution of our group management accounting system, which we view as providing a uniform language and set of operating procedures. Our basic philosophy is that each company is unique and must design and develop its own management accounting system. Nevertheless operating as a group of companies does require some common language and procedures and we have found that the cost structure analysis has been particularly useful in drawing matters together at the centre, and allowing us to develop group policies. There is a delicate balance to be struck here between the need to maintain the individuality of companies and need to develop common procedures for the group.

Case study no. 46 – aspects of corporate planning: 3 Setting financial objectives

Hardy Developments Ltd

As part of the development of corporate planning in Hardy Developments, detailed discussions had taken place on the subject of setting financial objectives for each division and for the company as a whole.

However, substantial differences of opinion existed. The main points expressed by the three divisional managing directors and the group financial controller are summarised below.

Divisional managing director, Star Components

In my view, return on capital employed is the main test of financial performance. In our division, the return on capital is 25 per cent, which must exceed the cost of capital for the group as a whole by a considerable margin. Divisions should be charged with the cost of capital which they use; I suggest a uniform rate for each division of 15 per cent. Divisions should then be judged by the amount of residual net income which they generate. On this basis, the electrical components division has done well in the last year. Divisional plans should clearly show the residual net income (i.e. after capital charges) which the division intends to produce. The overall objective of the group should be to maximise residual net income from all divisions. The implication of this is that, whenever possible, available funds should be channelled into the Star Components division.

Divisional managing director, civil engineering

The return on capital employed in my division is low at 2 per cent. However, I submit that this is an inappropriate measure of performance. At present, excess capacity exists in our industry and our sales of £5.5 million represent a very fine effort. We are taking steps, as shown in our divisional plans, to rationalise our activities but we are convinced that if we take a five-year period, satisfactory profits can be made, from pressure vessels. In my view our financial objectives should be to increase our market penetration and maximise our sales. It is likely that in five years' time there will be only two or three manufacturers in this field. At that point, the survivors will be in a strong position and our strategic plans should have in mind this long-term objective for Hardy Developments. Inappropriate short-term measures of performance might distract us from the long-term goal.

Divisional managing director, materials processing

We have particular problems in our division which do not exist elsewhere. We are in the middle of a major redevelopment programme of our manufacturing facilities. This involves installing automated foundry equipment which will substantially reduce our manpower requirements in the future. I estimate that it will take two years before we see the real benefits from this exercise. At the moment our return on capital employed is low in relationship to our competitors, but when our new plant is fully installed and operational we expect above average returns. There is sufficient data available within the foundry trade to calculate returns on capital employed. In my view, a reasonable financial objective would be to obtain the average return on capital employed for the industry, taking the future five-year period.

Group financial controller

I see the financial objectives of this company in terms of meeting the expectations of our shareholders. These expectations are conditioned by a number of factors:

1 our historic return on assets;
2 our historic dividend yield;
3 our historic earnings yield;
4 our historic price/earnings ratio;
5 the performance of companies which are considered to be comparable.

Our profit performance in the past has been somewhat spotty. But on the basis of past growth, we still have a high price/earnings rating on the Stock Exchange. In my view, we must determine the expectations of the shareholders and draw up our financial objectives to meet these expectations. Specific attention must be paid to future dividend policy, together with the cash flow and earnings growth necessary to support the market price of our shares. The implications are that the individual divisional plans and the overall group plans must meet a number of objectives. It is most unlikely that a single measure of financial performance will suffice.

Required
1 Evaluate the four views expressed in the case.

Commentary by Derek Moore and John Marsh

We often refer to this case when we wish to make the point that we are really a collection of quite different businesses and therefore we have a problem of deciding whether to apply to each company a single uniform method of measuring performance or whether a different measure or measures should be used for each company, taking into account its individual characteristics. A single uniform measure certainly has the attraction of simplicity and also provides a basis of comparison. However, we have found that such single measures need to be interpreted with some sensitivity and imagination, otherwise dysfunctional behaviour can be produced and poor decisions can be made.

The divisional managing director of Star Components mentions two measures: return on investment or capital employed and residual income. We know from talks to other companies that the majority use some version of return on investment (ROI). We prefer to use this measure as a tool of diagnosis rather than the single and therefore most important measure of performance. As a ratio, it deals with two factors critical to the success of any enterprise, profits and capital employed. However, the problems of definition are so severe that we have rejected it as our main measure of performance, although for internal reviews we encourage managers to make their own definitions and monitor the progress of the constituent elements.

Residual income is an amount rather than a ratio and is calculated by deducting a capital charge from profits. But major questions for us have been 'on what assets should the capital charge be levied; should different rates be charged for different classes of assets and should rate(s) be applied to fixed assets?' Our conclusion is that we must distinguish between the performance of the divisional manager and the performance of the division as an economic entity. So far as the divisional manager is concerned; he does not control the level of fixed assets in any meaningful sense since we certainly would not leave all investment decisions to the discretion of the divisional manager. We think that we should take the fixed assets as given (and thereby avoid some difficult measurement problems) and restrict the capital charge to controllable investment, which usually means the working capital of debtors, stock, minus creditors. We handle cash centrally and therefore exclude the item from our consideration. We control the investment in fixed assets by our capital budgeting system which helps us to examine projects and if necessary companies and divisions as economic entities. Here, decisions and action must be based on an evaluation of the discounted future cash flows of alternative causes of action, which is quite a different problem to that of evaluating the performance of an individual over a limited period. Conceptually, perhaps there is no difference between the individual manager and the economic entity in that ideally we would wish to judge a divisional manager according to the changes he personally has made to the future cash flows of his division over the period of review. Unfortunately we have not found a reliable measure for such future cash flows and therefore we have evolved a third measure, that is, 'controllable profit' which reviews the actual profits of the division after charging for the use of controllable capital against budgeted controllable profit.

The divisional manager, civil engineering, adds another dimension by arguing for non-financial measures such as market penetration and we have support for this view. We encourage our divisional managers to identify the key result areas of their individual companies, to develop key success factors associated with the key result areas and to develop appropriate measures. We recognise that the key result areas will change as circumstances change and therefore the measures of performance will need to change also. We have found that a great deal of our time is spent with divisional managers, discussing key result areas, as well as agreeing the budgeted amount of controllable profit.

How do we assess the amount of controllable profit? Well, certainly we build into our judgement the point made by the divisional managing director, materials processing, about the estimated future average return on capital employed for the industry. It is a subjective manner which takes into account how we think the environment will change in the short term, since our measure operates for one year. It follows from this that our measures take into account our view of the particular circumstances of the individual companies. We consider that there are significant weaknesses in using a single uniform standard as some companies do, for example 20 per cent on capital employed, when reviewing the short-term performance of our company and divisional managers.

Another factor, which enters into our subjective judgement of the controllable profit which we expect from a division, is the total profits, cash flow and dividends which are expected by our shareholders. This represents yet another financial objective and one of our key tasks at the centre is to ensure that all these financial and non-financial objectives fit together and reinforce each other. In some ways this is the most important (and most difficult) aspect of corporate planning.

Conclusion

As with our comments on cost analysis and as we have argued in other cases, we believe that each individual company in our group is unique and therefore different financial measures and standards of performance for the individual managers must be designed and developed. We see financial measures as being important but also being supplemented by other measures of the identified key success factors which themselves are derived from a determination of key result areas. We have a vision of clusters of measures for each individual company and for the group as a whole and we see these clusters changing in constituency and in relative importance as circumstances change. The design and development of these clusters of measures is perhaps the most difficult aspect of corporate planning; it is a strategic issue which must be handled at the centre of the group by the most senior executives.

Case study no. 47 – aspects of corporate planning: 4 Pricing policy

Hardy Developments Ltd

Recently the detail included under the 'pricing policy' report heading has come up for discussion at group headquarters between the chairman and his divisional managing directors, and back at the divisions between the managing directors and their executives.

To recapitulate, this report heading reads as follows:

Pricing policy

   (a) Overall attitude to pricing policy in respect of:
       (i)   price leadership
       (ii) buying into a market
   (b) Use of 'market price' as well as 'cost plus' approach
   (c) Pricing over the life of a product
   (d) Policy in regard to size of orders and volume requirements
   (e) Price in relation to the other economic variables to influence customer behaviour
   (f) Charging of special tools, development and pre-production costs
   (g) Influence of royalty or commission payments
   (h) Charging of distribution costs, packing and delivery

(j)   The impact of 'capital over time'
(k)   Volume/cost/profit relationships and the use of
      marginal cost information.

The discussion at group headquarters was stimulated by the
chairman's insistence that pricing policy was one of the main
pivots of the group achievements in the future and that this
should be the subject of a proper study. He contended that
quite apart from attention to operating efficiency and improvements needed in budgetary planning and control procedures, there needed to be clear policies on pricing, particularly bearing in mind the increased market possibilities
brought about by Britain's entry into the European Community. One divisional managing director replied that problems could be brought about by the introduction of stereotyped planning and control procedures throughout the group
and that it could be even worse if the same uniform approach
to pricing was adopted, particularly in view of the difference
between the divisions and the markets aimed at.

The discussion had ended with a resolution that each division should carry out its own study on pricing matters and
report back to group headquarters, stating as clearly as
possible:

1   what it considered to be a sound basic pricing policy
    for the division; and
2   the nature of any flexibility required in pricing
    arrangements.

Required
*1   Review the financial information required for the pricing
     study.*

Commentary by Derek Moore and John Marsh

There is no earthly reason why corporate planning should introduce rigidity; this danger exists only if group top management see and intend it to be a straitjacket which really would be quite unreasonable. Corporate planning is intended primarily to be a philosophy, to encourage logical thinking about the objectives of the enterprise as a whole and means of achieving those objectives, bearing in mind the constituent parts. And having said this, it really would be quite wrong to insist on a rigid group pricing policy.

But the report heading within the outline procedure document does offer individual divisions the opportunity to review, in a systematic way, most aspects of pricing policy, and then it does enable a dialogue between division and group about, what we agree, is a main pivot in encouraging demand and making profit.

First of all, the comment in the case about rigidity points to the need for an education and training task to be undertaken when one uses the inevitable 'procedures' of corporate planning. If there is any sort of reaction to the effect that such procedures are or may become stereotyped, the real intentions and practices need to be explained and demonstrated. Second, it is right and proper that there should be a comprehensive study of pricing matters within each division and it is our contention that such a study should be a regular feature of planning within an organisation. Changes within the organisation, but much more important, outside in the business, necessitate the regular scrutiny of pricing policy which is a patent mechanism for livelihood, survival and success. Reference to 'outside the business' means, of course, to aspects within the immediate product/market environment of the company, but also to the more general environmental aspects, economic and technological.

In addition there are some very useful headings of pricing policy which are worth particular study. Let us take the whole question of price leadership (a) and the need on occasions to buy into a market. Size in the particular field may dictate that one is followed by every other competitor on matters of price, but that really was not our position in any division. So that there is the question of who one follows, if one is to follow at all; linked with (e), there is the point that one may choose to carve one's own niche on the joint matters of price, delivery, quality, service generally and after-sales service. It is our contention that in the UK and even more so overseas, one can command better prices than are often thought possible, if one can offer satisfaction on the other variables already mentioned, and in particular, on delivery and quality. As a part of corporate planning one should decide where one's strengths lie, and they may lie in the area of price or one of the other variables which can substantially influence demand.

It is certainly necessary to consider the impact of (b) within one's own division, to attempt to ensure that one gets the best out of the cost factors and the market factors when pricing. In our case, the prices ruling in the foundries were much more market oriented than absorption cost oriented, because of the cut-throat nature of pricing in general, whereas in the newer fields of activity, such as electronics, a certain amount of work was chargeable on a cost-plus basis. Item (k) was relevant here, as was (d), and it is very much up to the individual unit to give careful thought both to the costing approaches to be used in pricing, and to the policy to be adopted when trying to break into a new market to secure a particular customer, retain a valuable market and also in relation to long-run and short-run work. By the way, there is nothing academic about the issues being talked over; we are amazed by the number of organisations we know where the most dreadfully rigid approaches are adopted in pricing and where reviews of policies in this area are non-existent.

The impact of 'capital over time' is a sadly neglected area, particularly relevant in situations where contracting-type production may mean jobs being on the shop floor for long periods or short periods, thus consuming capital over many months or a few weeks only. What one must attempt to reflect in prices as a directly attributable item is this use of capital, which is particularly important in these days of cash flow problems and high interest rates. This was particularly relevant in our James and Breasley Company, so that inevitably it was the cause of much discussion within that division.

All the other items within the report headings were studied, but other factors, too, such as exchange rate aspects, links between prices and credit terms, and the particular problems of pricing when confronted by possible contracts with government departments.

The divisional reports contained much food for thought both in the group and within the other divisions. We made all three reports available to all divisions, and we know that this was welcome and generated a lot of new thinking.

Conclusions

Sometimes it is necessary to generate and stimulate thought on particular problem areas from the group, and by means of the longer-term planning cycle. Price-fixing policy is a case in point (incidentally we do mean policy, not the hand-to-mouth practices). Pricing is such a significant factor in the achievement of business objectives and yet, like so many other 'policy' matters, it is often subordinated as a result of the short-term pressures. In other words, the urgent often takes precedence over the important. Having said that, one must not allow divisional management to think that pressure upon them to study important matters is a prelude to a rigid imposition from on high. Once again, the lesson arises that effective and efficient management accounting (for pricing in this case) depends upon a thorough understanding of all the relevant variables and their interactions.

16

Major financial issues since flotation

Second interview with Derek Moore and John Marsh

Question *Well, I have found the case studies to be most illuminating and I believe that I have learned a great deal from the descriptions and analyses of the financial control issues. I should like to bring matters up-to-date and ask what have been the most difficult financial problems which you have faced at the centre since obtaining your Stock Exchange quotation?*

Derek Moore I would identify two major issues: the first has centred on the question of company liquidity and the second has been concerned with the financial and accounting effects of inflation. Let us strt with the question of liquidity. We went through a very difficult period in 1974/75 as, of course, did almost every company, and the first thing we learned was that, whilst we needed to divisionalise our activities for profit responsibility, at the same time we had to instal very tight procedures for the central control of cash.

Question *How did the divisional managers react to this?*

Derek Moore Well, at first there was some resentment because they thought that we were giving them some autonomy but then taking it back, and constraining them so far as cash management was concerned. I can understand their point of view but I convinced them that, in a sense, as divisional managers, they were managers of 'ambiguity' because in the last analysis, they are *not* operating their own business and it is necessary to have tight control of cash and also capital expenditure for the group.

John Marsh   You will see that in addition to the dramatic changes externally caused by the increase in oil prices, we were in any case set on an expansion programme. This growth on its own would have needed to be financed and we considered that the first search for cash should start within the individual operating companies.

Question   *What sort of system did you adopt?*

John Marsh   Each company has its own bank account which is linked to the central bank account, and the companies are expected to comply with the two basic rules of cash management: deposit receipts as quickly as possible; and take as much credit as ethically possible in regard to payments to creditors and to overdrafts.

Question   *You encouraged the individual companies to arrange their own local overdraft facilities?*

John Marsh   Yes, at this stage we needed to ensure that we used our 'debt capacity' to the full so that individual companies were expected to make their own arrangements for working capital finance. At the centre we were interested in the overall group implications of this local short-term financing and also we needed to be ready to make arrangements for medium- and long-term finance.

Derek Moore   As chairmen of the individual companies, John and I were on the lookout for the early warning signals that a company had cash flow problems.

Question   *What were these early warning signals?*

John Marsh   As an accountant, my suspicions are immediately aroused if the regular accounts are produced late; if there is an absence of up-to-date financial information and if there are changes in accounting practice; for example the capitalising of intangible expenditure, which has the effect of inflating reported profits.

Derek Moore   For my part, I tend to be alerted by physical signs, for example an excessive build-up of stocks and work in progress or perhaps the under-utilisation of a workforce who are being retained to avoid the cost of terminating contracts of employment.

John Marsh   On the borrowing side, I look for signs of a slow or unsystematic payment of creditors, and also a build-up of preferential creditors. I examine leasing charges to see whether if capitalised, they would indicate an excessively high borrowing level. On the lending side I watch for signals of an excessive build-up of debtors.

Question *Having set up this early warning system and received some signals, what happens next?*

Derek Moore Well, this will depend upon the type, frequency and strength of the signal. I can take you into our companies where we have implemented tight credit control; and we have installed better stock-monitoring systems. We have paid attention to the identification and measurement of loss making segments and our debates on the Merry-dale case helped us there. We have reviewed our overheads in all companies, drawing on our experience in Star Components. We have sub-contracted assembly operations and we have closed transport and in-house servicing departments. These debates and decisions have involved John Marsh and his company financial men in providing relevant and reliable data.

Question *What is the main lesson you have learned from this experience?*

Derek Moore I should say that it is firstly that cash management starts in the individual companies. However, cash management itself reflects physical activities both inside and outside the company; and the control of these physical activities (and by implication their associated cash flows) raises not only operational issues but problems that go to the heart of the strategy of the whole group. Thus there is both a local operating dimension and also a central strategic dimension to the problem and we have found some difficulty in the simultaneous handling of both dimensions of the cash flow management problem.

Question *Let us now turn to the second major problem which you mentioned — the financial and accounting effects of inflation.*

John Marsh Well, we have considered some of the effects of inflation in our discussion of cash flow management. In our case, the difficulties were exacerbated since we were trying to expand during a period of inflation. Setting on one side the effects of expansion, in times of inflation, increased levels of debtors and stocks have to be financed in some way. If we compound the problem, as we have recently, with declining profit margins and a credit squeeze by the banks, then our cash flow management has been a key factor in our survival , yet alone success. We would argue that whether we have inflation, stagflation, recession or boom, cash flow management is a key factor in the running of any enterprise.

Question *What have been the particular problems of accounting for the effects of inflation?*

Derek Moore First of all we need to recognise that this is a problem of measurement; as such the solution will not in itself affect the physical circumstances of our companies, although clearly it might affect our view of how profitable we have been. Second, the solution will depend upon our definition of the problem — in our case do we wish to measure the effect of inflation on the results of our holding company reporting to the outside world? Or are we principally concerned with the management of our individual companies, each operating in its own unique environment subject to its own rates of inflation dependent upon the type of operations in which it is engaged? Our view is that first we need a measure to take into account the effects of inflation on the capital of the individual shareholder or proprietor. In this case we consider it appropriate to measure the maintenance of the purchasing power of the individual shareholder in relation to the general price level and this is the method we have used in examining the accounts of the holding company. This method will show, in a period of general price inflation, a gain from holding monetary liabilities and a loss from holding monetary assets. In some ways this accords with aspects which we wish to stress in the strategic management of the cash flows for the whole group. Incidentally, this method was recommended by the accounting profession in 1974/75 when the management of cash flows and the effects of the rate of inflation were particularly difficult to handle.

Question   *Is this method generally accepted by the business community?*

John Marsh   By no means. In fact the government set up the Sandilands Committee to consider the issues, which eventually dismissed the method described by Derek in its report on inflation accounting.

Question   *Why was this?*

John Marsh   The main argument of the Sandilands Committee was that the average movement of prices, and thus the rate of inflation, will vary for different individuals and entities according to the selection of goods and services which they buy. Thus a general index of price changes is of little practical use, as it does not measure the inflation which is relevant to any particular individual or entity, except by accident. The consequence of this argument is that accounts which are based on current purchasing power (CPP) do not show the value to the business of the company's assets, since the measurements produced are not specifically related to those assets, but relate to movements in the prices of other goods, usually covered in the official retail price index. The Sandilands Committee objected to the measure derived from a mixture of gains from operations and gains from holding monetary assets. Also the Committee argued that the measures of cost produced from CPP adjusted accounts did not measure the 'user cost' of long-term resources, particularly plant and inventory. So far as our individual companies are concerned we have been impressed by these arguments of Sandilands and we have encouraged each individual company to use the measurements which most closely take into account their particular type and mixture of assets and costs. This is in line with our general philosophy that the accounting system of an individual company should be designed to take into account its particular characteristics. With this problem, it has meant devising specific indices for the particular types of assets used by individual companies. We think that this is logical, since for individual companies we wish to know how well they have used their particular collections of assets (and liabilities). For the group as a whole, we consider that we need to produce measurements for the individual shareholder to inform him regarding the changes in purchasing power of his equity compared with the changes in the general purchasing power of money. We have concluded that we need different measurements for different purposes.

Question   *Did the Sandilands Committee Report conclude all debate?*

Derek Moore   No. A whole industry has developed round this topic and the debate continues (as does inflation). In order to devise a workable solution, capable of being adopted by all organisations, yet another Committee, the Hyde Committee, has reported, recommending three main adjustments to historical accounts covering depreciation cost of sales and gearing. The depreciation adjustment represents the difference between the depreciation charge based on the current cost of fixed assets and that based on their gross book amount. The current cost of plant and equipment is calculated by reference to appropriate indices published by the Central Statistical Office (CSO). The cost of sales adjustment represents the difference between the current cost of stock and the amount charged in the accounts to compute the historical cost results. This adjustment is calculated using the average method based on indices published by the CSO. Finally, the gearing adjustment represents that part of the depreciation and cost of sales adjustments which are not attributable to the shareholders. We still prefer the current purchasing power method for the holding company accounts and we will still continue to calculate profits in that way. Of course as a public company we shall try to present our accounts in a way which satisfies our auditors and meets the existing recommendation on accounting practice of Statement of Standard Accounting Practice No. 16. But as you can see these recommendations have conflicted over the past ten years and we have strong opinions on which measurements are appropriate for the various aspects of our activities. I suspect that the debate is not yet finished and we shall continue to produce historical accounts, with an adjusted supplementary statement for many years to come. For management accounting purposes, we shall do as we have always done — what we think is fitting!

Question   *Well that's fighting talk and I see your point. Just one more question. Have you learned all there is to know from the Hardy group?*

Derek Moore   No. The environment is changing all the time, bringing fresh issues which we must face and to which we must adapt. For example, we anticipate that our international operations will expand considerably over the next five years and I predict that John and I will have to give this topic a fair amount of our attention. Why don't you come back in five years' time and we will tell you what we have learned?

Bibliography

Ansoff, H. I., (ed)., *Business Strategy*, Penguin, Harmondsworth, 1969.

Anthony, R. N. and Dearden, J., *Management Control Systems,* Irwin, Homewood, Illinois, 1980.

Anton, H. R., Firmin, A., and Grove, H. D., (eds.), *Contemporary Issues in Cost and Managerial Accounting,* Houghton Mifflin, Boston, 1978.

Bromwich, M., *Economics of Capital Investment,* Penguin, Hardmondsworth, 1976.

Bruns, W., De Coster, D., (eds.), *Accounting and its Behavioural Implications,* McGraw-Hill, New York, 1969.

Donaldson, G., *Strategy for Financial Mobility,* Harvard University, Boston, 1969.

Hague, D. C., *Pricing in Business,* Allen & Unwin, 1971.

Hofstede, G. H., *The Game of Budget Control,* Tavistock, London, 1968.

Lorange, P. and Vancil, R. F., *Corporate Planning Systems,* Prentice-Hall, Englewood Cliffs, N.J., 1977.

McCosh, A. M. and Scott Morton, M., *Management Decision Support Systems,* Macmillan, London, 1978.

National Association of Accountants, *Information for Marketing Management,* New York, 1971.

Pyhrr, P. A., *Zero-Base Budgeting,* Wiley-Interscience, New York, 1973.

Samuels, J. M. and Wilkes, F. M., *Management of Company Finance,* Nelson, Sunbury-on-Thames, 1975.

Sizer, J., (ed)., *Readings in Management Accounting,* Penguin, Harmondsworth, 1980.

Smith, J. E., *Cash Flow Management,* Woodhead-Faulkner, 1981.

Smith, J. E. and Ray, G. H., *Financial Aspects of Supervisory Management,* Nelson, 1976.

Solomons, D., *Divisional Performance: Measurement and Control,* Financial Executives Research Foundation, New York, 1965.

Welsch, G. A., *Budgeting: Profit Planning and Control,* Prentice-Hall, Englewood Cliffs, N.J., 1976.